Social Data Analytics

Amin Beheshti
School of Computing
Macquarie University, Sydney, Australia

Samira Ghodratnama
School of Computing
Macquarie University, Sydney, Australia

Mehdi Elahi
Department of Information Science and Media Studies
University of Bergen, Bergen, Norway

Helia Farhood
School of Computing
Macquarie University, Sydney, Australia

T0321394

CRC Press
Taylor & Francis Group
Boca Raton   London   New York

CRC Press is an imprint of the
Taylor & Francis Group, an **informa** business

A SCIENCE PUBLISHERS BOOK

First edition published 2022
by CRC Press
6000 Broken Sound Parkway NW, Suite 300, Boca Raton, FL 33487-2742

and by CRC Press
4 Park Square, Milton Park, Abingdon, Oxon, OX14 4RN

Library of Congress Cataloging-in-Publication Data (applied for)

ISBN: 978-1-032-19627-5 (hbk)
ISBN: 978-1-032-19631-2 (pbk)
ISBN: 978-1-003-26014-1 (ebk)

DOI: 10.1201/9781003260141

Typeset in Times New Roman
by Radiant Productions

Dedication

This book is dedicated to all optimistic, generous, courageous, forgiving, and kind mentors—the mentors who have positively influenced the lives of their students.

Foreword

This monograph addresses the extremely important and timely topic of social data analytics. Understanding social data is of paramount relevance in today's society. Virtually all organizations today face the challenge of improving and customizing their business's processes in order to become more competitive. Utilizing social data analytics provides and leads a set of tools and methodological improvements in an organizations' processes. Most organizations and even governments today talk about data science and data-driven computing and products. In order to truly become data-driven, social data analytics is a key ingredient, as this topic touches everything connected to the customers.

By now it has become clear that fully grasping social data is tremendously important for directing people, organizations, and even influencing societies at large. Gaining a deeper understanding and appreciation of data analytics also has a huge impact on policy decision-making on multiple levels. We can, therefore, say that to provide modern decision-making mechanisms and foundations, one has to truly master the whole life-cycle of social data analytics.

This book truly provides a deep level understanding of the subject matter. It does so by discussing all relevant aspects beginning from organizational aspects of social data, curating social data, analytics of social data for text, video, to summarizing social data and its storytelling.

It is with great pleasure that I recommend this book by profound experts in the topics addressed: Amin Beheshti, Samira Ghodratnama, Mehdi Elahi, and Helia Farhood. The book is written with great competence, care, and a level of mastery of the subject, which the authors have proven in their research throughout the years. I am certain that the reader will gain many valuable insights as well as practical guidelines for this topic. This book serves as a textbook as well as a reference guide for the topic.

I have thoroughly enjoyed reading this book, as the authors combine theoretical insights with practical relevance and show through real world examples how the topics discussed can be understood in depth. This approach chosen by the authors makes reading this monograph a joy to read, and you as the reader will benefit directly from this. The book is highly relevant for students and practitioners alike. Policy-makers can also gain much of insight in cultivating their understanding of the topics discussed. After all, social data analytics is of paramount relevance in today's interconnected world.

Schahram Dustdar

Professor of Computer Science, Head of the Distributed Systems Research Division, TU Wien, Austria

Preface

Many organizations see knowledge production from an ever-increasing amount of social data as an increasingly important capability that can complement the traditional analytics sources. Social data analytics can help organizations improve their processes, personalize their products, and discover hidden insights to their empower business performance. Examples include extracting knowledge and deriving insights from social data to improve government services, predict intelligence activities, personalize advertisements during elections and improve national security and public health. Understanding social data can be challenging as the analysis goal can be subjective, i.e., it depends on the analyst's perspective. In this context, social data analytics is considered an appropriate metaphor as it provides the backend to facilitate understanding and surfacing insights embedded within the data.

Considering various social data analytics needs and the critical role of social data in data-centric computing, we felt the need for writing this book. This book is a technical introduction to social data analytics to share the state-of-the-art research achievements and practical techniques of social data analytics in this modern world. Given that many "social data analysis" subjects such as querying and warehousing are covered well in the literature, the focus of this book will be on understanding the approaches that can be used to systematically engineer the data generated on Online Social Networks; and offering a common understanding of the concepts and technologies in social data analytics.

This book will cover a large body of knowledge in social data analytics, including Organizing, Curating, Summarizing, and analyzing social data, as well as challenges, opportunities, and applications of social data analytics in the age of big data and Artificial Intelligence. This book introduces basic social data analytics concepts, describes the state of the art in this space, and continues with deeper dives on modern techniques for curating and summarizing social data and storytelling with data and interactive visualization techniques. The book also reviews practical applications, including recommender systems, trust, and influence maximization.

Chapters Overview

We introduce concise and commonly accepted definitions, taxonomies, and frameworks for Social Data Analytics in Chapter 1. We briefly discuss the challenges in social data understanding, followed by the need to organize, curate, process, analyze, and visualize the huge amount of data and information generated every second on social data islands. We discuss the variety of data, from structured to semi-structured and unstructured, generated on social networks and discuss the state of the art challenges and opportunities in social data analytics. We cover a range of analytics from text to image and video, and introduce modern techniques such as storytelling with social data and interactive visualization.

Chapter 2 presents techniques for organizing the large amount of data generated on social data islands such as Twitter (Twitter.com/) and Facebook (facebook.com/). This is important as continuous improvement in connectivity, storage, and data processing capabilities allow access to a data deluge from the big data generated on open, private, social, and IoT (Internet of Things) data islands. This chapter will introduce technologies from relational to NoSQL database management systems. It will also discuss modern technologies, including Data Lakes which facilitate storing raw data and let the data analyst decide how to curate them later.

One of the main challenges in understanding social data is to transform raw data into actionable insights. To achieve this goal, it will be vital to prepare and curate the raw data for analytics. Data curation has been defined as the active and ongoing management of data through its lifecycle of interest and usefulness. To address the importance of social data curation in social data analytics, in Chapter 3, we focus on curation tasks including cleaning, integration, transformation, and adding value. This chapter will also discuss modern technologies including the Knowledge Lake, i.e., a contextualized Data Lake, that facilitates turning the raw data (stored in Data Lakes) into contextualized data and knowledge using extraction, enrichment, annotation, linking, and summarization techniques.

Every second, a tremendous amount of content in unstructured text format is generated on social networks. Text analytics and mining techniques can uncover insights such as sentiment analysis, entities, relations, and key phrases in unstructured data. In Chapter 4, we provide an overview of text analytics, followed by an introduction to basic text processing, Sentiment and Emotion Analytics, Topic Extraction, Opinion Extraction, Text Classification, and Information Extraction. We will also highlight the challenges and opportunities in social media text analytics.

Photo and video sharing on social networking services are now quite popular. A huge number of images and videos are posted every second on social networks. Social image an video analytics play an important role in extracting meaningful information and insights from photos and videos posted on social media. In Chapter 5, we provide an overview of image and video data analytics, followed by highlighting challenges and opportunities in the field. We discuss important topics, including image and video detection and recognition and storytelling with image and video data. We will also discuss modern topics such as analyzing and generating 3D posts on social media.

The ubiquitous availability of computing devices and the widespread use of the internet have continuously generated a large amount of data. For example, the amount of available data on any social network could be far beyond humans' processing capacity to properly process, causing what is known as 'information overload'. To efficiently cope with large amounts of information and generate content with significant value to users, we require identifying, merging, and summarizing information. In Chapter 6, we provide an overview of summarization techniques and discuss how social data summarization can help gather related information and collect it into a shorter format that enables answering complicated questions, gaining new insight, and discovering conceptual boundaries. We also focus on modern topics, including Time-aware, Personalized-aware, and Conversational Summarization of Social Data.

The business world is getting increasingly dynamic and inseparable from social data. As the scale of available social data grows ever larger, such data may hold tremendous amounts of potential value. In this context, insights need to be uncovered and translated into actions or business outcomes for deeper interpretations and better intelligence. To achieve this goal, data stories should combine data with narratives to reduce the ambiguity of social data, connect data with context, and describe a specific interpretation. In Chapter 7, we focus on advancing the scientific understanding of storytelling with social data. We define storytelling as an incremental and interactive process that enables analysts to turn insights into actions. We will discuss the related work in this domain and highlight the importance of enabling analysts to communicate analysis findings, supporting evidence and evaluate the quality of the social data stories.

The rapid growth of social networks has resulted in an enormous amount of social data generated every day. The massive volume, variety, and velocity of social data has led to undesired effects such as information pollution for online users. This has caused the users to feel desperate when navigating social networks and exposed them to choice overload when making certain choices among unlimited alternatives. Social Recommender Systems are digital tools that can tackle these problems through building personalization in social environments by exploiting user preferences learned from the data users generate in their online activities. In Chapter 8, we provide an overview of recommendation techniques along with challenges and opportunities in the field. We discuss important topics, including content recommendation, social, collaborative filtering, trust-aware recommendation, group recommendation, and application domains.

Finally, Chapter 9 provides an overview of social data analytics applications, including: personality detection from social data, understanding bias in social media, social Trust, improving sales and marketing (e.g., creating successful campaigns with social media marketing analytics), influence maximization (e.g., to identify influencers for your brand and industry), situational Awareness (e.g., discover trending topics), social media audience segmentation, social media information discovery (e.g., from Topic trends to Sentiment ratio), linking social media performance to business and revenue growth, and performance analysis of the industry.

Who is This Book for?

In writing this book, we have had a wide range of audiences interested in social data analytics in consideration. We have tried to cover topics of interest from academics (professors, researchers, and research students), professionals (managers, data scientists, analysts, and software engineers), and practitioners in understanding and employing social data analytics methods and techniques. This book is a comprehensive textbook on social data analytics, and therefore, could be a valuable reference for academics, professionals, and practitioners.

To Professors. You will find this book useful for various courses, from an undergraduate course in data science and analytics up to a graduate course in social data analytics. We have provided considerably more material than can fit in a typical one-term course. Therefore, you can think of the book as a buffet from which you can pick and choose the material that best supports the course you wish to teach.

To Research Students and Researchers. We hope that this textbook provides you with an enjoyable introduction to the field of social data analytics. We have attempted to correctly classify state-of-the-art, describe in-depth technical problems and techniques/methods, and highlight future research directions in social data analytics.

To Professionals and Practitioners. You will find this book helpful as it provides a review of state of the art in social data analytics, its applications, along with challenges and opportunities. The wide range of topics in this book makes it an excellent handbook on social data analytics. Most of the methods that we discuss in each chapter have great practical utility: Social Data Analytics Challenges and Opportunities in Chapter 1, Organizing Social Data in Chapter 2, Curating Social Data in Chapter 3, Social Media Text Analytics in Chapter 4, Social Media Image and Video Analytic in Chapter 5, Summarizing Social Data in Chapter 6, Storytelling with Social Data in Chapter 7, Social Data and Recommender Systems and the Future of Personalization 8, and Social Data Analytics Applications in Chapter 9.

Contents

Social Data Analytics: Challenges and Opportunities

1.1 Understanding Social Data

An Online Social Network (OSN) platform is a networking service which enables people to build social relationships with other people who may have same career, education, background, interest, goal, and more. To achieve this goal, Online Social Networks enable users to communicate by posting information, comments, messages, images, and more. Examples of social networks include Twitter[1], Facebook[2], Linkedin[3], Instagram[4], TikTok[5], and Clubhouse[6]. Two main elements of a social network include an *Information-Item* (e.g., a tweet on Twitter or a post on Facebook) and a *Social Actor* (e.g., a person/organization who has an account on Twitter/Facebook). A social actor is a conscious, thinking individual who has an account on a social network such as Facebook and can shape their world in a variety of ways by reflecting on their situation and the choices available to them on social networks. An information item in a social network may contain structured information such as an id (unique identity of the information item), a source (the utility used to post the information item), a user (who posted the information item), and coordinates (the

---

[1] https://Twitter.com/.

[2] https://www.facebook.com/.

[3] https://www.linkedin.com/.

[4] https://www.instagram.com/.

[5] https://www.tiktok.com/.

[6] https://www.clubhouse.com/.

geographic location of this item). However, an information item may also include unstructured data such as text (the actual UTF-8 text of the status update), image, audio, and video.

In this context, the discovery, interpretation, and communication of meaningful patterns in social data (i.e., Social Data Analytics) could be a challenging task and may include:

- **Data Science** and Analytics, the goal here is to examine the information item that a social user posted. This may include: Text Analytics (e.g., to examine the text that a social user has posted), Natural Language Processing (e.g., to understand, analyze, manipulate, and process the text that a social user has posted), Image Processing and Analysis (e.g., to extract meaningful information from images posted by a social user) and more.
- **Social Science** and Analytics, the goal here is to study the communities on online social media and the relationships among individuals/groups within those communities. This will help us to understand how social users behave and influence the world around us.
- **Cognitive Science** and Analytics, the goal here is to study the intelligence, personality, behavior, and attitude of individuals/groups on online social media [58]. This could significantly contribute to personalizing the recommendations or analyzing behavioral disorders in Online Social Networks (to help in suicide prevention, school bullying detection, and extremist/criminal activity prediction).

The combination of data, social, and cognitive analytics will enable understanding, analyzing, measuring, and interpreting the data, topics, and ideas posted online social media as well as the relationships among social users on such networks. To achieve this, it is essential to characterize variables that grasp and encode information, thereby enabling to derive meaningful inferences from social data [37, 69]. Social data is useless unless processed in analytical tasks from which humans or downstream applications can derive insights. In this context, the main research problem would be to understand the social data. To properly understand the social data, we need to implement the following:

- *Organizing Social Data*: this step deals with a variety of data ranging from structured to semi-structured and unstructured data. It involves organizing data using technologies from relational to NoSQL database management systems and Data Lakes [61].
- *Processing Social Data*: this step deals with the organization and manipulation of large amounts of social data, and may involve operations including validation, curation, sorting, classification, calculation, interpretation, and transformation of data. The main challenge in processing social data is the large volume of data generated from various sources. As an example, consider Twitter[7], where approximately 12TB of data is generated every day on Twitter. Accordingly, processing a simple query such as "Calculate the count of the number of tweets

---

[7] https://Twitter.com/.

(per day) for a list of different countries" on a single computer may take several days/weeks/months. In this context, Big Data platforms such as Apache Hadoop[8] are required to support the real-time processing of social data.

- *Curating Social Data*: this step not only involves cleaning social data, but also includes efforts to understand the content and context of the social data [62, 67]. In particular, data curation is the process of transforming raw data into contextualized data. It includes all the tasks needed for principled and controlled data creation, maintenance, and management, together with the capacity to add value to the raw data. Social data curation may involve: Identifying relevant data sources, Ingesting data and knowledge, Cleaning, Integration, Transformation (Normalization and aggregation), Adding Value (e.g., Extraction, Enrichment, Linking, Summarization) [63].
- *Summarizing Social Data*: this step helps with efficiently coping with large amounts of social data, to generate data summaries with significant meaning to users. This step is vital to social data analytics. The amount of available information on any given topic on online social media is far beyond humans' processing capacity to manage, e.g., due to information overabundance and irrelevant obtained information. Data summarization facilitates gathering related information and collecting it into a shorter format that enables answering complicated questions, gaining new insight, and discovering conceptual boundaries. Social data summarization aims to identify and highlight the critical aspects of one or multiple input document(s) within a defined size limit.
- *Visualizing Social Data*: this step enables a better understanding of the trends, outliers, and patterns in social data. Several techniques from simple visualization (e.g., using visual elements such as charts, graphs, and maps) to advanced approaches (e.g., storytelling with data [67] and interactive visualization [590]) could be leveraged to facilitate understanding social data and analytics results. These techniques can help us make sense of trillions of records and information items in social data, generated every second.

1.2 Organizing Social Data

The continuous improvement in connectivity, storage, and data processing capabilities allows access to a data deluge from the big data generated on social data islands. Social data analytics for insight discovery is a strategic priority for modern businesses. This process heavily depends on properly organizing the large data generated on online social media platforms every second. Organizing social data may involve processes to persist and categorize social data to make it more usable. Persistence is the continuance of an effect after its cause is removed [44]. In computer science, data persistence means that the data survives after its creation has ended. In other words, for a data store to be considered persistent, it must be written

---

[8] Hadoop [641] is an open-source framework that uses a simple programming model to enable distributed processing of large data sets on clusters of computers.

to non-volatile storage. Ingesting and persisting vast amounts of social data (varying from the semi-structured data generated on Twitter to unstructured data such as images generated on Instagram, videos generated on Youtube, and audios posted on Clubhouse) being generated continuously, is challenging and may require a different approach to distributed data storage that is designed for large-scale clusters. Typical properties of social data include wide physical distribution, diversity of formats, independently-managed, and heterogeneous semantics.

1.2.1 Social Data Volume

Social data volume refers to the vast amounts of data generated every second on Online Social Networks. Social data is large scale, never ending, and ever changing, and arrives in diverse forms from diverse sources at irregular time intervals. Therefore, the main challenge would be to store the vast amounts of social data generated every second. To deal with the high volume of social data, with the aim to support scaling applications, there are two main approaches that can be used: (i) *Scale Up*: Keep the same number of Systems/Servers, but migrate each system to a larger System. For example, changing from a server with 16 CPU cores and 1 TB storage system to a server with 64 CPU cores and a 100 TB storage system; and (ii) *Scale Out*: When the workload exceeds the capacity of a server, the workload is spread out across several servers. This technique, also referred to as Clustering, supports scaling applications that have a loosely coupled architecture. In particular, it is cheaper to buy ten 100 TB storage systems than it is to buy a single 1 PB storage system.

1.2.2 Social Data Variety

Social data variety refers to the different types of data (from structured to semi-structured and unstructured) generated on Online Social Media.

Structured Data is highly organized and easily decipherable by an algorithm. Structured data can be easily defined by a schema, i.e., a structure described in a formal language supported by the database management system to facilitate organizing and interpreting information. Relational database management systems [144] (RDBMSs) typically support organizing structured data and require creating a schema for data before writing into the database, which is called Schema-on-write. Example of structured data generated on Online Social Networks includes the record of a user on a social network.

Unstructured Data is information that either does not have a pre-defined data model or is not organized in a pre-defined manner. Examples include text, audio, video, images, and analog data. NoSQL database management systems [144] normally support organizing unstructured data and do not require creating a schema for data before writing into the database, which is called Schema-on-read. Example of unstructured data generated on Online Social Networks includes the text of a tweet posted on Twitter or an image posted on Instagram.

Semi-structured Data is a form of structured data that requires a high-level schema to understand the data structure. However, this schema may describe some unstructured data embedded in the high-level structure. As an example, consider a tweet in Twitter which has schema describing attributes such as an id (unique identity of the tweet), source (the utility used to post the Tweet), user (the user who posted this Tweet), coordinates (the geographic location of this Tweet), text (The actual UTF-8 text of the status update), as well as entities that have been parsed out of the text of the Tweet such as hashtags, URLs, and media.

Traditional data management systems required very predictable structured formats for the data, and supported relational data with a fixed schema. Today, social data is generated in diverse forms from diverse sources. To handle the volume and variety of such data, semi-structured data formats such as JSON[9], Avro[10], and XML[11] have become the standard to store and exchange semi-structured data. In particular, semi-structured data does not require a prior definition of a fixed schema. The schema can evolve over time, and new attributes could be added at any time. Moreover, semi-structured data may contain hierarchies of nested information.

1.2.3 Social Data Velocity

Social data velocity refers to the rate at which new social data enters the system as well as the rate at which the social data must be processed. In the past, social media applications used to capture only the data about the main entities, such as posts and user information. But recently, social media applications started to capture user activities such as capturing every click in searching, browsing, and comparing. This, in turn, will heavily increase the velocity of the social data. The velocity of social data processing can be broken down into Streaming and Feedback Loop.

- *Streaming*: Social networks are quickly becoming the primary medium for sharing news and discussing what is happening in the world. For example, Twitter is now considered one of the fastest news sources in the world, as it produces rich data streams for immediate insights into ongoing matters and the conversations around them. Stream processing, i.e., a big data technology that focuses on the real-time processing of continuous streams of data in motion, is now supported by many big data platforms such as Apache Kafka[12], Amazon Kine-

---

[9] https://www.json.org/.

[10] https://avro.apache.org/.

[11] https://www.w3.org/standards/xml/core.

[12] https://kafka.apache.org/.

sis[13], Microsoft Azure Stream Analytics[14], Apache Flink[15], and IBM Streaming Analytics[16].

- *Feedback Loop*, i.e., a process in which the outputs of a system are circled back and used as inputs, is an important step in analyzing the data to produce actionable results. As an example, the browsers started to capture users' activities on the client-side, send that information to recommendation engines, with the goal to personalize the services for each user. For example, visit a Website to book a flight to travel to Australia, later when you log in to your social media account, e.g., Instagram or Facebook, you may see advertisements for cheap flights to Australia. In particular, this process may use customer activity and feedback, to create better recommendations.

1.2.4 Social Data and Metadata

Metadata is the data that provides information about other data, which can help users correctly understand the data. Metadata (e.g., descriptive, structural, and administrative metadata) can be generated manually or automatically. Tracing is a mechanism to generate metadata. For example, when we use our cell phone, a set of algorithms can trace our movement (location services), what Apps[17] we are using, and how frequently. Or, a social network App can trace the activities of a user, including: which days of the week and what time of the days the user is more active, what sort of content the user liked or reshared, and what type of people (e.g., from personality, behavior and attitude viewpoints) the user is following.

Metadata can help in generating the story of a digital object from the present time back to its derivation, i.e., provenance [77] (the documentation of an object's lifecycle), including: who created the file, on which system (e.g., IP address), and when; how the digital object evolved over time and more. Provenance has an important role in understanding social data and discovering facts and insights in novel applications, such as: (i) tracking down fake news on social media; (ii) understanding bias in social media; (iii) social Data and Trust; (iv) improving sales and marketing, e.g., create successful campaigns with social media marketing analytics; (v) influence maximization, e.g., to identify influencers for your brand and industry; (vi) Situational Awareness, e.g., discover trending topics; (vii) social media audience segmentation; (viii) social media information discovery, e.g., from Topic trends to Sentiment ratio; (ix) linking social media performance to business and revenue growth; and (x) performance analysis of the industry.

Chapter 2 of this book will present techniques for organizing the large amount of data generated on social data islands such as Twitter and Facebook. It will also

---

[13] https://aws.amazon.com/kinesis/.

[14] https://docs.microsoft.com/en-us/azure/stream-analytics/.

[15] https://flink.apache.org/.

[16] https://www.ibm.com/au-en/cloud/streaming-analytics.

[17] An App is an application, especially as downloaded by a user to a mobile device.

introduce technologies from relational to NoSQL database management systems; and discuss modern technologies, including Data Lakes, which facilitates storing raw data and let the data analyst decide how to curate them later.

1.3 Curating Social Data

The key principle and challenge in understanding the social data is to transform the raw data generated by social actors into curated data, i.e., contextualized data and the knowledge that is maintained and made available for end-users and applications. This process, known as data curation [65], can have a significant impact on business operations, especially when it comes to the decision-making processes within organizations [74]. Data curation involves cleaning social data and includes steps to understand the content and context of the social data. Data curation involves identifying relevant data sources, extracting data and knowledge, cleaning, maintaining, merging, enriching, and linking data and knowledge. For example, information extracted from tweets is often enriched with metadata on geolocation, in the absence of which the extracted information would be difficult to interpret and meaningfully utilize. Data curation thus acts as the glue between raw data and analytics, providing an abstraction layer that relieves users from time-consuming, tedious, and error-prone curation tasks.

To address the importance of social data curation in social data analytics, in Chapter 3, we focus on curation tasks including cleaning, integration, transformation, and adding value. This chapter will also discuss modern technologies, including the notion of Knowledge Lake, i.e., a contextualized Data Lake. Knowledge Lakes introduced to facilitate turning the raw data (stored in Data Lakes) into contextualized data and knowledge. A Knowledge Lake benefits from intelligent data science pipelines that include extraction, enrichment, annotation, linking, and summarization techniques [515, 591, 592].

1.4 Processing Social Data

Data processing, i.e., the manipulation of data by a computer, may include the conversion of data to machine-readable form, as well as the flow of data through the CPU and memory to output devices, aiming to produce meaningful information. Today, many science and engineering problems require large computational resources and cannot be executed on a single machine. Considering the large volume of social data, a set of techniques and programming models are required to access large-scale social data. This will facilitate extracting helpful information for supporting and providing decisions. Centralized system solutions such as Mainframe[18] and large

---

[18] Mainframes are computers used primarily by large organizations for critical applications; bulk data processing, such as: census, industry and consumer statistics, enterprise resource planning, and transaction processing. Modern mainframes can run multiple different instances of operating systems at the same time.

commercial Supercomputers[19] are very expensive and may not be accessible for many organizations to be used for processing social data.

Distributed computing is a field of computer science that studies distributed systems; and is introduced to address the large-scale computing challenge. In particular, distributed computing enables computers to share information as well as to processing tasks. A distributed system is a collection of independent computers that appear to the system's users as a single system. The main advantage of distributed systems over centralized systems is that a collection of microprocessors offers a better price/performance ratio than centralized systems such as mainframes. This, in turn, will provide a cost-effective way to increase computing power. A distributed system may have a higher total computing power than a mainframe. Additionally, in a distributed system, the computing power can be added in small increments. Advances in distributed computing offered solutions such as Cluster, Grid, and Cloud computing that aim to provide High-performance computing (HPC) on a small scale and at a lower cost [532]. A cluster is a collection of parallel or distributed computers that are interconnected using high-speed networks, such as gigabit Ethernet. Grid is a system that coordinates resources that are not subject to centralized control, using standard, open, general-purpose protocols and interfaces to deliver nontrivial qualities of service. Cloud computing refers to both the applications delivered as services over the Internet and the hardware and system software in the data centers that provide those services. Cloud computing is a model for enabling on-demand network access to a shared pool of configurable computing resources (e.g., networks, servers, storage, applications, and services) that can be rapidly provisioned and released with minimal management effort or service provider interaction. Cloud computing provides three kinds of service: Software as a Service (SaaS), Platform as a Service (PaaS), and Infrastructure as a Service (IaaS).

Several software utilities were introduced to facilitate using a network of many computers to solve problems involving massive amounts of data and computation. For example, Apache Hadoop [641] provides a software framework for distributed storage and processing of big data using the MapReduce [161] programming model. In particular, Hadoop is a Java-based framework for distributing and processing large data sets across clusters of computers, and became a de facto standard for most Big Data storage and processing. Hadoop MapReduce is a programming model, where the model is a specialization of the split-apply-combine strategy for data analysis. MapReduce supports processing big data sets with a parallel, distributed algorithm on a cluster, i.e., a set of loosely or tightly connected computers that work together so that, in many respects, they can be viewed as a single system. MapReduce is inspired by the map and reduce functions commonly used in functional

---

[19] A supercomputer is a computer that is at the frontline of current processing capacity, particularly speed of calculation. Supercomputers are used for scientific and engineering problems (high-performance computing), data crunching, and number crunching, while mainframes are used for transaction processing. Supercomputers play an essential role in the field of computational science: weather forecasting, climate research, oil and gas exploration, and molecular modeling.

programming[20]. Other examples include Spark (a high-speed, open-source processing and analytics engine ideal for large quantities of real-time data) and Kafka (an open-source stream-processing platform).

1.5 Summarizing Social Data

The amount of available information on any given topic is far beyond humans' processing capacity. To efficiently cope with large amounts of information and generate content with significant value to users, we require identifying, merging, and summarizing information. Data summaries can help gather related information and collect it into a shorter format that enables answering complicated questions, gaining new insight, and discovering conceptual boundaries. Summarization approaches create the best representation of the original data, enabling efficient storage, quick browsing, and retrieval of an extensive collection of data without loss [99]. However, there is no unique definition for summarization, meaning it can be understood based on the goal of the application or user. For example, summarization can be defined as the process of reducing the size of data or finding the important part(s) of data while eliminating redundant or non-relevant data. The most general definition for summarization is the automatic mechanism of generating brief and condensed representations of the important content [396]. However, defining what is essential in this definition is a challenging and subjective task. Even for a human expert, producing a summary is a complicated text [241, 243]; consequently, it is even more challenging for machines that do not understand the text. The machine should be able to have the ability to understand texts and produce summaries using background knowledge suitable for humans.

Summarizing high-volume content generated daily by users scattered globally provides valuable insights beneficial for different real-world applications. While social data includes images, videos, and text, most shared and spread data is in the form of text data such as posts, comments, or messages. Text data is required to be summarized and transformed into machine-readable forms to be utilized for practical purposes. Produced summaries are represented in different formats, including text or graphical forms like histograms or pie charts which analyze the data. While statistical representations can effectively capture various specific parameters from extensive social media data, a noise-free textual summary is preferable in most usages of social media analysis.

Generated text data in social platforms have various formats and structures. For instance, tweets from Twitter, posts on Facebook, pins on Pinterest[21], posts on Tum-

---

[20] It is a declarative programming paradigm, which means programming is done with expressions/declarations instead of statements.

[21] https://www.pinterest.com.

blr[22], and check-ins on Foursquare[23] and Yelp[24] are all different regarding their format. Nevertheless, their content values are as important as a formal document, if not more than that. The reason is that social media data is instantaneous, time-sensitive, and topically relevant, and delicate to the world's concerns. The most significant difference among various platforms is the users' language and the length of generated text data. For instance, the language in LinkedIn, Yelp, or Reddit is more formal. Their structure is well-formed according to linguistic grammar and formality than on Facebook, where user-generated content expresses emotion context-specific content. The amount of generated text data in Yelp or Reddit is also substantial compared to Twitter or Facebook. Another aspect of social data which makes it different from a formal document is the sensitivity to chronological recency. Therefore, focusing on the most chronologically significant set of social interactions is necessary for proposing a summarization technique. Scale is another aspect that affects the performance of summarization approaches. Consequently, standard natural language processing tools such as parsing, Parts of Speech Tagging (POS), and Named Entity Recognition (NER) are not applicable for social text data.

A summarization approach for social data is required to work with dynamic, quick-to-change, and large-scale data streams. For example, using term frequency as a relevancy measure in a summarization system is very common. However, the size of the input document should be large enough to detect essential concepts. Instead, trending phrases specified by users, such as a hashtag, are used to define the importance of text [177]. Besides, the short-length textual content in social media data exhibits sparse contextual information, resulting in new text classification, clustering, or information extraction challenges. Moreover, the purpose of summarizing social media has a significant impact on designing a summarization approach. For instance, event, sentiment, and opinion summarization are examples of social data summarization approaches.

The diversity of styles and formats, noise and redundancies within data, and dynamic and quick-to-change nature of produced data make social media summarization an exciting but challenging problem. Therefore, social media summarization varies according to the purpose of the summarization task. In Chapter 6, we will review the social data summarization problem from different perspectives. We categorize summarization approaches into two groups: summarization approaches for formal social data such as Reddit or LinkedIn, called 'generic' approaches, and summarization approaches for micro-blog data such as Twitter. We discuss micro-blog summarization approaches from various aspects, including time-based, event-based, and opinion-based approaches.

---

[22] https://www.tumblr.com/.

[23] https://foursquare.com/.

[24] https://www.yelp.com/.

1.6 Storytelling with Social Data

Many organizations see knowledge production from an ever-increasing amount of social data as an increasingly important capability that can complement the traditional analytics sources. Social data analytics can help organizations know their audience, e.g., behavioral analysis and personalization, and improve their processes. Understanding social data can be challenging as the analysis goal can be subjective, i.e., it depends on the analyst's perspective. In this context, storytelling is considered an appropriate metaphor as it facilitates understanding and surfacing insights embedded within the social data.

Storytelling with Social Data comprises of three main steps:

- *Curation*: As discussed in Section 1.3, data curation includes all the processes needed for principled and controlled data creation, maintenance, and management, together with the capacity to add value to data [43]. In the context of storytelling, we primarily focus on data curation as a process for data creation and value generation from social data. More specifically, we focus on curation tasks that transform raw social data (e.g., a tweet on Twitter) into contextualized data and knowledge include extracting, enriching, linking, and annotating social data.
- *Summarization*: As discussed in Section 1.5, data summarization focus on shortening a large dataset computationally, to create a subset that represents the most important or relevant information within the original content. Data summarization techniques aim to produce a "good" quality of summaries and may include tasks such as clustering, sampling, compression, histograms, and more; with respect to the role of these tasks in a variety of fields such as data mining. Some summarization techniques may also benefit from extracting information items from unstructured social data (e.g., extracting Named Entity, Topic, Phrase, Part of Speech, Keyword, as well as relationships among attributes, activities, and actions). Other summarization techniques may focus on extracting structures (e.g., List, Table, Tree, and Graph) from unstructured social data.
- *Interactive Visualization*: Data Visualization enables communicating effectively with social data and data summaries. Visualization is complementary to curation and summarization tasks and will enhance the discovery of connected entities, concepts, and topics.

In Chapter 7, we focus on advancing the scientific understanding of storytelling with social data. We define storytelling as an incremental and interactive process that enables analysts to turn insights into actions. We will discuss the related work in this domain and highlight the importance of enabling analysts to communicate analysis findings, supporting evidence and evaluate the quality of the social data stories.

1.7 Social Media Text Analytics

Individuals and businesses produce tons of unstructured text data every day. Organizing, categorizing, and capturing relevant information from textual data is a significant concern and challenge for companies. Text analysis is used for analyzing large and complex documents, including social media posts, forums, news, chats, surveys, and call transcripts, in an easy, speedy, and efficient way. Text analytic is the process of knowledge discovery or deriving meaning from text [574] with a broad application.

Text analytic approaches use machine learning, statistics, and linguistics to identify textual patterns and trends. Textual social data helps extract valuable insights given in various aspects that were not previously attainable in both scale and extent. Text analytic tools have influenced how industries work by improving product user experiences and making more agile and reliable business decisions. For instance, text mining and sentiment analysis tools enable companies to define and prioritize their customers' key pain points, resulting in responding to urgent issues in real-time, detecting a potential crisis and identifying service or product flaws to increase customer satisfaction. Moreover, monitoring shifts in sentiment provides insights around industry inclinations and financial markets for managing risks, specifically for business investments spread across various sectors, which is a high priority for companies. However, textual data in social media presents new challenges due to the distinct features, including time sensitivity and unstructured text format [66]. Some social media Websites, including Twitter, restrict the length of user-generated content to a specific word or character number limit. For instance, Twitter limits the length of each tweet to 140 characters, making people more effective and quick with their interaction in social media applications. However, the ubiquity of short-length text on social media builds new challenges, making traditional research in text analytics ineffective, such as information extraction, text classification, text clustering, and sentiment analysis.

A general framework for knowledge discovery from a large corpus of the text includes: (i) text preprocessing, (ii) text representation, and (iii) knowledge discovery using natural language processing techniques. Natural Language Processing (NLP) aims to understand natural language using artificial intelligence and linguistics. The foundation of many text mining algorithms, including information retrieval, information extraction, text classification, and summarization, is some basic NLP techniques, such as part of speech tagging, syntactic parsing, and other linguistic analysis [375]. Information Retrieval (IR) aims to find the required information. Hence, IR approaches focused principally on facilitating information access rather than analyzing information and finding hidden patterns [436]. However, Information Extraction (IE) is the process of automatically extracting information, which serves as the first step for other text mining algorithms, which include feature selection, feature extraction, and named entity recognition (NER) [541]. Text summarization is a profitable text mining approach that gives a concise overview of a large document or a collection of documents on a topic [240, 242]. Different supervised and unsupervised approaches have been used for this purpose [60, 244, 245].

Applying traditional techniques for processing social textual data is not possible. Therefore, text analytic methods need to be designed for social textual data specifically. In this book, we introduce various text analytics methods designed for extracting insights from textual social data. We discuss different text analytic tasks used for social textual data in detail, including event detection, text classification, social data tagging, topic modeling, sentiment, and opinion extraction, and linking metadata to textual data.

The volume and velocity of textual data contained in social media provides many event detections and tracking opportunities. Event detection is the task of monitoring data sources to discover the existence of an event [405]. It has many beneficial applications, specifically during a disaster or crisis, such as the occurrence of an earthquake or tsunami. In addition to event detection, monitoring and tracking events' changes and evolution over time is another interesting research direction. User-generated text social content and the network's structure provide a rich source of information for monitoring events.

Social tagging is the process of associating tags to an entity using for managing and searching through Internet-based applications. Social tagging services provide an opportunity to generate a large volume of tagging data, useful mining information on the Web. However, the tagging services provide keyword-based search. Topic modeling is an unsupervised machine learning-based text mining technique that reveals hidden topical patterns across the document collection. In other words, it projects document collections to a topic space by finding a group of words that best represent the information in a collection. Classifying or assigning predefined tags or categories to unstructured text is a primary task in the natural language processing field. It facilitates further processing, including organizing, browsing, and categorizing text data for delivering valuable insights. Automatic text classification reduces error compared to human annotating since people are biased.

1.8 Social Image and Video Data Analytic

Social media profoundly influences people's social life. Customer decision-making can be affected by this technology, allowing customers to make more informed decisions. Studies have revealed that young people in a variety of fields rely on social media for knowledge. In general, the information you get through social media sites is reliable, up-to-date, and easily accessible. There is a critical lack of a technique for understanding and analyzing Internet data among governments, commercial researchers, and organisations [359]. The quantity of images shared on social media each day has risen dramatically. As visual data is more likely than a word to be shared, it has become the most effective way to disseminate information to a large audience [128].

If you are collecting social data, images are preferable to text since they give more context. Data coding by hand is impractical with large data sets. However, variables may be readily recorded in a picture. Using images rather than text makes expressing information about an organization or medical policy easier and faster. Furthermore, it is a fact that emotions dominate human behavior in the great majority of instances, and visuals elicit these responses more powerfully than words. Humans utilize images to provide visual assistance for evaluating multidimensional political situations to discover the problematic issues behind them. Because visual information is more likely to catch people's interest and support their study than written content, it may be used to aid independent decisions.

Images can aid in the preparation of data for the promotion of certain research projects. Photos, for instance, can offer data on demographic and socioeconomic features of people and places when surveys are not possible to conduct in such places. In locations with inconsistent data that are hard to observe over time, photos might help demonstrate economic growth. To illustrate the level of violence or better scaling demonstrations, images may even assist us in measuring theoretical concepts. The Internet and social media are mainly responsible for producing and transmitting a significant volume of visual data. Social data analytics will enable organizations to observe the universe through their consumers' eyes. Accordingly, organizations can benefit from insights driven from social data analytics to demonstrate how their decisions impact consumer sentiments.

Existing technologies for data analysis have several drawbacks. As an example, most contemporary algorithms do not do any picture processing directly, and they mainly focus on evaluating captions. Consequently, the information being given is quite restricted. Face recognition from social media images, on the other hand, will aid visual data analytics. Increasing biometric security and policing capabilities are attractive to government officials because of the apparent benefits. Data and enhanced precision in testing ideas will be more readily available, scientists predict. Large amounts of visual posts are also processed by Artificial intelligence (AI) enabled image analytics, and photo theories to: discover trending hashtags from visual data, analyzing the character of users via social media profile photos, measuring and proving the Return On Investment (ROI), acquiring online news by finding the context behind images, analyzing visual data on social media to market an enterprise, and analyzing images from social media to promote public health [385].

Given today's abundance of images and content, a system for parsing enormous volumes of social media visual data is required. Photographs, as opposed to simple text, need the use of technical features to recognize and differentiate objects [316]. People's ideas, views, and behaviors may be seen locally and worldwide via social media and information sources, which provides an excellent resource. The information obtained from social media gives us a better knowledge of how individuals interact with their environment, which opens up lots of new possibilities in various fields. There are still prejudices in who has access to social media, what they need it for, and why it has grown so rapidly. These biases and the likelihood that these data may impact information system security experts make it difficult for them to extract valuable information from this data. Images gleaned from social networking sites provide both opportunities and challenges. People are more inclined to take photographs or videos and share them with others in an accident to properly educate them of what is occurring, significantly if an occurrence might substantially harm the infrastructure.

Images and videos on social media give many possibilities for gaining rapid information important to disaster response modifications. According to studies, the general public depends on social media to communicate emergency information regarding catastrophes, such as early notifications, warnings, and damage assessments for infrastructure, including roads, houses, and bridges [299]. Due to the widespread use of social media, defining today's culture has never been more critical. This is due to the explosion in the Internet exchange of visual information spawning a new culture. These images portray various philosophies of life as well as feelings. According to recent research, visual data from social media platforms may better understand clients and deliver better service. Furthermore, this approach might provide academics with helpful information on how environmental regulations have been received in the past and how they would be received in the future (e.g., climate regulation) [567]. Visual data may be utilized for several commercial objectives by businesses that use social media, covering communications, the selling of virtual goods, market research, personnel management, and the administration of business operations. It is impossible to keep up with social media since what's hot now may be obsolete tomorrow [324].

When it comes to the challenges in this field, automation, data collection, and administration are the most pressing concerns. Analytics of data is laborious to do despite the advantages listed above. There are many different types of material on social media, such as pictures, videos, and text messages, some of which do not adhere to standard Web protocols, such as headlines or graphical data that accompany these pieces. As a result, the majority of conventional data analysis methods designed for common online data are inadequate for social media research [299]. Working with visual data on social media comes with various challenges, such as decreasing information overload. There are several ways to acquire visual data from social media. Analyzing vast volumes of visual data generated in disaster zones is challenging. After a disaster, humanitarian organizations are usually tasked with looking through photos and videos for any important information that could have been captured on film. On the other hand, some social media images are raucous and disorderly, and they contain a lot of pointless and unnecessary information. Nobody has the time to go through all of this not relevant information and figure out what is significant [299].

Social media is also a place where misinformation may be spread through the use of fake information that is often provided for entertainment or promotional reasons. The public needs to recognize that validating the data obtained from social media pictures is an untapped resource. Obtaining location data for photos shared on social media is also a major challenge. Since most social media visual material does not include geolocation information, computer vision researchers have been challenged to develop a working prototype. As a result, they have attempted to identify GPS locations from pictures or streaming videos. Due to the rapid expansion of social media, various internal regulations have been implemented for social media use and have become increasingly relevant for information system security experts.

As a social scientist, one of the most critical challenges in computer vision is recognizing and identifying items in photographs and videos and tracking the movements of people and things over time. Searching for and categorizing objects in pictures is what is meant by the term "object detection". Detecting objects from social data images, might provide opportunities to improve classifications and to detect locations from social posts. Image recognition necessitates the assignment of labels to objects. Face detection identifies the locations of individual faces in a photograph. Detecting objects in this scenario is as simple as keeping an eye out for people's faces. In addition, 3D postings grab the viewer's attention and entice them to participate in social media activities. Uploading 3D photos is one of the finest ways to improve a company's business and increase younger audiences' interaction with their brand on social media; since 3D data may give more information than 2D images.

1.9 The Future of Personalization

The ever-growing production of social data has brought up a wide range of opportunities while posing particular challenges to individuals, societies, and businesses. The good side of the story is the availability of an enormous volume of data indicative of user preferences that social networks can exploit to provide interesting digital content tailored to users' needs [187]. The massive catalog of choices available for the users, potentially creates several unintended issues such as *Choice Overload*. Personalization and recommendation systems can address these issues by filtering out irrelevant content in social networks and generating recommendations of social content according to the preferences of the users [517, 519].

Social Recommender Systems are modern instances of such tools specifically designed to support online users when navigating in social networks and choosing the right content to consume. These systems actively observe the user behaviors, build user models, and generate a shortlist of the most relevant social content accordingly. The recommendations are then presented to the users through the designed interface of the social network. More particularly, social recommender systems are smart tools designed to operate in social networks and create (or enhance) the personalized experience of the users through the adoption of a wide range of approaches, including two major classes, i.e., *Collaborative Filtering (CF)* and *Content-based Filtering (CBF)* approaches [9, 304]. These approaches have been already applied in a wide range of application domains including the education domain [191], tourism [102], media domain [166], fashion domain [627], and even food domain [606].

The former class primarily focuses on utilizing the user preferences (e.g., likes/ dislikes, clicks, and ratings) provided by a large community of users, while the latter class focuses more on the exploitation of the item content (e.g., title, description, and genre). The classical collaborative filtering approaches compute the user-to-user or item-to-item similarities based on the co-rating patterns and exploit them for the recommendations. *Matrix Factorization (MF)* is a more complicated type of collaborative filtering [346, 347] that models users and items with a set of latent factors computed according to preferences data elicited from a large network of users.

Approaches within the content-based filtering class, put more emphasis on the exploitation of the item content and measuring the user preferences associated with a set of features describing the content. The content features can represent either a high-level or low-level description of the item content. In both cases, the content is modeled with a Vector Space Model associated with these features. A common technique in this category uses *K-Nearest Neighbors (KNN)* to measure the content similarities among items and then recommend items similar to those a user liked before [581]. For example, collaborative filtering may suffer from several challenges, such as the *Cold Start* problem, which happens when the recommender system has insufficient data to learn the user preferences and build recommendations accordingly. In reality, this problem can be intensified if a large number of users have provided little or no information about their personal preferences.

A noveler category of *Hybrid* recommendation approaches combines collaborative filtering with content-based filtering to enable social recommender systems to address the limitations of both approaches, when generating a more robust form of recommendation [106]. While this type of recommendation approach plays a significant role in improving the performance of the recommendation, other factors can still influence the quality of the recommendation. Some examples of such influential factors are the quantity, the distribution, and the quality of the preference data as the building blocks of user-profiles built by the system. Indeed, the more informative the available user preferences are, the higher the recommendation accuracy is. Hence, it is essential to keep acquiring new and valuable preferences from the users to maintain or improve the quality of the recommendation. This is especially true for the *Cold Start* stage, where a new user or a new item is added to the system [183, 199]. In such a scenario, the system has not yet obtained any data describing the tastes and preferences of the new users and hence may fail to generate relevant recommendations for them. Similarly, there might be a considerable number of items added to the system catalog, and none of the users have yet provided any feedback for them [184, 327].

Consider YouTube[25] as a notable example of a popular social network; there exist billions of users where a large subset of them are content creators. Such users constantly upload videos, reportedly, in the volume of thousands of hours (of videos) within a single minute. Social networks in this scale typically utilize advanced Machine Learning models to perform preference elicitation in addressing the above-noted challenges [197, 410]. Accordingly, they may explicitly request the new users to provide more of their preferences, e.g., by adding ratings or comments to several items carefully selected by the system and identified as the most informative ones [196, 216]. In such a case, the users (typically the new users) provide their preferences for such items enabling the system to build their initial profiles. This process is commonly referred to as the *Active Learning* [196, 528].

---

[25] https://youtube.com.

Cognitive Recommender System [69], introduced as a new type of data-driven, knowledge-driven, and cognition-driven Recommender Systems. Such Recommender Systems may benefit from learning algorithms such as, Personality2Vec [66] to enable the analysis of a customer's personality, behaviour, and attitude to facilitate the understanding of a user's preferences, detect changes in user preferences over time, and predict user's unknown favorites. They also enable exploring adaptive mechanisms to enable intelligent actions within the compound and changing environments. Chapter 8 describes more the above-noted topics and provides a comprehensive discussion on the latest research findings relevant to the research field of personalization and recommendation systems. The chapter begins with a discussion on an overview of the field and continues with discussing a range of important research works relevant to social recommendations, e.g., trust-aware recommendation [239], context-aware recommendation, and group recommendation. The chapter further extends the discussion by listing the most popular application domains and provides an overview of the specific characteristics of the data collected within those domains, and future potentials for personalization and recommendation approaches.

1.10 Social Data Analytics Applications

The rise of new social media has resulted in a notable growth of social data during the last few years. Social data comes in many different forms and textures and may be used to extract a wide range of information. Trust networks, sentiment data, and personality characteristics are examples of this type of information. As a result, a wide range of applications has emerged, resulting in substantial alterations in people's social life as well as several new economic prospects. For example, social data has been leveraged in developing customization tools, resulting in values that improve the customer experience while increasing revenue. We discuss several key elements of social data and potential applications, such as:

- *Social Data and Trust*: For several applications, social data may be a valuable source of information. Members of social media, for example, can form a vast network that represents the possible trust linkages among themselves. Social contagion refers to the spread of ideas and attitudes among those linked together because of trust relationships like these [135].
- *Bias in Social Data*: Recent studies have examined the possibility of social data being biased. It is possible to trace this kind of bias back to many fields. Thus, it may be seen from various angles. Bias is often defined as a departure from the norm, showing the presence of any statistical trends in social data [153, 218]. Biases in social data may be a result of how the data are gathered in social settings. According to the results of a recent study, biases may be divided into two categories: data biases and algorithmic biases [423].
- *Personality Detection from Social Data*: There is a predictable and consistent impact of people's personalities on their behaviors. Personality is a psycholog-

ical concept that refers to a person's recurring patterns of behavior and social communication [104]. This approach takes into consideration people's emotional, interpersonal, cognitive, behavioral, and incentive styles. It has been shown that personality has an impact on people's decisions and wants [313]. Individuals with similar personality qualities have activities that are common to both of their traits; thus, they are intricately connected [512]. Social media platforms may also be used to identify people based on their personality features. As an illustration, several studies have presented methods for gleaning personality qualities about people from their online accounts [47, 250, 254, 499].

- *Sentiment Analysis of Social Data*: A growing number of researchers and businesses are interested in sentiment analysis using social media data. As a general term, sentiment analysis refers to using Natural Language Processing (NLP) techniques to extract the hidden feelings included in written views. Artificial intelligence (AI) methods capable of identifying the polarity within textual data are widely used in sentiment analysis, an automated procedure. Such polarity may be found in the sentiment gleaned from user data, whether it is good or negative. Such remarks can be analysed to find hidden clues, possible strengths and flaws of particular items and notify the relevant firms.
- *Personalization with Social Data*: Personalization tools have become more important in the age of rapidly developing social networks when it comes to producing customization for the e-commerce business [492]. Without customization, choosing what to buy has never been more complex due to the fast growth of items and services offered by online retailers [326]. When it comes to solving this issue, personalization tools may significantly enhance the purchasing experience for customers by displaying product information, summarizing user comments, and making fair comparisons between various options. Modern algorithms based on AI approaches are often used in personalization tools to thoroughly analyze social data to learn about the individual tastes of users and provide recommendations appropriately [17].
- *Sales and Marketing (Create Successful Campaigns with Social Media Marketing Analytics)*: Even more subjective data suggests that social media analytics is beneficial for firms and marketing in general. Thus, companies may utilize social media data research to improve brand awareness by gaining knowledge of current industry trends and patterns. There are several advantages to adopting business analytics, including more profits from customers, lower operational expenses, and better results from marketing initiatives [81]. Using social media analytics, organizations can better understand their consumers' beliefs and behaviors and gauge the effectiveness of their online marketing campaigns. Additionally, it is anticipated that the knowledge gained would inspire new ideas for building a company's brand and keeping customers engaged with it. Organizational effectiveness benefits include faster time to market, higher levels of participation, greater agility in the supply chain, and better results from marketing campaigns. Since they use "soft" criteria, it is hard to say how they will affect financial outcomes. Social media analytics services will alter as a result of each of these driving forces.

- *Influence Maximization (Identifying Influencers for Your Brand and Industry)*: Social media networks has the potential to play significant roles both Sociologically and economically. Social networks provide new methods for delivering information to users, opening the door for many new applications. There are currently several applications that make extensive use of the massive increase of information available on the Internet and social networks, such as market research, product marketing, and identifying well-known individuals. Finding strategies to maximize the impact of each group member has been increasingly popular in recent years [586]. Influence maximization identifies the group of persons in a social community who maximizes the projected spread of influence throughout society by concentrating on this group. The social graph has dominated the research on this issue, but other forms of data, such as historical information, are just as important. This challenge seeks the people with the highest clout on social networks to aid your search for the most influential users. The research of influence propagation has also been carried out in regard to an extensive social network to assess the likelihood of knowledge diffusion. Each node in the social network is given a threshold using this method.
- *Situational Awareness (Discover Trending Topics)*: Using social media networks appears to be a key source of recent, true details on big news events, quickly giving a wealth of information. Social media posts on flooding catastrophes are tracked using text and image analysis. The use of social media is being scrutinized to see if the results achieved in one environment correspond to those achieved in another [333]. Several natural disasters in the last few decades have incurred enormous economic, ecological, and social consequences. The unpredictable nature of catastrophic occurrences makes it challenging to maintain comprehensive situational awareness to aid emergency response. Opinion polls are a tried-and-true method for gauging public sentiment following natural disasters, but they have limitations, are expensive, and are time-consuming. Thanks to social media, academics now have access to alternative data on widely debated topics. People may now publicly share their opinions and discuss current events, including natural disasters, on social media [325].
- *Social Media Information Discovery (from Topic Trends to Sentiment Ratio)*: Social media is an essential part of online businesses, which run on the Web and can be viewed via mobile and desktop devices. Because of the increasing number of people using social media, there is a growing need for methods and tools for analyzing large amounts of data. For example, sentiment analysis may be used to get an advantage from all of the publicly available user-generated content [27]. The major objective of marketing today is having a technology that can quickly discover information, such as what the news press is saying about a firm or a product Some well-known goods get a lot of press coverage, but the limits of basic grouping and simple summarization of known references make them difficult to evaluate. Using humans to read and summarise information quickly and cost-effectively is not viable to fulfill demand [251].
- *Linking Social Media Performance to Business and Revenue Growth*: Many people today use social media sites like Facebook and Twitter to collaborate,

network, and share information. Numerous businesses are turning to these tools to discover new markets and revenue streams. In reality, these resources are underutilized since there is no apparent connection between the performance of a firm and the resources it generates from these places. According to the conclusions of this investigation, company owners and financial advisors stand to gain from the information provided [475]. Businesses now use social media to revolutionize many aspects of their operations, from marketing to sales to economics to customer service. Client data collection and analysis have played a critical role in businesses' capacity to provide consumers with tailored services and goods due to these technologies. Online Apps, services, and tools are the major means people utilize social media to stay in touch with one another and share information. You may use social media to find out whether people desire your goods and to launch new innovative marketing tactics like word of mouth and viral marketing [258].

- *Performance Analysis of the Industry*: The use of social media for market analysis in the disciplines of economics and machine learning has become increasingly popular. Contrary to popular belief, most research demonstrates that social media concerns have an influence on the stock market as well [309]. Marketers use social media platforms to connect with current and potential customers. Companies must connect with customers if they are to offer information, engage with customers, learn, and meet societal needs. The use of social media can help you build a more extensive supplier network and improve the number of new contacts you make. The capacity to make better judgments is aided by the availability of additional social media outlets [644].

1.11 Goals, Structure, and Organization

Social data analytics have become a vital asset for organizations and governments. Applications may include anything from improving services and processes to understanding customer needs and personalizing recommendations. This book will focus on the important role of social data in data-centric computing and will cover a large body of knowledge in analyzing and understanding social data. Given that many "social data analysis" subjects such as querying and warehousing are covered well in the literature, the focus of this book will be on techniques for systematically engineering the social data to prepare them for analytics.

In particular, this book will cover a large body of knowledge in social data analytics, including organizing, curating, summarizing, and analyzing social data, as well as highlighting challenges, opportunities, and applications of social data analytics in the age of big data and Artificial Intelligence (AI). This book starts by introducing basic social data analytics concepts, describes state of the art in this space, and continues with deeper dives on different modern techniques for curating and summarizing social data as well as storytelling with social data and interactive visualization techniques. The book also provides a review of practical applications, including recommender systems, trust, and influence maximization.

Chapters Overview

Organizing Social Data. Chapter 2 presents techniques for organizing the large amount of data generated on social data islands such as Twitter and Facebook. This is important as continuous improvement in connectivity, storage, and data processing capabilities allow access to a data deluge from the big data generated on open, private, social, and IoT (Internet of Things) data islands. This chapter will introduce technologies from relational to NoSQL database management systems. It will also discuss modern technologies, including Data Lakes which facilitate storing raw data and let the data analyst decide how to curate them later.

Curating Social Data. One of the main challenges in understanding social data is to transform raw data into actionable insights. To achieve this goal, it will be vital to prepare and curate the raw data for analytics. Data curation has been defined as the active and ongoing management of data through its lifecycle of interest and usefulness. To address the importance of social data curation in social data analytics, in Chapter 3, we focus on curations tasks including cleaning, integration, transformation, and adding value. This chapter will also discuss modern technologies including the Knowledge Lake, i.e., a contextualized Data Lake that facilitates turning the raw data (stored in Data Lakes) into contextualized data and knowledge using extraction, enrichment, annotation, linking and summarization techniques.

Social Media Text Analytics. Every second, a huge amount of content in unstructured text format is generated on social networks. Text analytics and mining techniques can uncover insights such as sentiment analysis, entities, relations, and key phrases in such unstructured data. In Chapter 4, we provide an overview of text analytics, followed by an introduction to basic text processing, Sentiment and Emotion Analytics, Topic Extraction, Opinion Extraction, Text Classification, and Information Extraction. We will also highlight the challenges and opportunities in social media text analytics.

Social Media Image/Video Analytics. Photo and video sharing on social networking services are now quite popular. A considerable number of images and videos are posted every second on social networks. In this context, social image and video analytics play an important role in extracting meaningful information and insights from photos and videos posted on Online Social Networks. In Chapter 5, we provide an overview of image and video data analytics, followed by challenges and opportunities in the field. We discuss important topics, including image and video detection and recognition and storytelling with image and video data. We will also discuss modern topics such as analyzing and generating 3D posts on social media.

Summarizing Social Data. The ubiquitous availability of computing devices and the widespread use of the Internet have continuously generated a large amount of data. For example, the amount of available data on any social network could be far beyond humans' processing capacity to properly process, causing what is known as 'information overload'. To efficiently cope with large amounts of information and generate content with significant value to users, we require identifying, merging, and summarising information. In Chapter 6, we provide an overview of summarization techniques and discuss that social data summarization can help gather related information and collect it into a shorter format that enables answering complicated questions, gaining new insight, and discovering conceptual boundaries. We also focus on modern topics, including time-aware, opinion-based, and event-based summarization of social data.

Storytelling with Social Data. The business world is getting increasingly dynamic and inseparable from social data. As the scale of available social data grows ever larger, such data may hold tremendous amounts of potential value. In this context, insights need to be uncovered and translated into actions or business outcomes for deeper interpretations and better intelligence. To achieve this goal, data stories should combine data with narratives to reduce the ambiguity of social data, connect data with context, and describe a specific interpretation. In Chapter 7, we focus on advancing the scientific understanding of storytelling with social data. We define storytelling as an incremental and interactive process that enables analysts to turn insights into actions. We will discuss the related work in this domain and highlight the importance of allowing the analysts to communicate analysis findings, supporting evidence and evaluate the quality of the social data stories.

Social Data and Recommender Systems. The rapid growth of social networks has resulted in an enormous amount of social data generated every day. The massive volume, variety, and velocity of social data have led to undesired effects such as information pollution for online users. This has caused the users to feel desperate when navigating social networks and exposed them to choice overload when making certain choices among unlimited alternatives. Social Recommender Systems are digital tools that can tackle these problems through building personalization in social environments by exploiting user preferences learned from the data users generate in their online activities. In Chapter 8, we provide an overview of recommendation techniques along with challenges and opportunities in the field. We discuss important topics, including content recommendation, social, collaborative filtering, trust-aware recommendation, group recommendation, and application domains.

Social Data Analytics Applications. Finally, Chapter 9 provides an overview of novel applications of social data analytics, including personality detection from social data, understanding bias in social media, social Data and Trust, improving sales and marketing (e.g., create successful campaigns with social media marketing analytics), influence maximization (e.g., to identify influencers for your brand and industry), situational Awareness (e.g., discover trending topics), social media audience segmentation, social media information discovery (e.g., from Topic trends to Sentiment ratio), linking social media performance to business and revenue growth, and performance analysis of the industry.

2

Organizing Social Data

2.1 From Data to Big Data

In computing, data is information that has been translated into a form that is efficient for storage and processing. In social networks, this information can be generated on various islands of data, e.g., on Twitter[1], Facebook[2], Linkedin[3], Instagram[4], Tik-Tok[5], and Clubhouse[6]. This data can be in different formats, from text and image to audio and video. For example, when we take a photo using our cell phone, open a social network account, or post a piece of news on social media, we are generating data. From the storage point of view, data can be:

- *Structured Data*, e.g., the record of a user on a social network, is highly organized and easily decipherable by algorithms. Structured data can be easily defined by a schema, i.e., a structure described in a formal language supported by the database management system to facilitate organizing and interpreting information. Relational database management systems [144] (RDBMSs) typically support organizing structured data and require creating a schema for data before writing into the database, which is known as Schema-on-write.
- *Unstructured Data*, e.g., the text of a tweet or an image posted on Instagram, is the information that either does not have a pre-defined data model or is not or-

---

[1] https://Twitter.com/.

[2] https://www.facebook.com/.

[3] https://www.linkedin.com/.

[4] https://www.instagram.com/.

[5] https://www.tiktok.com/.

[6] https://www.clubhouse.com/.

ganized in a pre-defined manner, such as text, audio, video, images, and analog data. NoSQL database management systems (RDBMSs) [144] typically support organizing unstructured data and does not require creating a schema for data before writing into the database, which is known as Schema-on-read.

- *Semi-structured Data*, e.g., a Tweet on Twitter, is a form of structured data that requires a high-level schema to understand the data structure. However, this schema may describe some unstructured data embedded in the high-level structure. As an example, consider a tweet in Twitter that has a schema describing attributes such as: id (unique identity of the tweet), source (the utility used to post the Tweet), a user (the user who posted this Tweet), coordinates (the geographic location of this Tweet), text (The actual UTF-8 text of the status update), and entities (e.g., entities which have been parsed out of the text of the Tweet such as hashtags, URLs, and media). Traditional data management systems required very predictable structured formats for the data, and supported relational data with a fixed schema. Today, social data is generated in diverse forms from diverse sources. To handle the variety of such data, semi-structured data formats such as JSON[7], Avro[8], and XML[9] have been introduced as a standard, to store and exchange semi-structured data. In particular, semi-structured data does not require a prior definition of a fixed schema, and the schema can evolve over time, and new attributes could be added at any time. Moreover, semi-structured data may contain hierarchies of nested information.

2.1.1 Big Data

Big data refers to our ability to collect and analyze the ever-expanding amounts of data and metadata that we are generating every second! Organizing, Curating, Processing, Analysing, and Presenting this data is challenging and of high interest. Big data [537] is different from a large dataset. We have had supercomputers to deal with processing and analyzing a large data set. In particular, Big data can be seen as a massive number of small data islands from Private (Personal/Business), Open, Social, and IoT[10] (Internet of Things) Data [64].

Typical properties of big data include: wide physical distribution, diversity of formats, non-standard data models, independently-managed and heterogeneous semantics. Organizing, curating, analyzing, and presenting this data is challenging and of high interest. For example, as illustrated in Figure 2.1, consider a motivating scenario in a police investigation process, such as the Boston Marathon bombing[11]. In

---

[7] https://www.json.org/.

[8] https://avro.apache.org/.

[9] https://www.w3.org/standards/xml/core.

[10] The Internet of Things describes physical objects, that are embedded with sensors, processing ability, software, and other technologies, and that connect and exchange data with other devices and systems over the Internet or other communications networks.

[11] https://en.wikipedia.org/wiki/Boston_Marathon_bombing.

this scenario, the police investigator may need to understand the big data generated on various private, social, open, and IoT data islands, analyze them, and link them to historical police data. This is quite important, as modern police investigation processes are often highly complex, data-driven, and knowledge-intensive [63, 74]. Understanding and analyzing big data will facilitate communicating analysis findings, supporting evidence, and making decisions in this context. Figure 2.1 illustrates a big data problem scenario in policing [548].

Fig. 2.1 A scenario in police investigation, to understand the big data problem.

2.1.2 NoSQL: The Need for New Database Management Systems

Social data is large-scale, never-ending, ever-changing, and arrives in diverse forms from various sources at irregular time intervals. Therefore, the first challenge would be to store the vast amounts of social data generated every second (*Volume*), which contains increasingly different types of data (*Variety*), and generated at high speed (*Velocity*). To deal with the high volume of social data, with the aim to support scaling applications, two main approaches could be used:

- *Scale Up*: Keep the same number of Systems/Servers, but migrate each system to a larger System. For example, changing from a server with 16 CPU cores and a one TB storage system to a server with 64 CPU cores and a 100 TB storage system.
- *Scale Out*: When the workload exceeds the capacity of a server, the workload is spread out across several servers. This technique, also referred to as Clustering, supports scaling applications that have a loosely coupled architecture. In particular, it is cheaper to buy ten 100 TB storage systems than it is to buy a single 1 PB storage system.

Velocity, refers to the rate at which new data enters the system as well as the rate at which the data must be processed. In the past, social media applications used to capture only the data about the main entities, such as posts and user information. But recently, social media applications started to capture user activities such as to every mouse click in searching, browsing and comparing. This, in turn, will heavily increase the velocity of the social data. The velocity of social data processing can be broken down into:

- *Streaming*: Social networks are quickly becoming the primary medium for sharing the news and discussing what is happening in the world. For example, Twitter is now considered one of the fastest news sources globally, as it produces rich data streams for immediate insights into ongoing matters and the conversations around them. Stream processing, i.e., a big data technology that focuses on the real-time processing of continuous streams of data in motion, is now supported by many big data platforms such as Apache Kafka[12], Amazon Kinesis[13], Microsoft Azure Stream Analytics[14], Apache Flink[15], and IBM Streaming Analytics[16].
- *Feedback Loop*, i.e., a process in which the outputs of a system are circled back and used as inputs, is an essential step in analyzing the data to produce actionable results. As an example, the browsers started to capture activities on users on the client-side, send that information to recommendation engines, with the goal to personalize the services for each user. For example, visit a Website to book a flight to travel to Australia; later, when you log in to your social media account, e.g., Instagram or Facebook, you may see advertisements around cheap flights to Australia. In particular, this process may use customer activity and feedback to create better recommendations [69, 651].

From the Variety point of view, the structured, semi-structured, and unstructured data generated on social media can be organized in various database management systems. For example, information stored in Relational Database Management Systems (RDBMS) is known as structured data because it is represented in a strict format and has a specific Schema. RDBMSs use concepts such as Entity, Database, Tables, Rows, Columns, Primary Keys, Foreign Keys, and Joins to ensure that all data follows the structures and constraints specified in the schema. In an RDBMS, social data can be: (i) stored as a collection of tuples that groups attributes; and (ii) visualized as tables, where the tuples are the rows, and the attributes form the columns. Tables can be related to each other through specific columns, and each row in a table has at least one unique attribute. Structured Query Language (SQL) can be used to query and analyze the data persisted in a relational database. However, aiming to organize the social data, Relational Databases may have several challenges, including:

---

[12] https://kafka.apache.org/.

[13] https://aws.amazon.com/kinesis/.

[14] https://docs.microsoft.com/en-us/azure/stream-analytics/.

[15] https://flink.apache.org/.

[16] https://www.ibm.com/au-en/cloud/streaming-analytics.

- Storing large volumes of social data that often have little to no structure could be challenging and expensive.
- Scaling Out and making the most of cloud computing and storage could be challenging and expensive.
- Relational Databases will slow down Agile sprints.

The above challenges highlight the need for a new generation of database management systems that are not based on the traditional Relational Database Model. To address this need, NoSQL databases are introduced as non-tabular databases that scale-out easily and can persist large amounts of data, supporting from unstructured to semi-structured and structured data. The main types of NoSQL databases include:

- *Key-Value Databases*, which are conceptually the simplest of the NoSQL data models, where data will be stored as a collection of Key-Value pairs. The *key* is an identifier for a value, and can be anything such as Text, Document (XML/J-SON), or Image. The Key-Value Database does not attempt to understand the content of the value, and it is the role of the application to analyze and understand the content. It is essential to highlight that there are no Foreign Keys used in Key-Value Databases, and relationships cannot be tracked among keys at all. This feature greatly simplifies the work that the Database Management System (DBMS) must perform, making the Key-Value DB extremely fast and scalable. In such a database, Key-Value Pairs are typically organized into BUCKETs. A Bucket can roughly be thought of as the Key-Value Database equivalent of a table in RDBMSs. Key-Value must be unique within a bucket, but they can be duplicated across buckets. All queries are performed using the bucket and the key, which means it is impossible to query the data based on anything in the value component of the key-value pair. Operations on Key-Value databases are relatively simple and include GET (read), STORE (insert/update) and DELETE operations. Examples of Key-value databases include: Dynamo[17] (developed by Amazon), Riak[18] (developed by Basho), Redis[19] (developed by Redis Labs), and Voldemort[20] (developed by LinkedIn).
- *Document Databases*, are conceptually similar to Key-Value Databases, and can be considered as a sub-type of Key-Value Databases. The main difference is that the $Value$ component can only contain semi-structured documents, where the document can be in any encoded format, such as XML and JSON. Unlike Key-Value Databases, the Document Databases do attempt to understand the content of the Value; that is why the documents provide a semi-structured format to support understanding a high-level schema. Document Databases group documents into logical groups called Collections. Documents may be retrieved by specifying the collection and the Key, as well as the content of tags. Examples of document databases include: MongoDB[21] (developed by Mon-

---

[17] https://aws.amazon.com/dynamodb/.

[18] https://riak.com/.

[19] https://redis.io/.

[20] http://www.project-voldemort.com/voldemort/.

[21] https://www.mongodb.com/.

goDB, Inc.), CouchDB[22] (developed by Apache), OrientDB[23] (developed by OrientDB, Ltd.), and RavenDB[24] (developed by Hibernating Rhinos).

- *Column-oriented Databases*, stores the data in blocks by column instead of by rows. This type of database: (i) works very well for systems that are primarily used to run queries over few columns but many rows, as is done in many reporting systems and data warehouses; and (ii) would be inefficient for processing transactions since Insert, Update and Delete activities would be very disk intensive. Examples of Column-oriented databases include: HBase[25] (developed by Apache), Cassandra[26] (developed by Facebook), and Hypertable[27] (developed by Hypertable, Inc.).

- *Graph Databases*, are a NoSQL database designed based on the graph theory to store data about relationship-rich environments. Graph is a mathematical and Computer Science field that models relationships (edges) among objects called nodes. Modeling and storing data about connections is the focus of Graph Databases [70]. The nature of social data is very well fit to be represented and persisted using graphs. For example, Facebook introduced a social graph to map the relationships among users in social media. Facebook also introduced a Graph Search to support semantic search over the Facebook social graph. Graph Databases, similar to relational databases, are Aggregate Ignorant. This means that the data is not collected/aggregated around a central topic or entity (unlike Key-Value, Document, and Column family databases). In particular, aggregate ignorant models do not organize the data into collections based on a central entity. Therefore, data about each topic will be stored separately, and joins are used to connect individual pieces of data (often called SHARDs). A database shard is a horizontal partition of data in a database or search engine. Examples of Graph databases include: Neo4J[28] (developed by Neo4J), ArangoDB[29] (developed by ArangoDB, LLC.), and Graphbase[30] (developed by FactNexus).

2.2 Capturing Social Data

Multiple methods are available for capturing social data. In modern enterprises, data services play an essential role in capturing social data [114, 267, 513, 659]. For example, when an enterprise wishes to controllably share social data (or related insights) with its business partners, via the Internet, it can use data services to provide

---

[22] http://couchdb.apache.org/.

[23] https://orientdb.org/.

[24] https://ravendb.net/.

[25] https://hbase.apache.org/.

[26] https://cassandra.apache.org/.

[27] https://www.hypertable.com/.

[28] https://neo4j.com/.

[29] https://www.arangodb.com/.

[30] https://graphbase.ai/.

mechanisms to find out which information can be accessed, what are the semantics of the data, and how the data can be integrated from multiple enterprises. In particular, data services are "software components that address these issues by providing rich metadata, expressive languages, and APIs for service consumers to send queries and receive data from service providers" [114].

A Web service, i.e., a method of communication between two electronic devices over the Web [35], can be specialized, as a data service, to encapsulate a wide range of data-centric operations. These operations need to offer a semantically richer view of their underlying data to use or integrate entities returned by different data services [114, 659]. Microsoft's Windows Communication Foundation (WCF) data-services framework[31], which enables the creation and consumption of data services for the Web, and Oracle's Data Service Integrator (ODSI[32]), which provides a wide array of data services designed to improve data access from disparate data sources for a wide range of clients, are the two of several commercial frameworks that can be used to achieve this goal.

In this context, Service Oriented Architecture (SOA) applications [35] will often need to invoke a service to obtain data, operate locally on that data, and then notify the service about changes that the application wishes to make to the data. For example, the Open SOA Collaboration's Service Data Objects (SDO) specification [513] addresses these needs by defining client-side programming models, e.g., for operating on data retrieved from a data service and for XML serializing objects, and their transmission changes back to a data service [114]. In particular, the capturing data is bound to various rules imposed by data owners. The consumers should find and select relevant data services and utilize the data 'as a service'.

Data as a service (DaaS) is based on the concept that the data can be provided on demand to the user, regardless of geographic or organizational separation of provider and consumer [609]. In particular, data services are created to integrate and enable a collection of data sources in an easy way. These services can be used in mashups, i.e., Web applications developed starting from contents and services available online, to use and combine data from two or more sources to create new services. In particular, data services will be integral for designing, building, and maintaining SOA applications. For example, Oracle's ODSI supports creating and publishing collections of interrelated data services, similar to Data-Spaces.

Data-Spaces are an abstraction in data management that aims to manage many diverse interrelated data sources in enterprises in a convenient, integrated, and principled fashion. Data-Spaces are different from data integration approaches because they provide base functionality over all data sources, regardless of how integrated they are. For example, a Data-Space can provide keyword search over its data sources. More sophisticated operations (e.g., mining and monitoring certain sources) can be applied to queried sources in an incremental, pay-as-you-go fashion [269]. Data-Spaces Support Platforms (DSSPs), have been introduced as a key

---

[31] http://msdn.microsoft.com/en-us/data/bb931106.

[32] https://www.oracle.com/middleware/technologies/data-service-integrator.html.

agenda for the data management field and to provide data integration and querying capabilities on (semi-)structured data sources in an enterprise [269, 543].

Cloud has become a new universal platform for data storage and management, and a new class of data services introduced for providing data management in the cloud [626]. In practice, data warehousing, partitioning, and replication are well-known strategies to achieve the availability, scalability, and performance improvement goals in the distributed data management world. Moreover, database-as-a-service is proposed as an emerging paradigm for data management in which a third-party service provider hosts a database as a service [267]. Data services can be employed on top of such cloud-based storage systems to address challenges such as availability, scalability, elasticity, load balancing, fault tolerance, and heterogeneous environments in data services. For example, Amazon Simple Storage Service (S3[33]) is an online public storage Web service offered by Amazon Web Services[34].

2.3 Organizing Social Data

Organizing social data requires arranging data in a coherent form and systematizing its retrieval and processing. In today's modern enterprises, related social data comes from many sources and can be used for multiple purposes. The social data inputs are enormous and need to be organized and stored for processing. Organizing social data is challenging as (over time) new data sources are becoming accessible, data streams change, and data usage (how we use and process social data) evolves. Even, the historical social data is not necessarily static and unchanging. Another challenge is the size of social data, where there is a need for big data platforms and techniques to process vast amounts of unstructured data. For example, only on Twitter, there are around 6000 tweets sent every second, which is close to half a billion tweets each day, and that is equal to 12 TB of tweets generated each day[35].

To organize the social data, the first step is gathering and integration of social data sources from various, potentially heterogeneous, systems and services. In general, this step involves several phases [65]: (i) pre-processing: is required to detect errors and inconsistencies of heterogeneous event logs; (ii) transformation and cleaning: depending on the number of data sources and their degree of heterogeneity of the social data, a large number of data transformation and cleaning steps may have to be executed; (iii) verification: the correctness and effectiveness of a transformation workflow should be tested and evaluated; and (iv) curation: data transformations deal with schema/data translation and integration, and with filtering and aggregating social data to be prepared for adding value and contextualization. To address the importance of data curation in social data analytics, in Chapter 3, we focus on curations tasks including cleaning, integration, transformation, and adding value. This chapter will also discuss modern technologies including the Knowledge Lake, i.e., a

---

[33] https://aws.amazon.com/s3/.

[34] http://aws.amazon.com/.

[35] https://www.oberlo.com/blog/Twitter-statistics.

contextualized Data Lake that facilitates turning the raw data (stored in Data Lakes) into contextualized data and knowledge using extraction, enrichment, annotation, linking and summarization techniques.

The next step is providing techniques to extract, enrich, and contextualize items and entities from social data. In this context, most information items in social data (such as keywords, phrases, named entities, and topics) could be potentially interconnected through background and domain-specific knowledge that can provide rich semantic information. Accordingly, such information items and their relationships can be modeled using graphs to understand the social data properly. For example, Facebook introduced social graph modeling and graph search[36] to extract hidden insight from the Facebook data. Since graphs form a complex and expressive data type, methods are needed to organize and index the graph data. Existing database models, including the relational model, lack native support for advanced data structures such as graphs [71, 73]. In particular, as the graph data increases in size and complexity, it becomes essential that a database system can manage it. There are several approaches for managing graphs in a database. A line of related work extended a commercial RDBMS engine. For example, Oracle provides a commercial DBMS for modeling and manipulating graph data [14]. Some other works [80] used general-purpose relational tables to support graph structure data, e.g., triplestore, which is a special-purpose database for the storage and retrieval of RDF [14] (Resource Description Framework).

A new stream of work used MapReduce [161] for processing vast amounts of unstructured data in a massively parallel way. Hadoop [641], the open-source implementation of MapReduce, provides a distributed file system (i.e., HDFS[37]) and a high-level language for data analysis, i.e., Pig[38]. For example, a new stream of work [71] introduced a framework and a set of methods to support scalable graph-based OLAP analytics over big data, stored in open, private, and social data islands. The proposed platform facilitates the analytics over large graphs by summarizing the graph and providing multiple views at different granularity [241, 243].

2.4 Warehousing Social Data

To analyze social data, it is possible to collect the captured and organized data into a data warehouse, using extract, transform, load (ETL) tools. Then we can leverage Online analytical processing (OLAP) technology to organize large databases and support complex analysis [71]. In this context, the social data warehousing presents interesting challenges [353]: (i) outsourcing: developing ad-hoc solutions for warehousing and reporting on social data is not a sustainable model; (ii) social data abstraction: social data may contain spatial, temporal, cultural, and contextual details. Accordingly, the separation between the external interface of objects and internal

---

[36] https://developers.facebook.com/docs/graph-api/.

[37] http://hadoop.apache.org/.

[38] http://pig.apache.org/.

data handling and manipulation could provide more insight and facilitates analytics; (iii) social data evolution: social data analytics relates to the process of gathering, storing, and analyzing that social data. This is quite important as a social data's content, and context could evolve as it is shared and viewed by different social users over time.

Considering the challenges mentioned above, and in the domain of social data analytics, it is essential to devise a method to minimize the impact of changes and quickly modify and re-test the ETL (extract, transform, and load) procedures and the warehouse model. To address these challenges, the notion of Knowledge Lake [62, 65] presented as the foundation for intelligently warehousing social data by automatically curating the raw data and preparing them for deriving insights. To support warehousing for social data, there is a need to provide users with a way to model the abstraction. This will help to understand the high-level applications. Moreover, there is a need for an ETL mechanism that, based on similar social data generated on different social data islands, specify how the abstracted social data for each island of data (e.g., Twitter or Facebook) is populated and maintained. To populate the social data warehouse, it is necessary to first extract the data from the different sources into the landing tables of the staging area. In this context, data services can play an essential role in capturing, organizing, and warehousing related social data.

2.5 Social Data Provenance

Metadata is the data that provides information about other data, which can help users correctly understand the data. Metadata (e.g., descriptive, structural, and administrative metadata) can be generated manually or automatically. Tracing is a mechanism to generate metadata. For example, when we use our cell phone, a set of algorithms can trace our movement (location services), what Apps we are using, and how frequently. Or, a social network App can trace the activities of a user, including: which days of the week and what time of the days the user is more active, what sort of content the user liked or reshared, and what type of people (e.g., from personality, behavior and attitude viewpoints [66, 67]) the user is following. Metadata can also help in generating the story of a digital object from present time back to its derivation, i.e., provenance [77] (the documentation of an object's lifecycle), including: who created the file, on which system (e.g., IP address) and when, and how the digital object evolved over time and more.

Prior work on modeling and representing provenance metadata [77, 129, 223] (e.g., lineage, where-provenance, why-provenance, dependency-provenance, how-provenance, and provenance-traces models) model provenance as a directed acyclic graph [14], where the focus is on modeling the process that led to a piece of data. They present vocabularies to model activities and their causal dependency, i.e., the relationship between an activity (the cause) and a second activity (the effect). The second activity is understood as a consequence of the first. For example, the Open

Provenance Model (OPM) [440] (which proposed to design a standard graph data model and vocabulary for provenance), presents graph nodes as:

- *data artifacts*: defined as a product of human intelligence and effort, and is classified as tangible such as a physical object, and intangible such as a digital representation of an object;
- *processes*: defined as an action or series of actions performed on or caused by artifacts, and resulting in new artifacts), and *agents* (i.e., contextual entity acting as a catalyst of a process, enabling, facilitating, controlling, affecting its execution such as people and services);
- *Relationships*: defined as relations between sets of information items. There are five causal relationships recognized in OPM: a process 'used' an artifact, an artifact 'was generated by' a process, a process 'was triggered by' a process, an artifact 'was derived from' an artifact, and a process 'was controlled by' an agent.

In a dynamic world, social data changes, so the graphs representing data provenance evolve over time. It is crucial to be able to reproduce a piece of social data or the process that led to that social data for a specific point in time. For example, this could be a critical application in *understanding fake news*. Achieving this goal requires modeling *time* as a first-class citizen in the provenance models. Times, intervals, and versioning can be essential in understanding provenance graphs as the structure of such graphs evolves. To address this challenge, Temporal Provenance Model [72, 78] has been introduced to highlight the need for explicit representation of temporal information in provenance models. TPM offers an efficient approach for analyzing and querying provenance information with respect to time. In particular, TPM introduced a time-aware graph data model for provenance and a query language to query and analyze these graphs.

To facilitate summarizing large provenance graphs, in TPM, two concepts are introduced: (i) *timed folder*, i.e., a placeholder for a group of inter-related time-evolving entities; and (ii) *timed path*, i.e., a placeholder for the set of entities that are related to each other through transitive relationships. These relationships may evolve over time, e.g., to show the evolution of the historical path of an information item (such as a post on Facebook) to its origin. Timed folders can be used to: (i) store and represent the result of provenance queries over TPM graphs, e.g., retrieving the provenance graph of snapshots of objects or group of related objects over time; and (ii) partition TPM graphs into various temporal phases which can simplify the discovery of temporal relationship among provenance graph entities over time. Timed paths can be used to store and represent the results of path queries over TPM graphs, e.g., derivation queries that retrieve historical path(s) from an object to its origin over time. Timed folders and paths show their evolution for the time period they represent and can be used for further querying.

Provenance has an essential role in understanding social data and discovering facts and insights in novel applications. This may include tracking down a fake news on social media, understanding bias in social media, improving sales and marketing (e.g., create successful campaigns with social media marketing analytics), influence maximization (e.g., to identify influencers for organizations' brand and industry), situational Awareness (e.g., discover trending topics), social media audience segmentation, social media information discovery (e.g., from topic trends to sentiment ratio), linking social media performance to business and revenue growth, and performance analysis of the industry. In the following sections, we study the related work in provenance into three main areas: provenance representation, temporal graphs and databases, and graph query languages:

2.5.1 Provenance Representation

Many provenance models [77, 129, 223] have been presented in several domains (e.g., databases, scientific workflows, and the Semantic Web), motivated by notions such as influence, dependence, and causality. For example, why-provenance models have influences that a source data had on the existence of the data. Where-provenance focuses on the dependency to the location(s) in the source data from which the data was extracted. How-provenance represents the causality of an action or series of actions performed on or caused by source data. Open Provenance Model [440] focuses on the causality dependency among data artifacts, the process which generates them, and a contextual entity or entities acting as a catalyst of the process. Temporal Provenance Model (TPM) [72, 78] introduced a graph data model for organizing a set of entities as graph nodes and time-aware relationships as edges of the graph. In TPM, entities and relationships are represented as a directed graph $G_{(\tau_1, \tau_2)} = (V_{(\tau_1, \tau_2)}, E_{(\tau_1, \tau_2)})$, where $V_{(\tau_1, \tau_2)}$ is a set of nodes representing instances of entities in time or timed folder/path nodes added to the graph between a time period of τ_1 and τ_2, and $E_{(\tau_1, \tau_2)}$ is a set of directed edges representing relationships among nodes. It is possible to capture the evolution of the graph $G_{(\tau_1, \tau_2)}$ between a time period of τ_1 and τ_2. Such a temporal model could be a good solution fit for collecting and exchanging metadata in social networks.

Discovering historical paths through provenance graphs forms the basis of many provenance query languages. In ProQL [328] a query takes a provenance graph as an input, matches parts of the input graph according to path expression, and returns a set of paths as the result of the query. PQL [283] uses a semi-structured data model for handling provenance and extends a query language for traversing and querying provenance graphs. NetTrails [684] proposes a declarative platform for interactively querying network provenance in a distributed system, in which query execution performs a traversal of the provenance graph. RDFProv [123] is an optimized framework for scientific workflow provenance querying and management. Missie et al. [433] present a provenance model and query language for collection-oriented workflow systems (e.g., Taverna). They emphasize querying the provenance of the collection of activities. These related activities are not considered as first-class objects in the proposed graph. Moreover, they do not support modeling, querying, and analyzing the evolution of a group of related entities over time.

2.5.2 *Temporal Databases and Graphs*

Time is an essential aspect of all real-world data, and it is critical to model the temporal dimension of social data and metadata. Considering time as an additional dimension in social data will directly affect the process that led to that data, i.e., its provenance. Temporal databases enable retrieving multiple snapshots (versions) of data artifacts at different points in time [435]. However, a temporal database does not capture necessary information for social data provenance, such as activities performed on the data, agents acting on the data, and the relationships among different versions of artifacts at various points in time. Annotation techniques [171] represent another perspective to model temporal relationships. In this technique, system entities are (optionally) labeled with time offsets. This method considers well-designed systems of interacting components and analyzes data within a specific narrow domain. Using temporal annotations will loosen the semantics of time, as the timestamp of data would capture the state and time for a snapshot but not the temporal evolution history of the artifact and the version of the artifact at each point in time.

In recent years, a plethora of work [429] has focused on temporal graphs since, in many applications, information is best represented and stored as graphs. The focus of temporal graphs is to model evolving, time-varying, and dynamic networks of data. They capture a snapshot of various states of the graph over time. For example, Ren et al. [507] proposed a historical graph structure to maintain analytical processing on such evolving graphs. Moreover, authors in [507] proposed approaches to transform an existing graph into a similar temporal graph to discover and describe the relationship between the internal object states. In Temporal Provenance Model (TPM) [78], a temporal provenance model is proposed to capture the provenance of time-sensitive data where this data can be modeled as a temporal graph. Also, the set of proposed abstractions in TPM provides efficient mechanisms for time-aware querying of temporal provenance graphs.

2.6 Data Lakes

The production of knowledge from ever-increasing amount of social data is seen by many organizations as an increasingly important capability that can complement the traditional analytics sources [75]. In this context, modern data-oriented applications deal with various types of data - unstructured, semi-structured, and structured - such as tweets, documents, videos, and images. For example, consider a police investigation application. Once a crime has been reported, an investigator will need to deal with a wealth of digital information generated through social networks, blogs, online communities, and mobile applications, which forms a complex Data Lake [548]: a collection of datasets that holds a vast amount of data gathered from various data islands. As another example, consider an analyst interested in analyzing the Government Budget through engaging the public's thoughts and opinions on social networks [65]. To achieve this, the analyst may need to deal with a wealth of digital information generated through social networks, blogs, online communities, and mobile applications, which forms a complex Data Lake [61]. In the Data Lake, organizing and indexing the growing volume of internal data and metadata is challenging and requires a vast amount of knowledge to deal with dozens of new databases and indexing technologies.

In particular, for an analyst who is dealing with the data layer for organizing, indexing, and querying different types of data - from structured entities to be stored in relational databases to large volume of open data to be organized using appropriate NoSQL databases such as MongoDB[39] - various skills and experiences may be required:

- How to store information items (from structured entities to unstructured documents)?
- What technology to use for persisting the data (from Relational to NoSQL databases)?
- How to deal with the large volume of data generated continuously (from Key-value and document to object and graph store)?
- How to trace and persist information about data (from descriptive to administrative)?
- What technology to use for indexing the data/metadata?
- How to query the Data Lake (from SQL to full-text search)?

The notion of a Data Lake has been coined to address this challenge and to convey the concept of a centralized repository containing limitless amounts of raw (or minimally curated) data stored in various data islands. The rationale behind the Data Lake is to store raw data and let the data analyst decide how to curate them later.

2.6.1 Data Lake as a Service

The Data Lake as a Service was introduced as a centralized repository that runs on a cloud computing platform and provides access to a set of databases as-a-service. CoreDB [61] is a good example of the Data Lake as a Service. CoreDB is an open-source complete database service that powers multiple relational and NoSQL (key-/value, documents, and graph stores) database-as-a-service for developing Web data applications, i.e., data-driven Web applications. It powers relational, NoSQL (key-/value, document, and graph stores), and full-text search queries through a simple REST API. CoreDB enables analysts to build a Data Lake, create relational and NoSQL datasets within the Data Lake and CRUD (Create, Read, Update and Delete) and query entities in those datasets. CoreDB exposes the power of Elasticsearch[40], a search engine based on Apache Lucene[41], to support a powerful index and full-text

---

[39] https://www.mongodb.com/.

[40] https://www.elastic.co/.

[41] https://lucene.apache.org/.

search. CoreDB has a built-in design to enable top database security threats (Authentication, Access Control, and Data Encryption) along with Tracing and Provenance support. CoreDB weaves all these services together at the application layer and offers a single REST API to organize, index, and query the data and metadata in a Data Lake. Figure 2.2 illustrates the architecture and the main components of the proposed Data Lake as a Service in CoreDB.

2.6.2 Index and Federated Search

A database index allows a query to efficiently retrieve data from a database. In Data Lakes, indexes are related to specific datasets but should be managed together to facilitate the federated search over the Data Lake. Federated search is a technique that can be used to search multiple data sources in the Data Lake at once. With federated search, it would be possible to retrieve information from data islands in the Data Lake (from relational to NoSQL) with just one query. To achieve this goal, techniques such as full-text search can be used for searching a single computer-stored document or a collection in a full-text database. Full-text search is distinguished from searches based on metadata or parts of the original texts represented in databases (such as titles, abstracts, selected sections, or bibliographical references). Search engines such as Elasticsearch[42] can be leveraged in a Data Lake to provide a distributed, multitenant-capable full-text search engine. Data Lakes can expose the power of Elasticsearch without the operational burden of managing it by developers. In particular, when the user enables indexing while creating a dataset, the entities will be automatically indexed for powerful Lucene[43] queries. The Lucene engine examines all of the words in every stored data object as it tries to match search criteria. Considering that Elasticsearch is a search engine based on Lucene, it is also possible to search queries such as Wildcard, Fuzzy, Proximity, and Range in a Data Lake [61].

A Data Lake may enable the power of standard SQL with full ACID transaction capabilities for querying data held in relational databases and NoSQL databases [144]. For example, it is possible to send a SQL query to be applied to the datasets created in the Data Lake. To achieve this, it is possible to leverage Apache Phoenix[44] to take the SQL query and compile it into native NoSQL store APIs. Moreover, to support queries that need to join data from multiple datastores in the Data Lake, it is possible to leverage technologies such as Apache Drill[45]. For example, the analyst may be required to join a tweet collection stored in MongoDB with a location entry (e.g., Australia) stored in MySQL. That, to support such queries over the Data Lake, the developer requires to co-locate Apache Drill and the datastores on the same nodes in the cluster.

---

[42] https://www.elastic.co/elasticsearch/.

[43] https://lucene.apache.org/.

[44] https://phoenix.apache.org/.

[45] https://drill.apache.org/.

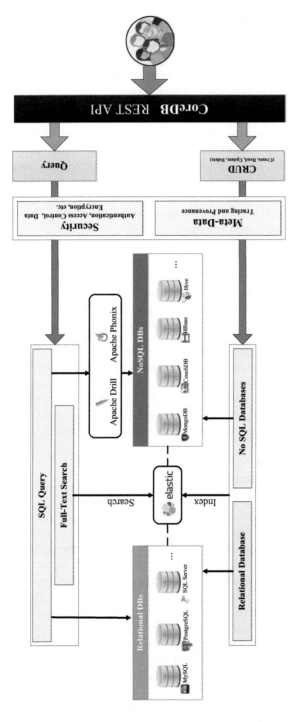

Fig. 2.2 The architecture and the main components of the proposed Data Lake as a Service in CoreDB [61].

2.6.3 Security and Access Control

Database servers and Data Lakes are essential systems in virtually all organizations. They store critical information that is vital for organizations. Data Lakes should have a built-in design to support top database security threats, such as:

- *Weak Authentication* [42], i.e., cryptographic authentication between previously unknown parties without relying on trusted third parties. User authentication methods and technologies include: Password-based, Multi-factor, Certificate-based, Biometric, and Token-based authentication. Poor or missing authentication schemes allow an adversary to anonymously execute functionality within the Data Lake and unauthorized access information, using different types of unauthorized access such as: Tailgating, Collusion, Pushing, Passbacks, Fraudulent Use of Cards, and Door Propping; and
- *Weak system configuration* [298], i.e., a flaw in security settings, such as failing to auto-encrypt files, could leave the entire Data Lake vulnerable to an attack. Denial-of-service (DoS) and distributed denial-of-service (DDoS) attacks, Man-in-the-middle (MitM) attacks, Phishing and spear-phishing attacks, Drive-by attack, Password attack, SQL injection attack, Cross-site scripting (XSS) attack, Eavesdropping attack, and Malware attack.

In particular, a Data Lake should support identification and Authentication requirements, System Privilege and Object Access Control, and Data Encryption. For example, each user may be identified and authenticated by the database system and has different access levels (e.g., create, read, update, and delete) to system entities by supporting Roles, Responsibilities, and Privileges, System and Object Privileges. Privileges are typically provided directly to users or through roles.

2.7 Concluding Remarks and Discussion

Many organizations see knowledge production from an ever-increasing amount of social data as an increasingly important capability that can complement the traditional analytics sources. This process heavily depends on properly organizing the large data generated on online social media platforms every second. Organizing social data may involve processes to persist and categorize social data to make it more usable. Organizing social data is a challenging task, due to the high volume, variety, and velocity of social data. This chapter reviewed various database management technologies from relational to NoSQL and data warehouses as the foundation for data analytics. We highlighted the importance of data services and discussed modern technologies such as Data Lakes which facilitate storing raw data and let the data analyst decide how to curate them later. Data Lake as a Service facilitates managing multiple database technologies and enable weaving them together at the application layer. This will heavily reduce the system set up phases and enable the analyst to focus on the conceptual layer and novel applications.

Cloud computing-based data warehousing technologies such as Snowflake[46], of-fers a cloud-based data storage and analytics service, i.e., Data Warehouse as a Ser-vice. The main difference between a Data Lake and a Data Warehouse is that Data Lakes designed to store raw data (Structured, Semi-Structured, Unstructured data) however, data warehouses can only store processes data (Structured data). More-over, Data Lakes are designed for low cost storage but data warehouses are expen-sive for large data volumes. In particular, Data Lakes are highly agile (configured and re-configured as needed), and data warehouses are less agile (fixed configura-tion). From the user point of view, data scientists and analysts will use the raw data stored in Data Lakes to understand the raw data and breath semantics and struc-tures to the raw data. The new structured and processed data will then be stored in a data warehouse, and business analysts will use data warehouses for advanced analytics and insight discovery. The next chapter will focus on social data curation and techniques to transform raw data into actionable insights.

---

[46] https://www.snowflake.com/.

3

Curating Social Data

3.1 Social Data Curation: Cleaning, Integration, and Transformation

Social technologies have transformed businesses from a platform for private data content consumption to where social network workers actively contribute to content production and opinion-making. For example, governments started to extract knowledge and derive insights from vastly growing social data to improve their services [63]. A key challenge in analyzing social data is to understand the raw data generated by social actors and prepare it for analytic tasks [65, 69]. For example, tweets in Twitter are generally unstructured (contain text and images), sparse (offer a limited number of characters), suffer from redundancy (the same tweet re-tweeted), and prone to slang words and misspellings. In this context, it is vital to transform the raw social data (e.g., a tweet on Twitter or a Post on Facebook) into contextualized data and knowledge. This task, known as data curation, involves identifying relevant data sources, extracting data and knowledge, cleansing (or cleaning), maintaining, merging, enriching, and linking data and knowledge.

The primary step in social data curation would be to clean and correct the raw data. This is vital as, for example, in Twitter with only 140 characters to convey your thoughts, social workers usually use abbreviations, acronyms, and slang that cannot be detected using automatic Machine Learning (ML) and Natural Language Processing (NLP) algorithms [15]. Accordingly, information extracted from tweets is often enriched with metadata on geolocation, in the absence of which the extracted information would be difficult to interpret and meaningfully utilize. Data curation thus acts as the glue between raw data and analytics, providing an abstraction layer that relieves users from time-consuming, tedious, and error-prone curation tasks. This section discusses main curation tasks, including identifying relevant data sources, ingestion, cleaning, extracting data and knowledge, maintaining, merging, enriching, and linking data and knowledge.

3.1.1 Identifying Relevant Data Sources

The first step in data curation is to identify relevant data sources. Social network services, such as Facebook and Twitter, may serve as critical data sources and platforms. Social science research has revealed new information on social phenomena, such as how friendships are formed and how interests spread, with the help of Online Social Networks. Choosing relevant data sources to achieve a particular analysis goal is essential since new data repositories are being published daily. Two significant samples of this step include linked data and knowledge bases.

Linked Data and Semantic Web

One way to understand linked data is as simple as utilizing the Web to connect pieces of data from several sources (as reported by Bizer et al. [91]). In simple terms, linked data means using machine-readable data (e.g., in formats such as RDF[1] (Resource Description Framework) and URI[2] (Uniform Resource Identifiers) to connect datasets to other data sources and then make that data public. The data can be published using Web applications protocols such as HTTP[3] (HyperText Transfer Protocol). Semantic platforms, e.g., OWL[4] (Web Ontology Language), can be used to facilitate knowledge representation. Expanding on the Linked Data concepts, a dataspace, or shared repository, brings together all of the essential data sources into one place [277]. Also as discussed in Chapter 1, a dataspace will facilitate large-scale data integration challenges.

Knowledge Bases

The common understanding of a Knowledge Base (KB) comprises a collection of ideas, instances, and connections among items. In particular, a Knowledge Base consists of a set of concepts organized into a taxonomy, instances for each concept, and relationships among the concepts and instances. Wikidata[5], Yago[6], Google-

---

[1] https://www.w3.org/RDF/.

[2] https://en.wikipedia.org/wiki/Uniform_Resource_Identifier.

[3] https://en.wikipedia.org/wiki/Hypertext_Transfer_Protocol.

[4] https://www.w3.org/OWL/.

[5] https://www.wikidata.org.

[6] https://github.com/yago-naga/yago3.

KG[7], and DBPedia[8] are examples of a Knowledge Base. A Knowledge Base can formulate the knowledge in a specific domain (e.g., health, finance, and education) and can be considered as an asset for domain analysts. For instance, companies such as Google and Microsoft employ a set of domain-specific KBs to comprehend and answer customer inquiries. Companies such as Amazon[9] and Walmart[10] use KBs to facilitate item classification for their e-commerce purposes. And similarly, Siri[11], the Apple[12] company's voice assistant, makes use of KBs to analyze and answer questions. Using a large KB to power various applications, Spotify[13] offers music recommendations, playlist creation, fingerprinting, and audio analysis.

3.1.2 Ingesting Data and Knowledge

The process of acquiring and importing data for immediate use or storage into a database is called data ingestion. Data is either streamed in near real-time or absorbed in batches [64]. Modern technologies such as cloud computing and the Internet of Things (IoT) enabled the generation of huge amounts of data, making the ingestion a challenging task. To handle real-time data ingestion, there are several technologies available. For example, Hortonworks Data Flow[14] (HDF) enables ingesting and tracking data as it is flowing.

During the ingestion process, several data sources are likely to be considered. As data sources begin to pile up, the processing may begin to get increasingly complex. For a long time, processing data required no extra tools, since the quantity of data was not very large. However, advancements in technology, enabled us to generate vast amounts of information and made data processing and storage a challenging task. The data ingestion is the first phase of the data management process, in which data is prioritized and organized for additional processing. Significant benefits of data ingestion include [412, 659]: (i) Efficient production: Companies spend a great deal of time doing an in-depth data analysis and moving data from several sources, but a data intake procedure allows for faster data retrieval and frees up time to concentrate on other priorities; and (ii) Process data in batches or live. Data is saved based on time intervals that vary depending on when the batch was created. Regardless of the various data formats or protocols, data are ingested automatically.

Concerning unstructured data from Open Data Cube (ODC), Kim et al. [338] describe ingestion as getting and importing data for usage or keeping it in a database for rapid use. There are three primary phases of ingesting satellite data, and they are

---

[7] https://developers.google.com/knowledge-graph/.

[8] http://wiki.dbpedia.org/.

[9] https://www.amazon.com.

[10] https://www.walmart.com/.

[11] https://www.apple.com/au/siri/.

[12] https://www.apple.com/.

[13] https://www.spotify.com/.

[14] https://hortonworks.com/.

done using the open data cube platform. To catalog metadata, it is vital to index datasets. The ingestion procedure follows soon after and gives customers access to data sets they can utilize out of the box in Open Data Cube. Python modules provide numerous advantages in various ways for creating metadata if YAML[15] metadata is used. According to Negru et al. [452], ingesting data, which is relevant to water monitoring infrastructure systems used in smart cities, the ingestion layer is in charge of handling the data acquisition and import process, for usage in storage or real-time notifications. For the first use case, data is first put into batches and then ingested. The second scenario is real-time ingestion, which means data will be consumed as it is being released. The data ingestion process involves the intake of two stages and data routing to the proper storage engine. As discussed in Chapter 2, if we're working with sensor data, we can ingest them in a temporal-spatial database. Moreover, in addition to HDFS, data sources such as Oracle's database for sensor and GIS data, NoSql for key-value data, text and tabular store for semi-structure data, and other variations may also be used.

In real world scenarios, ingestion may involve both taking and absorbing. Data ingestion may be used with data that is stored in a database or in a Hadoop Distributed File System [641]. Data can be delivered in real-time or compiled to be delivered later. If ingested immediately, it will be imported as is because data is transferred from the source in real-time. When data is imported in discrete blocks at frequent periods, it is consumed in batches [203]. To manage the massive quantity, immense velocity, and staggering diversity of data, the ingestion layer must be capable of filtering out the noise. To achieve this goal, several operations on data will be performed to ensure they are fit for the new environemt. Accordingly, the ingestion layer should have the following fundamental components [203]:

- Detecting the variety of data (from structured to unstructured) and assign them to relevant data types.
- Examining corporate information as it comes in.
- Performing constant validation and investigation.
- Removing noise using ways of cleansing and limiting disruptions.
- Performing data de-normalization or synthesis may be necessary to effect the change. Compression means squeezing data till its relevance remains intact. Compression should not impact the analysis.

3.1.3 Data Cleaning

Social data has become an extremely significant resource for corporate sectors. Several technological advances, such as social media trends, IoT, and smartphone capabilities, create and digitize a great deal of previously inaccessible data. Because of the massive growth in data, chances to identify new business models have opened up. Still, new data quality and methods are needed to extract information because

---

[15] https://yaml.org/.

the data comes from many sources. Deciphering data and deciding what is significant while coping with the unknown is a challenging task. Data analytics will be compromised by errors, missing data, miscoding, and other problems that exist in raw data sets. A lack of diligent maintenance might lead to incorrect analytics and dubious findings. The data quality process determines the information a data set may have. More and more, data cleansing methods are used to achieve this goal. In particular, data cleaning is crucial for working with and interpreting data. The data scientist's first priority is to ensure good data quality. For example, it is challenging to use regression models without having built a robust data cleaning process. This comprises of doing an identity search, evaluating the integrity of the data, sorting its information, and addressing data quality concerns by categorizing them and giving them significance [145, 306].

Data Cleaning deals with eliminating inaccurate, incomplete, poorly structured, or duplicated data from a database. Many established organizations have now understood the necessity of incorporating data analytics into their business for improved offerings and services. To enhance results and productivity, companies may make use of social data to get valuable insight. Several tools exist to work with massive datasets, but these are riddled with flaws. And not only does an organization requires the capacity to gather information without making mistakes or being incomplete, but it is also quite common for that information to be ignored. This type of data is commonly considered unclean, and for those who wish to achieve better outcomes, cleaning it is a real challenge. Several methods have used machine learning to automate the data cleaning process and to accomplish more work with less human input.

Data cleaning may include detecting and correcting flaws in data. For error detection, a significant number of papers present Integrity Constraints (ICs) that capture data errors. A violation is defined as a group of data values that, when taken collectively, breaks specific internal guidelines and, thus, can be deemed an error. Nevertheless, ICs cannot distinguish if a piece of data has been manipulated from the correct information; making it difficult for ICs to offer assistance with finding correct data. Recently, new criteria [625] has been presented that can identify which values are incorrect, given adequate information. Data repair strategies have been developed, and some of them can be used for data repair. Many examples of work rely on confidence levels provided by users for determining the course of repair or using master data. To infer data about missing information, and probable sources of errors, statistical inference is explored. To guarantee the validity of fixes, users must be consulted beforehand. Few related examples of work have also studied how to efficiently fix and repair data using rule-based systems [591, 592]. Although the importance of data quality and its many varied contributions have been rising, there is still no off-the-shelf product for automatically discovering and fixing mistakes and issues in the raw data, even though data cleaning tools are rather robust. The programming interface makes it possible for data analysts to establish numerous data quality criteria with which they may universally identify flaws in data, as well as how to repair the data via a specified code class [597].

Data cleansing must include these significant phases: First, the goal is to identify quality concerns and draw regression tasks to map the chosen data sources. It is critical to understand the data you have picked in the second step, where the goal is to identify data quality concerns. The third stage, in data cleansing, involves discovering and removing different elements. There is an in-depth discussion of each data quality concern, as follows [145]:

- Missing value: When one variable or attribute is missing, it is called a missing value. When incorrect measurements, transfer issues, or incomplete surveys are at fault, missing values could be found in the data.
- Outlier: The concept of an outlier is also relevant to both univariate and multivariate observations. A measure is labeled as an outlier when it deviates significantly from other measures. In other words, an outlier is a data point that differs considerably from other observations.
- High dimensionality: A dataset may be considered high-dimensional when it has a significant number of characteristics [335]. Regression models tend to over-fit in this scenario, which leads to a decline in performance.
- Redundancy: Data redundancy occurs when the same piece of data is stored in two or more separate places. It can be a problem since it leads to many instances of data, which can be disadvantageous to classifier performance [100].
- Noise: Noisy data are data with a large amount of additional meaningless information called noise. In particular, noise is unwanted data items, features, or records which don't help in explaining the feature itself or the relationship between the feature and the target. Noise may cause the algorithms to miss out on important patterns in the data.

3.1.4 Data Integration

Data integration involves combining data residing in different sources and providing users with a unified view of them. Data Integration may involve the procedure of converting data between differing formats. Many data management and data warehousing solutions have integrated Extract-Transform-Load (ETL) technology to help with data integration, migration, and transfer [173]. These technologies are adopted to manage enormous data quantities, but their versatility is not suited to semi-structured or unstructured data. Because of the diverse nature of the data generated on various sources, data integration and interoperability are massive challenges for organizations. It follows that integration and interoperability demand a multi-pronged strategy. Collecting data from several different sources is advantageous since it may be used to help understand more insights about the data. This requires the collection of information from many sources, which should be put together in various ways. Hundreds of terabytes of data are generated daily by large companies like Facebook, Google, and Twitter. A merging of two large sources of data would require special attention to data integration and interoperability since massive data interchange will be required from two businesses, e.g., each company may have distinct data management practices before merging. There are several complications associated with integrating and inter-operating of large datasets. These problems are crucial to note as below [317]:

- Accommodate scope of data: A new difficulty might be overcoming the sheer size of the data and establishing new business units.
- Data Inconsistency: Data consistency refers to whether the same data kept at different places does or does not match. Inconsistency is generally compounded by data redundancy. In particular, inconsistency happens when the same data exists in different formats in multiple tables, but redundancy happens when the same piece of data exists in multiple places in the database.
- Query Optimization: Effective query optimization is the core feature of data integration. It uses data dependencies (i.e., information about multiple attributes as the result of combining data residing in different sources) to generate more efficient optimization plans.
- Inadequate Resources: Lack of appropriate economic resources, shortage of qualified personnel, and expensive implementation expenses might make the deployment of data integration difficult. To get their work environment running better, every company has to think about a trade of between cost and time, as data integration could be a time consuming and expensive task.
- Scalability: When new data is integrated with existing data, scalability problems may emerge. As numerous updates and adjustments go via legacy systems to adapt to new technology, organizational changes may improve legacy systems efficiency.
- Implementing support system: Organizations must build a support system in every data integration stage, and a training program is required to teach employees (e.g., to handle error monitoring).
- Extract, Transform, Load (ETL): Integrating data from one or more sources into a centralized repository could be quite challenging, as the source data, as well as its context, could be different compared to the transformed data. To address this challenge, ETL was introduced as a data integration process that combines data from multiple data sources into a single, consistent data store that is loaded into a data warehouse or other target system.

3.1.5 Data Transformation

Data transformation, i.e., the process of converting data from one format into another, is a fundamental aspect of most data management tasks such as data integration. In this process, the data could be transformed using filtering and transformation techniques. To facilitate this process, it is important to have simple representations of the data, but for optimal usage, the representations should be filled with meaning. Data transformation may be used for: smoothing out or contouring the rough data, summarizing or generalizing the raw data, and normalizing the data to make it fit in with a broader range. Data transformation may include [64, 241, 243]: (i) Smoothing, to reduce, cluster, and predict noisy data; (ii) Normalization, to minimize data redundancy and to ensure only related data is stored in each dataset; (iii) Feature construction, to transform a given set of input features to generate a new set of more relevant features to enable accurate prediction; (iv) Aggregation, to gather data from multiple sources and combine them into a summarized format; and (v) Generalization, to create a broader categorization of data in a dataset. For example, this process can replace relatively low-level values (e.g., depression) with higher-level concepts (e.g., mental disorder) in the health domain.

Data quality is essential to ensure the value and importance of data and the effect of the transformations. Data transformation is simply the translation of data between two formats. In comparison, data migration describes moving data from one system to another, where a significant number of data transformation and cleaning stages must be performed. Conflict management, validation, rectification, and standardization are all instances of transformation types. To design a robust data transformation model, it is necessary to describe and attach the required metadata at its creation. Such details include, for example, the origin of data, the type of data, whether it is schema-less or structured, when it was created, and other pertinent information. In this context, provenance [77] (discussed in Chapter 2) plays a vital role in understanding the origin of data. To save bandwidth and storage space, it is crucial to spot insufficient data early in the creation and collection processes. These phases inherently impact the quality and hence need management and control [594].

3.2 Social Data Curation: Adding Value

Social networks have been studied fairly extensively in the general context of analyzing interactions between people, and determining the important structural patterns in such interactions [15]. One of the main challenges in this domain is to transform social data into actionable insights. It will be vital to prepare and curate the raw social data for analytics to achieve this goal. Data curation has been defined as the active and ongoing management of data through its lifecycle of interest and usefulness [224]. Data curation includes all the processes needed for principled and controlled data creation, maintenance, and management, together with the capacity to add value to data [43, 74]. In Section 3.1, we introduced the importance of the maintenance and management of social data over time.

In this section, we primarily aim at introducing data creation and value generation from social data. More specifically, we focus on curation tasks that transform raw social data (e.g., a Tweet in Twitter) into contextualized data and knowledge includes extracting, enriching, linking, and annotating social data. This task is essential as, for example, information extracted from social items, such as tweets in Twitter, is often enriched with metadata on geolocation, in the absence of which the extracted information would be difficult to interpret and meaningfully utilize. Data curation thus acts as the glue between raw data and analytics, providing an abstraction layer that relieves users from time-consuming, tedious, and error-prone curation tasks. Current approaches in data curation rely primarily on data processing and analysis algorithms, including machine learning-based algorithms for information extraction, item classification, record-linkage, clustering, and sampling [119]. For example, these algorithms can be used to extract named entities from tweets, link them to entities in a knowledge base (e.g., Wikidata[16]), and classify tweets into a set of predefined topics (e.g., using Naive Bayes classifier [119]).

These algorithms are undoubtedly the core components of data-curation platforms, where high-level curation tasks may require a non-trivial combination of several algorithms [37]; e.g., An IBM Watson question-answering system uses hundreds of various algorithms for producing an answer [219]. Modern data analytic platforms provide scripting-based, rule-based, and query-based languages for describing data curation pipelines over data sources [168]. Examples of these languages in Academia include [65]: Data Extraction Language (DEL[17]), as well as AQL (query-based Information Extraction language). Examples of these languages from Industry include Google Cloud Dataflow[18], Amazon Kinesis[19], and eBay QL.io[20]. General-purpose languages include: R[21], Scala[22], Python[23], and their extensions. Rule-based languages [143] use regular expressions, dictionaries, and taxonomies to specify user-defined classification, information extraction, and entity-matching tasks [108]. Overall, even sophisticated professional programmers and data scientists are regularly forced to resort to understanding different low-level programming libraries to create and maintain complex data curation pipelines [168].

Set of related work [65, 495, 631] on Semantic Web and semantically oriented data warehousing solutions aim to establish a semantic layer on top of heterogeneous metadata, where the goal is to breathe meaning into information extracted from raw data. Many of these approaches focused on creating, enriching, or reusing Knowledge Graphs (KGs), i.e., large Knowledge Bases (KBs) containing a wealth of information about entities (e.g., millions of people, organizations, places, topics, events) their relationships. Existing KBs [583] (e.g., Wikidata[24], YAGO[25], DBpedia[26], KnowItAll[27], BabelNet[28], ConceptNet[29] and DeepDive[30]) include both manually and automatically curated knowledge bases. These approaches can be used

---

[16] https://www.wikidata.org/.

[17] https://www.w3.org/TR/data-extraction.

[18] https://cloud.google.com/dataflow.

[19] https://aws.amazon.com/kinesis/.

[20] https://github.com/ql-io.

[21] https://www.r-project.org/.

[22] https://www.scala-lang.org/.

[23] https://www.python.org/.

[24] https://www.wikidata.org/.

[25] https://github.com/yago-naga/yago3.

[26] http://wiki.dbpedia.org/.

[27] http://projectsWeb.cs.washington.edu/research/knowitall/.

[28] http://babelnet.org/.

[29] http://conceptnet.io/.

[30] http://deepdive.stanford.edu/.

in enriching/annotating the raw data and, therefore, would be an excellent asset for the curation pipeline. For example, cognitive applications, knowledge-centric services, deep question answering, and semantic search and analytics can deeply benefit from the domain knowledge [58, 65].

Another line of related work [579, 671], focus on data integration, especially in ETL (Extract, Transform, and Load) systems, data federations, data cleaning, schema integration, and entity deduplication. However, there has been little work on collecting all of the curation components into an extensible and scalable curation system. For example, Apache UIMA[31] facilitates the analysis of unstructured content but does not consider the domain knowledge to contextualize the extracted information. A recent work, DataSynapse [65], addressed this challenge with the goal to provide an extensible, scalable and interactive framework to enable analysts to utilize a variety of different algorithms (i.e., features in our terminology) and use them in a composite manner.

Finally, there has been considerable work on curating open data. These works provide domain-specific solutions for different curation tasks, including leveraging crowdsourcing techniques to extract keywords from tweets in Twitter [68], Named entity recognition in tweets [523], linking entities for enriching and structuring social media content [608], and sentiment analysis and identifying mental health cases on Facebook [529]. However, there have been very few works on presenting a general-purpose approach that can be used for curating social data: this will enable the analysts to link the contextualized data and knowledge generated on different social networks, uncover hidden patterns and generate insight.

3.2.1 Extraction

Information Extraction (IE) is the task of automatically extracting structured information from unstructured/semi-structured machine-readable documents [76]. The first step in information extraction from social data includes pre-processing input documents to cast them into plain text. Tools such as *Boilerpipe*[32] and *Jsoup*[33] can be used for pre-processing such documents. After the pre-processing step, it is possible to extract various features from social data items, including [65]:

- *Schema-based features.* This category is related to the properties of a social item. For example, according to the Twitter schema[34], a tweet may have attributes such as text, source, and language; and a user may have attributes such as username, description, and timezone.
- *Lexical-based features.* This category is related to the words or vocabulary of a language such as Keyword, Topic, Phrase, Abbreviation, Special Characters (e.g., '#' in a tweet), Slangs, Informal Language and Spelling Errors.

---

[31] https://uima.apache.org/.

[32] https://github.com/kohlschutter/boilerpipe.

[33] https://jsoup.org/.

[34] https://developer.Twitter.com/en/docs/Twitter-api/v1/data-dictionary/object-model/tweet.

- *Natural-Language-based features.* This category is related to entities that can be extracted by the analysis and synthesis of Natural Language (NL) and speech. This may include Part-Of-Speech (e.g., Verb and Noun), Named Entity Type (e.g., Person, Organization, and Product), and Named Entity (i.e., an instance such as 'Scott Morrison'[35] of the entity type *Person*).
- *Time-based features.* This category is related to the mentions of time in the schema of the item (e.g., 'tweet.Timestamp' and 'user.TimeZone' in Twitter) or in the content of the social media posts (e.g., in Twitter the text of a tweet may contain '7 Nov 2021').
- *Location-based features.* This category is related to the mentions of locations in the schema of the item (e.g., in Twitter 'tweet.GEO' and 'user.Location') or in the content of the social media posts (e.g., in Twitter the text of a tweet may contain 'Sydney'; a city in Australia).
- *Metadata-based features.* This category is related to a set of data that describes and gives information about the social items and actors. For example, it is important to know the number of followers (followersCount) and the number of friends (friendsCount) of a social actor, as well as the number of times a social item has been viewed (viewCount), liked (likeCount), or shared (shareCount); or the sentiment [444] of the content posted on a social network.

In social data feature extraction, we may deal with low-level features as deployable, small, and modular services. Examples of low-level features in the category of "extraction" include [65, 76]: Named Entities, Keywords, Synonyms, Stem, and Part-of-Speech. Since APIs are akin to functions that are applied on features, through the use of APIs, lower-level features can easily be cascaded to produce higher-level features, and so on. As an example, we focus on Entity Extraction task [76], i.e., techniques that can be used to locate and classify atomic elements in text into predefined categories such as the names of persons, organizations, locations, expressions of times, quantities, monetary values, and percentages. This task is a key part of an information extraction system that supports robust handling of proper names essential for many applications, enables pre-processing for different classification levels, and facilitates information filtering and linking. In particular, entity extraction/identification consists of three subtasks: identifying entity names, temporal expressions, and number expressions, where the expressions to be annotated are 'unique identifiers' of entities (organizations, persons, locations), times (dates, times), and quantities (monetary values, percentages).

Most research on entity extraction systems has been structured as taking an unannotated block of text (e.g., "Obama was born on August 4, 1961, at Gynecological Hospital in Honolulu") and producing an annotated block of text, such as the following[36]:

---

[35] https://en.wikipedia.org/wiki/Scott_Morrison.

[36] In this example, the annotations have been done using so-called ENAMEX (a user defined element in the XML schema) tags that were developed for the Message Understanding Conference in the 1990s.

$< ENAMEXTYPE = "PERSON" > Obama < /ENAMEX > wasbornon$
$< TIMEXTYPE = "DATE" > August4, 1961, < /TIMEX > at$
$< ENAMEXTYPE = "ORGANIZATION" > Gynecological$
$Hospital < /ENAMEX > in < ENAMEX$
$TYPE = "CITY" > Honolulu < /ENAMEX > .$

where, entity types such as person, organization, and city are recognized.

However, NER is not just matching text strings with pre-defined lists of names. It should recognize entities in contexts where category definitions are intuitively quite clear and in contexts where many grey areas are caused by metonymy. Metonymy is a figure of speech used in rhetoric in which a thing or concept is not called by its own name, but by the name of something intimately associated with that thing or concept. Metonyms can be either real or fictional concepts representing other concepts, real or fictional, but they must serve as an effective and widely understood second name for what they represent. For example, (i) *Person vs. Artefact*: "The Ham Sandwich (a person) wants his bill. vs "Bring me a ham sandwich.";(ii) *Organization vs. Location*: "England won the World Cup" vs. "The World Cup took place in England"; (iii) *Company vs. Artefact*: "shares in MTV" vs. "watching MTV"; and (iv) *Location vs. Organization*: "she met him at Heathrow" vs. "the Heathrow authorities".

To address these challenges, the Message Understanding Conferences (MUC) was initiated and financed by DARPA (Defense Advanced Research Projects Agency) to encourage the development of new and better methods of information extraction. The tasks grew from producing a database of events found in newswire articles from one source to the production of multiple databases of increasingly complex information extracted from multiple sources of news in multiple languages. The databases now include named entities, multilingual named entities, attributes of those entities, facts about relationships between entities, and events in which the entities participated. MUC essentially adopted the simplistic approach of disregarding metonymous uses of words, e.g., 'England' was consistently identified as a location. However, this is not always useful for practical applications of Named Entity Extraction, such as in sports. MUC defined fundamental problems in NER as follows: (i) Variation of named entities: for example, John Smith, Mr. Smith, and John may refer to the same entity; (ii) Ambiguity of named entities types: for example, John Smith (company vs. person), May (person vs. month), Washington (person vs. location), and 1945 (date vs. time); (iii) Ambiguity with common words: for example 'may'; and (iv) Issues of style, structure, domain, genre, etc. as well as punctuation, spelling, spacing, and formatting. To address these challenges, existing approaches to entity extraction proposed four primary steps [76], described as follows:

- **Format Analysis.** In this step, the goal is to identify and handle the formatting content embedded within documents that control how the document is rendered on a computer screen or interpreted by a software program. For example, HTML documents contain HTML tags specifying formatting information such as new line starts, bold emphasis, and font size or style. Format analysis is also referred to as structure analysis, format parsing, tag stripping, format stripping, text normalization, text cleaning, and text preparation.

- **Tokeniser.** Tokenization is the process of breaking a stream of text up into words, phrases, symbols, or other meaningful elements called tokens. This module is responsible for segmenting text into tokens, e.g., words, numbers, and punctuation. The list of tokens becomes the input for further processing, such as parsing or text mining.

- **Gazetteer.** The role of the gazetteer is to identify entity names in the text based on lists. These lists are used to find occurrences of these names in text, e.g., for the task of named entity recognition. Gazetteers usually do not depend on Tokens or any other annotation and instead find matches based on the document's textual content. As an output, this module will generate a set of named entities (e.g., towns, names, and countries) and keywords (e.g., company designators and titles).

- **Grammar.** This module is responsible for hand-coded rules for named entity recognition. NER systems can use linguistic grammar-based techniques as well as statistical models. Hand-crafted grammar-based systems typically obtain better precision at the cost of lower recall and months of work by experienced computational linguists. Statistical NER systems usually require a large amount of manually annotated training data.

3.2.2 Correction and Enrichment

A key challenge in analyzing social data is to understand the raw data generated by social actors and prepare it for analytic tasks. For example, tweets in Twitter are generally unstructured (contain text and images), sparse (offer limited number of characters), suffer from redundancy (same tweet re-tweeted) and prone to slang words and misspellings. In this context, correction and enrichment of social data could be vital in the data curation pipeline. Such a pipeline may include: (i) feature extraction, e.g., keywords and named entities; (ii) correction, e.g., correcting misspelling and abbreviation; and (iii) enrichment, e.g., leveraging knowledge sources and services to find synonyms and stems for an extracted/corrected keyword.

A recent work, CrowdCorrect [68], designed and implemented services to use the extracted features and to identify and correct the misspelling, jargons (i.e., special words or expressions used by a profession or group that are difficult for others to understand), and abbreviations. These services leverage knowledge sources and services such as WordNet[37], STANDS4[38] service to identify acronyms and abbreviations, Microsoft cognitive-services[39] to check the spelling and stems, and cortical[40] service to identify jargons. The result of this step (automatic curation) will be an an-

---

[37] https://wordnet.princeton.edu/.

[38] https://www.abbreviations.com/abbr_api.php.

[39] https://azure.microsoft.com/en-au/try/cognitive-services/my-apis/.

[40] https://www.cortical.io/.

notated dataset that contains the cleaned and corrected raw data. After the correction phase, the following approaches could be embedded to enrichment the corrected social data:

- *Schema-based Semantics.* It is possible to use knowledge services such as Google Cloud Platform[41], Alchemyapi[42], Microsoft Computer Vision API[43] and Apache PredictionIO[44] to extract various features from the social items properties. For example, if a tweet in Twitter contains an Image, it is possible to extract entities (e.g., people and objects) from the image.
- *Lexical-based Semantics.* It is possible to leverage knowledge sources such as WordNet[45] to enrich Lexical-based features with their Synonyms, Stems, Hypernyms[46], Hyponyms[47] and more.
- *NL-based Semantics.* It is possible to leverage knowledge sources such as Wiki-Data[48], Google-KG[49], and DBPedia[50] to enrich Natural-Language-based features with similar and related entities. For example, 'Malcolm Turnbull'[51] is similar to 'Tony Abbott'[52] (they both acted as the prime minister of Australia) but 'Malcolm Turnbull' is related to 'University of Sydney'[53] (the University where he attended and graduated). It is also possible to use techniques such as Coreference Resolution [76] to enrich named entities with their mentions. For example, 'Malcolm Turnbull' is a named entity of type person whose entity mentions include 'Malcolm Bligh Turnbull', 'Malcolm B. Turnbull', 'M. Turnbull', '29th Prime Minister of Australia' and more.
- *Geo/Temporal-based Semantics.* It is possible to leverage knowledge sources such as Wikidata and services (such as events and storyline mining [67]) to enrich time-/location-based features with time and location events. For example, if a tweet is posted from Australia, we can enrich it with all the events in that location. If a tweet is posted on, for example, '15 October 2021' we enrich it with all the events happening around that time frame. For example, suppose a tweet is posted on '3 May 2021' from any location within Australia. In that case, we enrich the tweet to be related to 'Australian Budget' as we know from

---

[41] https://cloud.google.com/.

[42] https://www.ibm.com/watson/alchemy-api.html.

[43] https://azure.microsoft.com/en-gb/services/.

[44] https://github.com/PredictionIO/.

[45] https://wordnet.princeton.edu/.

[46] A Hypernym is a word with a broad meaning constituting a category into which words with more specific meanings fall; a superordinate. For example, colour is a hypernym of red.

[47] A Hyponym is a word of more specific meaning than a general or superordinate term applicable to it. For example, spoon is a hyponym of cutlery.

[48] https://www.wikidata.org/.

[49] https://developers.google.com/knowledge-graph/.

[50] http://wiki.dbpedia.org/.

[51] https://en.wikipedia.org/wiki/Malcolm_Turnbull.

[52] https://en.wikipedia.org/wiki/Tony_Abbott.

[53] https://en.wikipedia.org/wiki/University_of_Sydney.

knowledge sources that the Australian Treasurer is handing the Budget on 3 May every year.

- *Metadata-based Semantics.* It is possible to use metadata-based features (such as followersCount and ShareCount) to calculate semantics such as the *influence* of an item or a social actor. These semantics will enable the analysts to get more insight from the social media posts and analyze the capacity to have an effect on the character, development, or behavior of other social users (e.g., in analyzing cases for social network recruitment and radicalization) [515].

3.2.3 Linking

Social data may be interpreted in many different ways. To make sense of this for a given context, it is highly beneficial that such data is linked with domain knowledge to produce contextualized knowledge. This can be supported by building a domain-specific knowledge base that provides a rich structure of relevant entities, their semantics, and relationships. A Domain Knowledge is a knowledge base that consists of a set of concepts organized into a taxonomy, instances for each concept, and relationships among the concepts, in a specific domain, such as health, banking, and education.

For example, consider a typical scenario for analyzing Urban Social Issues from Twitter related to the Government Budget in Australia. In this context, a domain-specific Knowledge Base representing a set of concepts related to the Australian budget organized into a taxonomy, instances for each concept, and relationships among these concepts would be a vital asset for analysts in this domain. To build this Knowledge Base, we first need to identify the list of budget categories (e.g., Health, Transport, Employment, Defense, Welfare, Economy, Trade, and Agriculture) and their related programs provided by Australian government data services[54]. Then for each category in the budget, we can construct a Knowledge Base. For example, let us focus on building a Knowledge Base for the category of Health that is related to the budget in Australia, by identifying popular concepts and instances related to this category. For example, we can identify the following concepts:

- People, from GPs and Nurses to health ministers and hospital managers.
- Organizations, such as Hospitals, Pharmacies, and Nursing Federation.
- Locations, states, cities, and suburbs in Australia.
- Health funds, such as Medibank, Bupa, and HCF.
- Drugs, such as Amoxicillin, Tramadol, and Alprazolam.
- Diseases, such as Cancer, Influenza, and Tuberculosis.
- Medical Devices, such as Gas Control, Blood Tube and Needle.
- Job titles, such as GP, Nurse, Hospital Manager, Secretary of NSW Health and NSW Health Minister.
- Keywords, such as healthcare, patient, virus, vaccine, and drug.

---

[54] http://data.gov.au/.

It is possible to develop APIs[55] to automatically extract instances of concepts in our example Knowledge Base from available online sources such as:

- extracting list of locations from auspost[56].
- extracting list of doctors from Australian doctors directory[57] (including GPs, specialists and nurses).
- extracting list of hospitals from myHospitals[58].
- extracting list of health funds from health-services[59].
- extracting list of Drugs from drug-index[60].
- extracting list of Diseases from medicine-net[61].
- extracting list of Medical Devices from FDA[62].
- extracting list of Job titles from compdata[63].
- extracting list of keywords from Australia national health and medical research council[64].

The next step would be to enrich the above-extracted items to breathe semantics into the Knowledge Base. For example, it is possible to develop APIs to enrich these items using Knowledge Bases such as: Wikidata[65], Google Knowledge Graph[66] and Wordnet[67]. For example, we can extract relationships from Wikidata to form a relationship graph [70], e.g., 'Royal North Shore Hospital' located-in 'St Leonards, Sydney, NSW, Australia'; and we can use Google KG API to link entities to Wikipedia, e.g., by using 'Jillian Skinner' as an input we have learned that 'Jillian Skinner' is-a 'person', linked-to '$https : //en.wikipedia.org/wiki/Jillian\_Skinner$'; was a member-of 'New South Wales Legislative Assembly'; and is-a 'New South Wales Minister for Health' for Australia. It is also possible to use Wordnet to extract synonyms and hypernyms for the extracted keywords related to health.

---

[55] An application programming interface (API) is a type of software interface, offering a service to other pieces of software. In particular, we can consider an API as a program that can be made available as a Web service. Projects such as ProgrammableWeb (programmableWeb.com/) introduced as an information source about the Web as a programmable platform and offer thousands of reusable APIs.

[56] http://auspost.com.au/postcode/.

[57] https://www.ahpra.gov.au/.

[58] https://www.myhospitals.gov.au/browse-hospitals/.

[59] http://www.privatehealth.gov.au/.

[60] http://www.rxlist.com/.

[61] http://www.medicinenet.com/.

[62] http://www.fda.gov/.

[63] http://compdatasurveys.com/compensation/healthcare.

[64] https://www.nhmrc.gov.au/.

[65] https://www.wikidata.org/.

[66] https://developers.google.com/knowledge-graph/.

[67] https://wordnet.princeton.edu.

3.2.4 Summarization

The amount of available data on any social network could be far beyond humans' processing capacity to properly process, causing what is known as 'information overload'. Moreover, data curation steps, including extraction and enrichment, will also add more details to the raw social data. To efficiently cope with large amounts of information and generate content with significant value to users, we require identifying, merging, and summarizing information. In this context, data summaries can help gather related information and collect it into a shorter format that enables answering complicated questions, gaining new insight, and discovering conceptual boundaries. In Chapter 6, we provide an overview of summarization techniques and discuss that social data summarization can help gather related information and collect it into a shorter format that enables answering complicated questions, gaining new insight, and discovering conceptual boundaries. We also focus on modern topics, including Time-aware, Personalized-aware, and Conversational Summarization of Social Data.

3.3 Knowledge Lakes

Organizing a vast amount of social data gathered from various data islands will facilitate dealing with a collection of independently-managed datasets such as Twitter, Facebook, and LinkedIn. The notion of a Data Lake [61] has been coined to address this challenge and to convey the concept of a centralized repository containing limitless amounts of raw (or minimally curated) data stored in various data islands. The rationale behind the Data Lake is to store raw data and let the data analyst decide how to cook/curate them later.

Complementary to Data Lakes, the notion of Knowledge Lake [62] was introduced as a contextualized Data Lake. In particular, a Knowledge Lake is a centralized repository containing virtually inexhaustible amounts of both data and curated/contextualized data that is readily made available anytime to anyone authorized to perform analytical activities. The term Knowledge here refers to a set of facts, information, and insights extracted from the social data. Knowledge Lakes can provide the foundation for big data analytics by automatically curating the raw data in the Data Lake and preparing them for deriving insights. As discussed in Section 3.2, we are able to provide services to automatically:

- Extract features such as keyword, part-of-speech, and named entities such as Persons, Locations, Organizations, Companies, Products and more, from raw social data;
- Enrich the extracted features by providing synonyms and stems leveraging lexical knowledge bases for the English language such as WordNet;
- Link the extracted enriched features to external knowledge bases (such as Google Knowledge Graph and Wikidata) as well as the contextualized data islands [66]; and

- Annotate the items in a data island by information about the similarity among the extracted information items, classifying and categorizing items into various types, forms, or any other distinct class.

Figure 3.1 illustrates the architecture and the main components of a Knowledge Lake. Technical details of these services and how to organize and curate the data in the Knowledge Lake can be found in [62][68]. As illustrated in the figure, the Knowledge Lake not only supports organizing and querying the data in the Lake, but also it provides a database security protection mechanism including authentication, access control, and data encryption for both data and the contextualized data (Security and Access Control). It also supports collecting and aggregating metadata (including descriptive, administrative, and temporal metadata and building a provenance [79] graph) for both data and the contextualized data.

Data curation activities are heavily dependent on the challenges of scale. To address this challenge, Knowledge Lakes should provide an extensible and scalable microservice-based architecture to enable applications to decompose into components and provide capabilities to wrap components as network services. This will allow dealing with large social data to scale to huge volumes by replicating processing pipelines over a cluster of networked nodes. For example, it is possible to leverage technologies such as Apache UIMA[69] to support the reuse and composition of independently-developed social data curation services, for example, keyword extraction, named entity detection, similarity comparison, and entity linking APIs.

3.4 Concluding Remarks and Discussion

A key challenge in understanding social data is to transform raw data into actionable insights. This is important as social data may be interpreted in many different ways, and it is important to prepare the raw social data for the specific needs of analysts. Therefore, curation and contextualization of raw social data would vital. Data curation has been defined as the active and ongoing management of data through its lifecycle of interest and usefulness. In this chapter, we highlighted the importance of social data curation in social data analytics, and focused on curation tasks including cleaning, integration, transformation, and adding value. We also discussed modern technologies including the Knowledge Lake, i.e., a contextualized Data Lake that facilitates turning the raw data into contextualized data and knowledge using extraction, enrichment, annotation, linking and summarization techniques.

---

[68] https://github.com/unsw-cse-soc/CoreKG.

[69] http://uima.apache.org/.

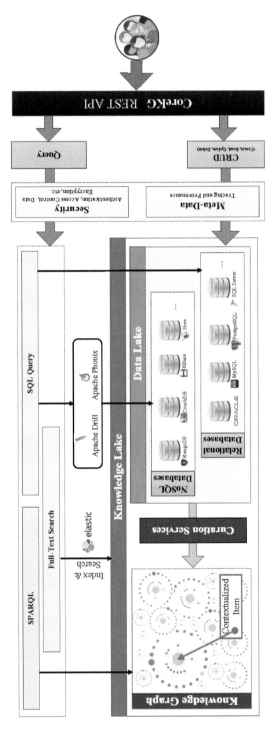

Fig. 3.1 Knowledge Lake Architecture [62].

New technologies such as Microsoft Azure Synapse[70], Google AI[71], Vertex AI[72], TensorFlow[73], IBM Cloud[74], and Amazon ML[75] offer scalable and extensible platforms for data scientists and analysts to facilitate the curation process and brings together not only enterprise data warehousing and Big Data analytics, but also Machine Learning (ML) and analytics as a service. These technology advancements highlight the importance of the data curation step in data science pipelines. Next chapter, will provide an overview on text analytic approaches by analyzing textual data features. It will also explain distinguished aspects of social textual data and its difference from traditional text analytic tasks, followed by categorizing text analytical tasks in social media from various viewpoints.

---

[70] https://docs.microsoft.com/en-us/azure/synapse-analytics/.

[71] https://ai.google/.

[72] https://cloud.google.com/vertex-ai.

[73] https://www.tensorflow.org/.

[74] https://cloud.ibm.com/.

[75] https://aws.amazon.com/about-aws/whats-new/2015/04/introducing-amazon-machine-learning/.

4

Social Media Text Analytics

4.1 Text Analytics: Overview

Text analytic approaches are used for analyzing large and complex documents, including social media posts, forums, news, chats, surveys, and call transcripts, in an easy, speedy, and efficient way. Text analytic is the process of knowledge discovery or deriving meaning from text [574] with a broad application using machine learning, statistics, and linguistics to identify textual patterns and trends. They enable extracting hidden insights by converting unstructured text data into a structured, machine-readable format.

Individuals and businesses produce tons of unstructured text data every day. Organizing, categorizing, and capturing relevant information from raw data is a significant concern and challenge for companies. On the other hand, it improves organizations' decision-making, leading to better business outcomes. Text analytic tools have influenced how industries work by improving product user experiences and making more agile and reliable business decisions. For instance, users' feedback is gathered through feedback systems, including long customer surveys, reviews, chatbots, and social media profiles. Text analytic tools such a sentiment analysis enable companies to define and prioritize their customers' key pain points, respond to urgent issues in real-time, detect a potential crisis, and identify service or product flaws to increase customer satisfaction. Moreover, monitoring shifts in sentiment provides insights around industry inclinations and financial markets for managing risks, specifically for business investments spread across various sectors, which is a high priority for companies. Text mining enables automating the decision-making process by revealing hidden potential patterns.

Text analytic approaches have also gained attention in the biomedical domain, where manual examination of medical research is expensive and time-consuming [241, 243]. Understanding natural human language has been challenging due to the high volume of data and unstructured format, requiring complex techniques for extracting insights. A set of statistical, linguistic, and machine learning techniques are usually required to represent and structure the textual content for research and business purposes. It incorporates various algorithms for text analysis, including information extraction, information retrieval, and machine learning algorithms such as supervised and unsupervised approaches.

Natural Language Processing (NLP) aims to understand natural language using artificial intelligence and linguistics. The foundation of many text mining and knowledge discovery approaches is based on basic NLP techniques, including syntactic parsing, part of speech tagging (POS), and linguistic analysis [63, 375]. Information Retrieval (IR) aims to find the required information. Hence, IR approaches mainly focus on accessing information rather than analyzing and mining data for discovering hidden patterns [436]. In contrast, Information Extraction (IE) is the process of automatically obtaining information, which serves as the first step for other text mining algorithms and includes feature selection, feature extraction, and named entity recognition (NER) [541]. Text summarization is a profitable text mining approach that produces a concise and comprehensive overview of a set of topic-related documents [240, 242]. Extractive and abstractive approaches are two main categories of summarization. Extractive summarization extracts information from original documents, however, abstractive summarization generates a summary [241]. Different supervised and unsupervised approaches have been used for this purpose [60, 244, 245]. New technologies and techniques have greatly empowered text analytics tasks in recent years, making it a trustable and cost-effective way to achieve efficiency, scalability, and performance. A general framework for knowledge discovery from a large corpus of the text includes: (i) text preprocessing, (ii) text representation, and (iii) knowledge discovery as depicted in Figure 4.1.

4.1.1 Text Preprocessing

Before applying any text mining approaches, text data needs to be prepared, known as preprocessing. Preprocessing is the core of any natural language algorithms that make documents more consistent and facilitate text representation and knowledge discovery. Preprocessing is the process of cleaning and converting unstructured text data into a machine-readable format using techniques such as language identification, filtering, tokenizing, part-of-speech tagging, chunking, lemmatization, stemming, and syntax parsing. Although it is proved that feature extraction [259] and feature selection [215] have a notable impact on the text mining process, the preprocessing step has a remarkable effect on the output. Uysal et al. [612] have examined the effect of preprocessing tasks, especially for text classification purposes.

Filtering is performed on documents to remove specific characters or words. For instance, removing stop words is a filtering technique. Stop words such as prepo-

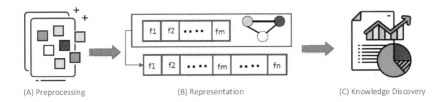

(A) Preprocessing   (B) Representation   (C) Knowledge Discovery

Fig. 4.1 A general framework for knowledge discovery from a large corpus of the text.

sitions or conjunctions are frequently used in the text content without adding semantic information. Similarly, words occurring quite often or rarely in the text can
not distinguish different documents; hence, they can be removed from the documents [569]. Tokenizing is the process of converting a text to a set of meaningful
units [637]. Lemmatization analyzes the morphology of words, aiming to put words
back to their dictionary form (lemma). Stemming is similar to tokenizing; however,
it transforms tokens to their stem, base, or root form. Therefore, words with variant
forms are considered equivalent.

Parsing focuses on understanding sentences' grammatical structure and tagging
them based on their grammatical role in sentences. Parsing strategies are categorized
into two groups, dependency parsing, and constituency parsing. The constituency
parsing breaks the text into sub-phrases, known as constituents for representing the
sentence structure. However, dependency parsing first detects the main words in
sentences. Then related words to the main words which modify their meaning are
extracted. Syntactic relationships allow interpreting sentence meaning, especially in
synthetic languages.

4.1.2 Text Representation

Text mining applications are required to rank various text units, including documents, paragraphs, sentences, and words, for more effective retrieval over extensive
collections. However, text data can not directly be fed into an algorithm. Besides,
machine learning algorithms require well-defined fixed-length vectors for both inputs and outputs. Therefore, a numeric representation of document collections is
required to evaluate each text unit and estimate its importance. Vector Space Model
(VSM) aim to represent documents as vectors to facilitate further processing extensive collections of documents [286].

Based on the application and input data, VSMs can be built in various ways.
For instance, for information retrieval problems, various features selection methods
are used such as (i) document frequency (DF) to count the number of the document that a word appears, (ii) information gain (IG) to measure the information
loss between presence and absence term in the document, and (iii) mutual information (MI). These approaches are used for dimensionality reduction of the text

data. This section discusses transforming ways to make numeric vectors, including handcrafted extracting feature, bag-of-words models, and embedding approaches.

4.1.2.1 Hand-Crafted Feature Extraction

Early traditional approaches in text mining used some handcrafted features for representing documents [65]. The process has two steps defining features and transforming text units based on specified features. Luhn [397] was the first to address the keyword frequency feature. Other features were later proposed, including cue words, title words, and sentence location [180]. Church et al. [138] proposed other new features such as sentence length cut-off, fixed phrases, paragraph features, thematic word features, and upper-case word features. Later, Hovy and Lin [378] verified that the position method is not applicable and efficient for all domains. Consequently, they proposed other features for sentence scoring, including term frequency-inverse document frequency (TF–IDF), cue words, sentence location, and longest common subsequences (LCSs) [500]. Many other features have also been proposed over the years. We categorized existing features into four groups, covering term-level features,sentence-level features,paragraph-level features and corpus-level features [421]. Table 4.1, Table 4.2, Table 4.3, and Table 4.4 present some important features in each group, with brief descriptions.

Features are applied individually or collectively according to the application and the proposed model. Typically, optimal results are obtained by combining various features. Rafael et al. [217] tried merging different word, sentence and graph level features for scoring sentences. Meena and Gopalani [422] evaluated available features and analyzed the results of combining different features. As discovered, find-

Table 4.1 Term-level features.

Feature	Description
Term Frequency	Frequent words mentioned in the document.
TF-IDF	Frequent words considering other terms.
Cue Words	Sentences includes cue words.
Title Similarity	Sentences containing words from the title.
Uppercase word	Sentences include upper-case words.
Positive Keyword	Frequent keywords occurring in the summary.
Negative Keyword	Keywords not frequently occurring in the summary.
Residual IDF	The residual IDF of a word.
Gain	Features based on hypothesising which moderately frequent words are most important in a document.
Term Co-occurrence	Clusters of important words are identified and weighted.
Query Score	Sentences are scored according to the number of query terms.
Synonyms	Synonyms are matched using WordNet or other tools.
Significant Word	Relative significance of words.
Title Similarity	Squares the number of common terms between a document's title and each sentence.

Table 4.2 Sentence-level features.

Feature	Description
Sentence location	Position of sentences determine the weights.
Semantic structure	Using a graph structure where node are sentences, and related sentences are recognised by edges between them.
Length Cut Off	Too short or too long sentences are eliminated.
Fixed Phrase	Sentences containing some fixed phrases, known as indicator phrases, are given priority.
Concept Signature	Topic words and the associated pairs are selected (co-occurrence feature).
Concept Count	Counts the concepts' occurrence instead of individual verbs and nouns.

Table 4.3 Paragraph-level features.

Feature	Description
Paragraph Position	Sentences are weighted according to their paragraph' position.
Optimal Position	A sequence of most important sentences are identified.

Table 4.4 Corpus-based features.

Feature	Description
Signature word	Frequency of word occurrence averaged across a large corpus is used.
Baseline Probability	Using baseline documents, we define a term's importance such that more frequent words have higher probability.
Document Probability	Estimates a term's likeliness of within a document.

ing the optimal feature set remains a challenge. One solution is to test different combinations of features and report the best feature for each document [421]. However, as the number of features increases, the approaches become less practical.

In addition to features, different models also have been suggested for recommending features. However, they optimize the feature based on a specific task. Fattah and Ren [211] proposed supervised models including genetic algorithms (GAs), probabilistic neural networks, feed-forward neural networks, mathematical regression, and a Gaussian mixture model for a text summarization problem. The authors used various features to train the summarization model, including sentence position, relative sentence length, positive and negative keywords, sentence resemblance to the title, named entity in the sentence, sentence centrality, numerical data, and aggregate similarity. Elsewhere, Prasad and Kulkarni [558] used word similarity among paragraphs, iterative query scoring, word similarity among sentences, as well as a format-based score, term frequency, cue words, and tile similarity as features to score sentences. Abuobieda et al. [6] further used title feature, sentence position, numerical data, sentence length, and thematic words. In another study, Mendoza et al. [426] used title similarity, sentence position, cohesion sentence length, and coverage as the features.

4.1.2.2 The Bag-of-words Model

Bag-of-Words (BoW) is another category for extracting features works for sentences and documents, which works based on statistical natural language processing where the text's linguistic structure is disregarded. The bag-of-words model is a representation model which transforms any text data into fixed-length vectors by counting the repetition of different mentioned words. In the BOW representation, text units such as sentences or documents are treated as an unordered collection of words using a fixed-length sparse vector containing word occurrence counts, ignoring grammar and even word order. However, the BoW representation has been shown to effectively capture topic information and long-range word-word correlation information [162]. The bag-of-words model mainly has two phases: (i) making a list of identified words and (ii) defining a scoring method for the presence of known words. The scoring method can be a simple binary value indicating the presence of words or a non-binary value presenting the frequency of different words in a document out of all the words. In the term frequency model, high-frequent words, which can be meaningless or general, are dominant in the document [25]. The Term Frequency–Inverse Document Frequency model (TF-IDF) aims to resolve the problem with scoring word frequency. In contrast to term frequency, Inverse Document Frequency evaluates and considers unique words over documents. The scores highlight distinct words and therefore enclose valuable information.

The bag-of-words model is simple, efficient, and very straightforward to understand and implement. Using the bag-of-words model as the feature vector in the classification task demonstrated outstanding results where the word frequency is used as a feature for training a classifier. However, it has some drawbacks. First, the vocabulary list needs to be designed carefully to manage the size to avoid sparse representation. Moreover, discarding word order ignores the context, which can potentially affect the knowledge discovery process. The range of vocabulary is a big issue faced by the bag-of-words model. For example, if the model comes across a new word it has not seen yet, the model will ignore it since it has not been seen yet. Bag-of-words models also ignore the semantics of the word.

Hash representation of known words is another category similar to the bag-of-words model. Words are hashed to corresponding integer indexes defined in the target hash space, called the 'feature hashing.' Hash representations are practical for a large text corpus with an extensive vocabulary list due to the flexibility in choosing the hash size. However, the challenge is choosing a hash space to support the vocabulary size. The specified hash space is required to reduce the collisions probability of hashed words and sparsity.

4.1.2.3 Embedding Model

Word embedding was introduced to tackle the drawbacks of the bag-of-words approach using a Neural Networks Language Model (NNLM) [83]. The assumption behind the model is that similar meaning occurs in the same context [273]. Therefore, word embedding is a vector representation of text such that words with similar meanings have same representation. Word embedding maps the words in unlabeled high dimensional text data to a vector of continuous values with low dimensional, capturing the internal semantic hidden information in the original feature space. Most NNLM-based approaches are unsupervised neural-based approaches with different architecture, including Convolutional Neural Network (CNN), Recurrent Neural Network (RNN), and Long-Short Term Memory (LSTM), and Restrict Boltzmann Machine (RBM) [58, 414]. The basis of all approaches is maximizing or minimizing the Log-Likelihood function. Based on the architecture, additional constraints need to be added to the model.

Log- Bilinear (LBL) model, SENNA, and Word2vec are some of the most representative examples of NNLM. is a statistical method for learning a continuous word embedding efficiently. Various architectures are used for generating the semantic representation of words. *Skip-gram* is a neural network model which works based on predicting the surrounding window of context words for a given word such that nearby context words are weighted heavily compared to more distant context words. To be more specific, having a sequence of training words $\{w_1, w_2, w_3, ..., w_T\}$, the objective of the word vector model is to maximize the average log probability defined in Eq. 4.1.

$$J = \frac{1}{T} \sum_{t=k}^{T-k} logp(w_t|w_{t-k}, ..., w_{t+k}) \qquad (4.1)$$

A multi-class classifier such as Softmax defined in Eq. 4.2 is usually used for the prediction task.

$$p(w_t|w_{t-k}, ..., w_{t+k}) = \frac{e^{y_{w_t}}}{\sum_i e^{y_i}}, \qquad (4.2)$$

where y_i is normalized log-probability for the output word i, computed based on Eq. 4.3.

$$y = b + Uh(w_{t-k}, ..., w_{t+k}; W), \qquad (4.3)$$

where U, b are the Softmax parameters. h is built using an average of word vectors derived from W. Stochastic gradient descent is mostly used to train the neural network-based word vectors via back propagation [432]. The embedding v_{w_t} is a continues vector representation of the word w_t contaning semantic information.

Word embedding broadly has been used in NLP applications and revolutionized this field. Pretrained networks are used to build word embedding, which is then fed as input data or the text data features directly, making it ready for subsequent knowledge discovery processes.

4.1.3 Knowledge Discovery

Vectorized representation of text corpus makes knowledge discovery possible. For instance, in text classification facilitates organizing and structuring any form of text to deliver essential insights driven from the text in many real-world scenarios as it assigns predefined tags or categories to unstructured text. Sentiment analysis algorithms use machine learning supervised and unsupervised approaches to interpret and categorize documents based on different sentimental categories. It can categorize documents based on opinion polarities such as positive, negative, neutral, or based on the writer's feelings and emotions, such as context and sarcasm. Sentiment analysis enables companies to categorize complaints and detect urgent requests, which require immediate action. Sentiment classifiers evaluate brand reputation over time, conduct market research, and improve services and products based on customer feedback. Topic analysis and intent detection are other examples of knowledge discovery problems using classification algorithms that automatically organize text by theme or subject.

Text extraction has also been used widely to select important parts of any given document, such as specific keywords containing information about brands, company names, product specifications, or prices. Named Entity Recognition (NER) is a text extraction approach that extracts predefined entities, such as people, organizations, and locations. Collocation is another task analysis technique to detect words that commonly co-occur, useful for discovering hidden semantic structures.

Generally, knowledge discovery techniques are divided into two main groups: (i) linguistic rules-based approaches and (ii) machine-learning models [591, 592]. Determining the appropriate method for a particular use case is essential to maximize the insights' efficiency and relevance value. However, machine-learning approaches recently could overcome rule-based systems in many scenarios. We elaborate each category in Section 4.1.3.1 and Section 4.1.3.2.

4.1.3.1 Linguistic Rules-based Models

The earliest approaches in text analytic tasks were based on extracting rules, known as rule-based methods, where despite the simplicity, they have been proven to work well [241]. Rules are applied to understand the structure of an arbitrary text by focusing on pattern-matching or parsing. Rule-based approaches work based on pattern matching strategy. Patterns are varied from simple boolean keywords to more complicated models composed over time by language experts based on the problems' requirements. The linguistic rules include using parts of speech, syntax-based rules about different topics, regions, or patterns about the presence of words. Rules-based approaches also include engineering grammars using a hand-crafted system by imitating human behavior in creating grammar structure [515]. The main benefit of rule-based systems is the flexibility in development. Besides, they can be updated quickly for adjusting to new known situations without the requirement for significant change to the core system. Moreover, tracking the rules' functionality is possible. Therefore, any reported mistakes can easily be found and adjusted, providing granular analysis. They can be promptly employed to a set of documents for fast analysis and are easy to understand.

However, some disadvantages make them impractical in many cases. They often serve to augment initial hypotheses rather than examine them with a more comprehensive view. Moreover, due to the variability of language, which makes it constantly changing, rules cannot consider how meaning can be represented differently. Rule-based systems often make rigid rules, missing the opportunity to concentrate on relevant information. In addition, designing complex grammar rules that match data requires expert knowledge, resulting in years of research. More importantly, humans create rules with inherent biases. Therefore, they are designed to recognize specific patterns. Besides, rules are required to improve continuously, taking linguistic experts to encode them manually. Sometimes designed rules become so complex that they may contradict each other.

To conclude, rule-based systems easily capture distinct language patterns by interpreting sentences and analyzing the relationships between words. Consequently, sentence-level tasks such as parsing and extraction are handled perfectly. An expected outcome is low precision with high recall. It demonstrates specific use cases are managed with high performance while it suffers from generalization.

4.1.3.2 Machine Learning-based Models

Machine learning-based algorithms have been extensively used in NLP to discover patterns from human-provided examples. Machine learning approaches work based on statistical techniques to discover the unique patterns in the corpus that can be extended for unseen data. Therefore, machine learning approaches significantly speed up the development of specific NLP systems' capability when sufficient training data is available, which is challenging in practice. Moreover, they can be adjusted easily to solve new problems in contrast to rule-based approaches.

Machine learning approaches are mainly categorized as unsupervised and supervised approaches. Unsupervised learning methods aim to uncover hidden structures of data without requiring a training phase. Clustering aims to group a collection of documents to improve retrieval and can be applied in different levels of granularity, including documents, paragraphs, sentences, or terms [39]. The large dimensionality and sparse feature space for text documents necessitate the need to design text-based clustering approaches. Text characteristics such as large dimensionality and sparse feature space necessitate specialized algorithms. Hierarchical clustering, k-means, and topic modeling are among the most common clustering algorithms used for text data.

Hierarchical clustering algorithms are distance-based clustering algorithms that use a similarity function to make a hierarchy in different levels [33]. The hierarchy is created in top-down (divisive approach) or bottom-up (agglomerative approach) fashion. In addition, there are different approaches to split or merge nodes of hierarchies. For instance, for agglomerative algorithms merging methods can be based on the highest similarity between any pair of documents (single linkage clustering), the average similarity between pairs of documents (group-average linkage clustering), or the worst-case similarity between any pair of documents in these groups (complete linkage clustering).

K-means clustering simply groups samples into k clusters. However, finding the optimal k is computationally difficult (NP-hard). However, various efficient heuristics are proposed to find a local optimum [101]. Besides, k-means is sensitive to initial points. Using another clustering algorithm such as agglomerative clustering algorithm to find the initial point is among the best strategies t solve this problem [323].

Topic modeling is a probabilistic clustering algorithm to build a soft clustering, where samples belong to different clusters by a membership value. A document is defined as a mixture of topics, where a topic is a probability distribution over words [578]. Probabilistic Latent Semantic Analysis (PLSA) [280] and Latent Dirichlet Allocation (LDA) [94] are among the main approaches in this category.

Supervised learning methods discover how to classify data by learning from the training data to predict unseen data, which vary from basic to more advanced text analysis techniques based on applications. Different machine learning algorithms have been used for text classification in separate communities, including data mining, database, machine learning, and information retrieval [434]. Classification tasks can be in a hard form that explicitly assigns a label to an instance or a soft form if a probability value is assigned to a sample. Multiple labels can also be assigned to a sample, known as multi-label classification [252].

Probabilistic classifiers are the most common approaches that work based on some probabilistic assumptions [533]. Despite its simplicity, the Naive Bayes algorithm is the most widely used classifier. It works based on Bayes's theorem and the conditional probabilities of words' occurrence. The main advantage of this algorithm that makes it popular is its applicability with less training data [416]. The class distribution of documents is modeled probabilistically by assuming the independence of different terms distribution. Two forms of Naive Bayes classifier are mainly used, the multi-variate Bernoulli model and the Multinomial model. Both models find the posterior probability classes based on the words distributions in the document. However, the Multi-variate Bernoulli model represents documents by a vector of binary features indicating the absence or presence of the words in the document. In contrast, the Multinomial model captures words frequencies using a bag-of-words model [573]. The Bernoulli model outperforms the Multinomial model for small vocabulary size.

The K-Nearest Neighbor (KNN) classifier is another simple classification model using distance-based measures to label samples based on similarity to their neighbors. The idea behind the mode is that similar samples with the same classes are close in feature space. If the model used k neighbors to infer a sample class, the model is called k-nearest neighbor [550].

The decision tree is a classifier that recursively splits the training data based on a defined attribute at each level [434]. The condition to split samples on each node for text data can be the presence or absence of a particular term in the document or other text attributed reported in Sec. 4.1.2.

Support Vector Machine (SVM) is a supervised learning classification algorithm with a broad application [175]. SVM, by default, is a binary linear classifier that makes decision boundaries based according to the linear combinations of the document features by finding a hyperplane with the maximum distance from samples of different classes. A sample with maximum distance from the hyperplane is called support vectors and defines the border of the hyperplane. Different variations of SVM are proposed for different tasks [467]. SVM is robust for high-dimensional data that makes it popular for text-based problems [286].

Finally, combining linguistic rules and different machine learning models produce the best results, known as hybrid approaches. Hybrid approaches use machine learning-based approaches as their core and apply rule-based strategies to enhance the prediction results. They complement each other in some very compelling ways, adding a serious edge to the overall architecture. Rule-based systems can be used flexibly in various ways and bring value and rigor to almost every stage of the ML pipeline, such as the feature engineering stage [69].

4.2 Social Data Text Analytics: Challenges and Opportunities

Social media applications, including micro-blogs such as Twitter, or discussion forums and blogs, are used frequently to share news, ideas, and events worldwide. They play a significant role in current Web applications, accounting for 50% of the top ten Websites based on statistics [295]. Consequently, they contain rich sources of information on human interaction and collective human behavior in different domains such as business, sociology, politic, economics, sociology, and computer science. Therefore, extracting meaningful information from social textual data provides unique opportunities for social media research and applications. Textual social data helps extract valuable insights given in various aspects that were not previously achievable. Generally, it helps measure specific values or insights in business and research. For instance, it detects key topics within any conversation. More importantly, the perception of how the content of the discussion or the sentiment has changed over time can be extracted, helpful for quantifying purchase intent and analyzing the consumer buying cycle. However, new challenges for mining social media exist due to the distinct features, including time sensitivity and unstructured text format.

4.2.1 Time Sensitivity

A unique feature of most social media services that affect analytical tasks profoundly is their real-time nature and the sensitivity to chronological recency. However, the frequency of activity is varied on different platforms. For instance, blog users post every few days; however, micro-blog and social network users update their profiles several times a day. This rapid generation of content in real-time provides valuable information for different purposes such as detecting a crisis, monitoring an event, and finding users' interested in various aspects useful for business purposes. Detecting and tracking information provenance extracted from users' communication in different locations is also a beneficial usage of the real-time nature of social media content [55]. For instance, Sakaki et al. [536] proposed an algorithm that analyzes the real-time interaction of events by monitoring tweets to discover a crisis such as earthquakes. However, due to the fast development of content and communication trends in social media, the text has changed, and consequently, different posts are not independent anymore [295]. Users are connected and influenced by their communities who have a relationship, reflecting the user's interests. For instance, if someone reports a problem with a product on social media, the reviews may change significantly due to the time-sensitivity of textual data in social media. Conversely, conventional text analytic techniques may not work for social text data.

4.2.2 Format and Style

Social media content has two main distinct characteristics; short length and unorganized structure. Some social media Websites, including Twitter, restrict the length of user-generated content to a specific word or character number limit. For instance, Twitter limits the length of each tweet to 140 characters, making people more effective and quick with their interaction in social media applications. However, the ubiquity of short-length text on social media builds new challenges, making traditional research in text analytics ineffective, such as information extraction, text classification, text clustering, and sentiment analysis. For instance, the short-length format of text in Twitter can not provide enough context data for practical similarity measures [491] which are fundamental in various text processing methods [288]. Another critical difference between traditional and social data is the content's quality and structure variance. Users in social media applications tend to use or invent acronyms or abbreviations, which make the interaction convenient. However, identifying the semantic meaning of these messages accurately is very challenging. Besides, the generated text in social media is noisy mainly. Moreover, the high variance in the quality of texts made by users, originating from people's attitudes, makes the other analytical tasks more complex than in other domains [20].

   In addition to the user-generated notions, there exist other non-content information specifically for each social media. For instance, on Twitter, users are allowed to utilize the '#' symbol, called a hashtag, for tagging information such as a keyword or subjects. Sometimes, it is also linked with an image or different regions of an image [672]. Therefore, text analytics in social media can use metadata from various aspects such as user profile, links, tags, content, and timestamp. There is extensive research using metadata used for detecting popular events [379], distinguishing breaking news or rumor [425], and finding overlaps communities in social network services [634].

4.3 Social Data Text Analytics

Applying traditional techniques for processing social textual data is not possible. Therefore, text analytic methods need to be designed for social textual data specifically. This section introduces various text analytics methods designed for extracting insights from social textual data.

4.3.1 Event Detection

Social text streams are the real world's sensors due to the real-time content generation feature of social media services [679]. Consequently, detecting real-world events or crises from social text data is necessary. The volume and velocity of textual data contained in social media provide many event detections and tracking opportunities.

Event detection is the task of monitoring data sources to discover the existence of an event [405]. It has many beneficial applications, specifically during a disaster or crisis, such as the occurrence of an earthquake or tsunami. Micro-blogging services provide a convenient way to communicate and distribute time-sensitive news and update during a crisis. Sakaki et al. [536] proposed an algorithm to examine the real-time interaction of events on Twitter used for earthquake-reporting systems in Japan. Each user is determined as a sensor for monitoring tweets posted about an event. The workflow to detect a target event has two phases: (i) using a trained classifier proper to classify tweets based on their content to predefined classes using features such as message length and keywords and (ii) building a probabilistic spatiotemporal model for identifying the event's location.

Detecting popular news, known as 'breaking news', is another important application of social media. Various news channels are fed daily news stories, that is hard for journalists and editors to rank them based on their priority which is possible through social media mentions [139]. Lee et al. [365] proposed a novel approach for detecting major news story headlines from the blogosphere daily, using features such as language mode, the news headline prior, and the query likelihood.

In addition to event detection, monitoring and tracking events' changes and evolution over time is another interesting research direction. User-generated text social content along with the network's structure provides a rich source of information for monitoring events. Lin et al. [379] proposed an approach for tracking popular events in online communities using various features. They employed the burstiness of user interest in addition to network structure. Using picture tags in addition to textual data is another approach for detecting events [127]. Another line of research in this category is using locational and temporal distributions of tag usage. Chen et al. [127] linked locational and temporal distributions of tags to related events and clustered them such that each cluster represents an event with similar distribution patterns in terms of time and location [127].

4.3.2 Social Data Tagging

Social tagging is the process of associating tags to an entity using for managing and searching through Internet-based applications. Social tagging services provide an opportunity to generate a large volume of tagging data, useful mining information on the Web. However, the tagging services provide keyword-based search. Therefore, it is challenging for a user to determine the associated resources quickly by searching tags. Besides, the keywords-based searching system fails to discover the semantic relationship between semantically related tags. Consequently, the output of the tag-based search module is not inadequate for users to identify their required resources for extracting insights. These challenges have attracted the research community to design more complex tag-based search services.

Tags features, including the short length and sparsity, make the design of an effective tag ranking algorithm challenging. Research on social tagging services mainly focuses on two main aspects: improving the quality of tag recommendation and employing social tagging resources for facilitating various applications. Sigurbjornsson and Van [568] proposed an advanced approach for supporting users during the tagging process in multimedia sharing sites. They assess tagging recommendation procedures for facilitating annotating tasks performed by users by recommending a set of tags linked to the photo. Yin et al. [664] proposed a probabilistic model for personalizing tag prediction tasks. Social tagging resources are fundamental for facilitating other Web applications such as browsing and search quality [279], Web object classification [666], and document recommendation [257].

4.3.3 Topic Modeling

People tend to express their idea about everything openly on social media. Therefore, extracting discussed topics in social media has extensive applications in the real world, such as management, marketing, and politics. Topic modeling is an unsupervised machine learning-based technique that reveals hidden topical patterns across the document collection. In other words, it projects document collections to a topic space by finding a group of words that best represent the information in a collection. It also enables annotating documents based on the extracted topics. Therefore, it facilitates further processes such as organizing, searching and summarizing text using annotated text data [74, 524]. In topic modeling, a document is defined as a probabilistic distribution over various topics. Each identified topic is also a probabilistic distribution over words.

Deerwester et al. [162] proposed an approach for topic modeling as a pioneer in this field. They improved the process of detecting relevant documents using terms of queries by proposing a semantic structure. Probabilistic Latent Semantic Indexing (PLSI) is another common topic modeling approach based on using polysemous words and domain-specific synonyms [281]. Among various algorithms, Latent Dirichlet Allocation (LDA) proposed by Blei et al. [94] has been widely used in different domains. LDA is a probabilistic topic modeling approach that combines the Dirichlet statistics distribution and the topic modeling process to detect discussed topics in a document set based on mentioning specific words considering their probabilities. LDA has been widely used in various applications, including identifying the recent academic inclination in literature [524]. Supervised LDA (sLDA) has also been proposed to improve LDA for labeled documents [524].

LDA has been extended in various ways to be compatible for identifying topics in social media with a broad application for social media community detection [417, 447]. For instance, Zhang et al. proposed a hierarchical model to find probabilistic community profiles in social networks by incorporating the Bayesian model induced from the LDA model, where communities in the social network are represented as latent variables. A distribution across the social space is defined for detecting communities [447, 675]. Another line of research for community discovery using the topic modeling concept was proposed by Liu et al. [389] where they modeled a framework using a Bayesian hierarchical approach. Li et al. [371] proposed a new model, called TTR-LDA, by combining LDA and Girvan-Newman community detection algorithm. They proved that users in the same communities are interested in a similar topic set. They also concluded that a topic could be divided into subtopics where each subtopic is spread across various communities.

Topic modeling approaches are also used in recommendation systems by combining traditional collaborative filtering approaches and probabilistic topic modeling to recommend scientific articles to online community users [524]. In another approach, Daud [156] proposed a model called Temporal-Author-Topic (TAT), which enables simulated model text, researchers, and time for specific research using the topic modeling approach and semantic-based intrinsic of words.

Nguyen et al. [455] proposed a model for finding out the desired topics to support products marketing in social networks using a content-based social network analyzer based on topic modeling. In another work, Vavliakis et al. [615] used the concept of topic modeling to extract important time-based events from Web documents on a large scale. Zhai et al. [673] was also incorporate large-scale topic modeling in MapReduce to detect topics from various languages.

Supervised topic modeling has also been proposed for micro-blogging services [285] where the authors improved the model's quality by training a topic model. The performance of the proposed model is significant to compare to other competitors. Lim et al. [376] applied a hierarchical Poisson-Dirichlet process (PDP) for topic modeling and a Gaussian process random function model for modeling social networks for Twitter, working in a complete Bayesian nonparametric way. Yang et al. [660] proposed another approach for topic modeling of Twitter text classification and other metadata sources of information. In a recent work by Ostrowski [466], he proposed a model combining classification and topic modeling applied to a filtered collection of Twitter messages in a single framework.

4.3.4 Social Data Text Classification

Classifying an unstructured text is a primary task in the natural language processing field. It facilitates further processing, including organizing, browsing, and categorizing text data for delivering valuable insights. Automatic text classification reduces error compared to human annotating since people are biased. However, text classification is a supervised approach, requiring extensive training data. Text classification is applied to different text formats, including short informal texts like tweets or chat-bot queries and longer documents such as emails, customer surveys, or reviews. Other NLP tasks mainly have a text classifier in part of their processes, such as sentiment analysis, intent detection, recommendation, spam detection, translation, and language detection. Therefore, text classification task in social media is mainly defined based on the application.

Using text classifiers provides scalability to any business needs by automating business processes. Among different applications of text classification, intent detection, identifying urgent issues, automating customer support processes are the most popular ones. Intent detection is used to classify customers' conversations to extract the reason behind feedback or complaints and route them to the corresponding department. Generating product analytics and intelligent customer services is among popular applications of intent detection or classification. Intent detection can also provide real-time analysis of users' generated content to take immediate action if required. Besides, businesses can follow their brand mentions constantly and in real-time and identify critical information and the changes over time. Businesses can also extract personalized and aspect-based sentiment reviews of their products and services on social media [66, 69].

Text classification approaches enabled various text analytic tasks for social text data. Various studies compared text classification techniques for different applications and datasets. For instance, Irfan et al. [300] evaluated various text mining techniques to explore multiple textual patterns from social media using machine learning and ontology-based algorithms. Patel et al. [480] also compared many classifiers discussed in Section 4.1.3.2 used for social text data, including Bayesian classifier, decision tree, support vector machine, k-nearest neighbor, and deep learning approach. Besides, Chirawichitchai et al. [132] examined various methods of feature weighting used for document classification problems. Viriyayudhakorn et al. [619] analyzed various thinking support engines and performed Word Article Matrix (WAM) to compute the association function applied on Wikipedia.

Another trend of research in this category has focused on the problem of classifying short stream texts in social media [329]. Lee et al. [364] proposed two approaches for classifying Twitter trending topics using the bag-of-words model and network-based classification, where the network-based classifier surpassed all other text-based classifiers. Sornlertlamvanich et al. [572] proposed a new method that used WAM combined with a cosine similarity measure for classifying text and tracking keywords for understanding social developments.

4.3.5 Sentiment and Opinion Extraction

The explosive growth of online social media content has recently received substantial attention to address automatic sentiment analysis. People openly express their opinions about various topics, including politics, sports, products, and news. Therefore, sentiment classification approaches enable extracting the feeling and emotion of the writer and opinion polarity such as positive, negative, and neutral. Businesses employ sentiment classifiers for various applications such as monitoring brands, exploring research, supporting customers, and analyzing their products.

Various approaches have been applied for sentiment analysis tasks, including rule-based and machine learning-based approaches. Sentiment classification are applied on different levels of granularity including document level [158, 474, 610] or the sentence level [228, 290, 339]. Both categories follow the same procedure on different levels. Opinion words or phrases are identified using approaches such as lexicon-based or rule-based. In lexicon-based approaches, a lexicon table is built where words are categorized as positive or negative evaluations. Then for determining the semantic direction, a distance measure is used to compare each opinion word and the product feature. On the other hand, rule-based approaches work based on each word's parts-of-speech (POS) tagging. Finally, co-occurrence patterns of words and tags are utilized to identify the sentiment.

Supervised and unsupervised techniques can be employed for sentiment analysis on social media data. Various text classification approaches discussed in Section 4.1.3.2 have been used for sentiment classification [474]. However, traditional research mainly focused on long text sentiment analysis such as reviews. Therefore, sentiment approaches are required to adjust for short texts such as micro-blogging messages. Recently, there has been lots of research in the area of sentiment classification that has targeted micro-blogging text data using approaches such as Naive Bayes, support vector machine, decision tree, random forest, Adaboost, and deep learning [311, 481, 688].

Bag-of-words model has also been widely used in sentiment classification or detecting opinion words combined with machine learning approaches. For instance, Pang and Lee [448] used bag-of-words to extract sentiment from online reviews about movies. In addition to the bag-of-words model, high-order n-grams are used for sentiment classification. As an example, Demitery et al. [86] proposed an embedding mechanism of n-grams for dealing with sparsity and dimensionality. Almatarneh and Gamallo [34] proposed a predictive model designed based on collected documents. They analyzed that the classifier result depends on various metrics, including selected features, parameter tuning, training phase, and the characteristic of the model to learn in a dynamic context.

Knowledge extracted from social media platforms such as Facebook, YouTube, and Twitter help various organizations and businesses to discover substantial clues about their services or brands to maximize customers' satisfaction level [52]. Besides, they can update their policies over time based on extracted feedback. It also helps them to consequently set up a trend increasingly for recommending personalized services or products [667].

4.3.6 Linking Textual Data and Social Metadata

Other forms of information are associated with textual information, which can significantly improve the result of text analytic methods, including classification and clustering. For instance, on Twitter, two posts can be associated via different ways such as authors' followers, followee, or retweeting, liking, or replying. Linked metadata such as hashtags or hyperlinks is the main feature in classifying Twitter messages. The semantic similarity of different posts is measured based on various indicators such as posting time, place, or author's profile. Facebook, Instagram, LinkedIn, and other social media sites are following the same trend. Therefore, a combination of link and text content has proved to extract the maximum information out of social media content.

Social media is a rich source of information in various forms that are not available in traditional text data. For instance, cosine similarity is a prevalent measure to estimate the similarity of two documents. However, in social media similarity of two different posts is estimated using two other features added to the text data, including *connectivity* and *structural similarity*. Connectivity is a measure indicating the possible paths to connect authors of documents. Structural similarity represents the shared numbers of neighbors.

Though links hold semantic information, it is very challenging to extract the information due to the multi-dimensionality of connections between users in social media [596]. To elaborate, users are linked based on different reasons and relations. Therefore, each link has a semantic meaning united with its corresponding latent dimensions in social data. Furthermore, traditional text analytic methods work based on local features, representing documents. However, extracting features for various types of network data is not possible [308]. To be more specific, an adjacency matrix used to represent a network would suffer from sparsity and dimensionality and consequently can not describe the relations properly. Moreover, labeling objects in social networks required for supervised learning methods is expensive and time-consuming.

Another important aspect of social media is its evolution over time. Therefore, networks constantly change by joining a new user, deleting friendship connections, or leaving the network. Consequently, community structure requires to be updated continuously. Therefore, integrating the most recent network information is required for different analytic tasks. Chakrabarti et al. [38] proposed a graph-based classification approach by incorporating features such as network evolution and edges pruning. Aggarwal and Li [18] followed the same procedure in addition to node classification using text content and links simultaneously. They used a random walk approach in addition to network content to make a robust model.

Link information has also been used in clustering [685] and topic modeling [588]. The authors proved that using a link and text information can lead to better results compared to other models based on only one of them [19].

4.4 Concluding Remarks and Discussion

Social media data, specifically text data, contains valuable hidden information that, if extracted, opens new horizons to transfer data to actionable knowledge. However, mining and summarizing social media data is challenging since it is noisy, unorganized, dynamic, distributed, and more importantly, short. In this chapter, we briefly introduced text analytic tasks. We explained the general framework for text analytic tasks, including text preprocessing, representation, and knowledge discovery. We elaborated more on social textual data properties and the need for specific methodologies to uncover hidden insights. Finally, we discussed recent advanced methods for different applications in social data, including event detection, sentiment analysis, opinion extraction, and social tagging. Existing preliminary progress in the social media text analytic research domain confirms the growing demand for new approaches customized for different social media services to tackle new challenges. There is a need to expand research and development in this field for exploring and understanding interaction patterns and human behavior, leading to more personalized approaches.

Social Data Analytics deals with a variety of data from text to image and video. Photo and video sharing on social networking services are now quite popular, and data analytics play an important role in extracting meaningful information and insights from photos and videos posted on social media. The next chapter, will provide an overview of image and video data analytics, followed by highlighting challenges and opportunities in the field. It will also discuss important topics, including image and video detection and recognition and storytelling with image and video data. We will also discuss modern topics such as analyzing and generating 3D posts on social media.

5

Social Media Image and Video Analytics

5.1 Image and Video Analytic: Overview

This chapter explicates an effective image and video content analysis of interactive social media, aiming to identify the characteristics of photo content posted across social media. Social media has a significant influence on people's social lives. It can have an effect on consumer behavior and opinions, such as allowing customers to make reasoned choices [69, 359, 515]. Around 79% of young people use social media daily. It has been shown that youth are looking to social media for information in several sectors [116]. Information from social media platforms is usually accurate, relevant, and available digitally. Governments, commercial researchers, and organizations need a method for interpreting and analyzing Internet data; in this way, meaningful information may be extracted from social data [359]. Every day, massive number of pictures are posted and shared on social media, and because visual data are more likely to get shared on social media compared to text, it is now a powerful method of distributing information to a wide audience [128].

Images provide supplementary information that makes them superior to text when conducting social data research. It is impossible to code data manually on enormous data sets, but an image can easily record variables. Images are more effortless and are quicker method for conveying a scenario. It is also true that in most cases, emotions strongly influence human conduct, and images grab these responses more forcefully than text. To identify the complicated issues that underlie images, humans use them to create a visual aid to evaluate multifaceted political matters. Individual decision-making can benefit from visual data since it is more likely to capture people's attention and help them learn rather than textual material. Images can help get information ready to promote specific research initiatives. For example, photographs can provide information about demographic and socioeconomic characteristics of both humans and areas when surveys are inaccessible. Photos are valuable in showcasing regions' economic progress lacking consistent statistics and are difficult to study over time. Social media data analysis enables marketers to see the world through their customers' eyes without the prejudice of being directly involved in the interactions. There are some limitations with existing analysis tools. For example, most current analytic tools do not process images directly, and only analyze the image captions. Yet, identifying faces from photos posted on social media will assist visual data analytics. The obvious advantages of increased biometric security and police powers are of interest to government leaders. The scientific community believes that improved data and increased precision in testing theories will be more readily available. In particular, image and video analytics can help in:

- Discovering trending topics from visual data: this may cover obtaining real-time updates from data on what companies are sharing, consumer ideas, and brand attitudes; and understanding what is driving the insight on Instagram so it can provide detailed insight for the sales teams and marketing. Finding actionable insights to discover trending stories and finding themes and feeling behind the industry from visual data could be another interesting application.
- Analyzing users' personality via a social media profile photo: It is quite interesting to know that there is a cognitive relationship between the personality of social users and the images that they post or interact with on social media [66]. To get an accurate idea of someone's character in an online setting, it is essential to concentrate on both their aesthetic and facial traits, as well as the variety in age and ethnicity found in their profile picture. Users with attractive and attentive online identities tend to post profile photographs with happy and bright expressions, while more creative types want a unique or more artistic look [58, 385].
- Measuring and proving the Return on Investment (ROI): to verify social ROI, we should rely on the visual data that has been posted on social media to quantify the generated revenue.
- Acquiring online news by identifying the image context: this task may include obtaining information about an image by analyzing the image and identifying various aspects, such as subjects, memes, scenes, faces, and emotions; and making sense of people's thoughts on news and understanding the content and context around the image.
- Analyzing visual data on social media to enhance marketing: This task may include perceiving logos and evaluating a few influential consumers; and creating ideas for marketing and monitoring brand awareness. Finding opportunities to engage with consumers, and earning how customers relate to the brand and the products through engaging at different times and intervals; and identifying consumer preferences and curious shopping behaviors by analyzing their social media postings.

- Analyzing social media images for public health: A study has revealed the ability to monitor public health issues such as the temporal patterns of influenza or obesity. A picture is worth a thousand words, and Instagram is a huge repository of visual data, so it is a perfect fit for the world of social media. It helps diagnose disorders related to lifestyle choices, such as obesity. Data about a given topic or subject can be found in several forms of media; often, this information might be more detailed in images compared to text [235]. Given the current amount of imagery material, a system to parse massive amounts of social media (visual) data is necessary. Technical details are needed to detect and distinguish items and facts in photographs in comparison to plain text [316].

This chapter focuses on these needs, aiming to extract and analyze the content of photos and videos posted on social media to provide valuable information. We introduce recent breakthroughs in computer vision and machine learning for object detection and recognition. One of the new approaches, informally known as deep learning, indicates considerable progress in learning from big data by using powerful hardware such as Graphical Processing Units (GPUs[1]). One major problem in computer vision that benefits social scientists is the ability to identify and recognize objects in photos and videos, monitor the movement of faces, and follow the movement of objects across time. Object detection is defined as finding items in pictures and classifying each object with a category. Classifications and locations can be discovered through the process of item detection. Recognizing images involves labeling items. Face detection algorithms are able to identify a face in an image. The method of determining the moving objects in a video is known as object tracking. Tracking objects plays a crucial role in computer vision applications, including robotics, surveillance, autonomous driving, and activity identification. This chapter will discuss such technologies, as well as highlighting the need for 3D posts, which recently attracted the attention of social users'. As 3D data can provide extra information compared to 2D images, uploading 3D images is one of the finest ways to enhance a company's business to increase audience engagement on social media.

5.2 Image and Video Analytic: Opportunities and Challenges

At both local and global levels, people's thoughts, beliefs, and behaviors can be seen through social media and information sources that present an invaluable treasure trove of knowledge. Data gathered through social media offers a deep understanding of how people relate to their surroundings [63]. Hence, it could provide many significant possibilities for usage in a wide range of applications. Even so, many sorts of biases in who has access to social media, what they use it for, the reasons for its dramatic increase, and how these data are likely to affect information

---

[1] A Graphics Processing Unit (GPU) is a chip or electronic circuit capable of rendering graphics for display on an electronic device. GPUs were originally developed for accelerating graphics processing; however, they are able to speed up computational processes for machine learning and deep learning algorithms [74].

system security professionals produce some barriers to being able to glean meaningful information from this data. In this section, we describe the opportunities and challenges that images from social media sources are provided.

5.2.1 Opportunities

If there is an emergency, people are more likely to record their experience in pictures or videos. They then share these media with others to better inform them of what is happening, as when an incident could cause significant infrastructure damage. During disaster relief efforts, most organizations find it hard to gather immediate knowledge of the current situation. It is frustrating to collect this information by traditional means as it is a costly and timely process. Social media provides abundant options to gain quick information relevant to making adjustments to catastrophe responses, using images and videos. Research shows that the general public relies on social media for several reasons, such as communicating urgent information about disasters, including early announcements, warnings, and damage assessments such as roads, buildings, and bridges [299]. In addition, social media platforms can serve as a source of information to collect data on the crowd's needs following a catastrophe. It has been discovered that certain real-world events, such as emergencies, are generally covered first by social media platforms such as Facebook and Twitter, while traditional media, such as newspapers and TV, are lagging behind.

The importance of characterizing today's modern culture increases by using social media. This is because a distinct culture is emerging from the explosive sharing of visual information online. These pictures communicate particular ways of life and emotions [564]. Research on Social Impact Assessment (SIA) can benefit from more data sources, such as digital photos in social media archives. In a more digital society, there are more ways to collect data for SIA. The word 'culturomics' embraces this large research subject that uses visual data from social media, which presents the collection as the concept of realizing culture. For some SIA applications, the visualizations are more robust if they contain more graphics [67]. Some of the approaches proposed to tie themes and traits together using image codes are statistical. The final landscape perception diagrams are perceptual rather than spatial, making them less sensitive to biases in the findings produced by differences in methods. An excellent illustration of this is to find out what aspects you can expect to change and understand how you might have associations with a specific value or activity via social media [564].

In particular, extracted images from social media data offer unique opportunities to test hypotheses created from social and psychological theories [393]. Since data on social media is constantly updating, data scientists typically need to watch the changes happen in real-time. A study of this kind, for example, investigated ideological differences in a variety of political and non-political situations by applying findings related to communication systems among ideological communities to a psychology hypothesis about why people have such beliefs. New theories related to the usage of visual data found on social media will provide the possibility of better understanding their customers and serving them more effectively. Additionally, this methodology could give researchers valuable insight into previous and future reactions to environmental regulation (e.g., climate regulation) [567]. For organizations using social media, visual data can be used for various business purposes, including communications, sales of virtual items, marketing research, human resource management, and management of internal processes. Social media is much more fluid and suitable area than is feasible; what could be current today could be gone tomorrow [324].

5.2.2 Challenges

The automation, gathering, and administration of visual data are the primary issues in this field. Despite the benefits above, data analytics is a difficult task. Many sorts of information, including photographs, videos, and text messages, can be found on social media, some of which are rather noisy and do not follow typical Web protocols, such as the news stories or graphical data that accompany these pieces. Because of this, most conventional data analysis methodologies developed for normal Web data are unsuitable for analysis of social media data [299]. There are several issues with working with visual data in social media. One of the major ones is reducing information overload. Despite how easy it is to collect photographs and videos from social media, the process of analyzing large amounts of visual data content, such as that created in disaster areas, is a difficult one. Humanitarian groups are frequently asked to review photographs and videos in the wake of an emergency for potentially relevant information. However, some social media photographs are noisy and chaotic and have a great deal of irrelevant and redundant content. Nobody has the time to dig through this clutter and identify relevant and important information [299].

It is also important to highlight that, false material can be posted on social media, e.g., for entertaining or advertising purposes, but it is also developed to propagate disinformation. If people want a quick humanitarian reaction, they should realize that verifying the gathered data from social media photographs is an under-explored area. Also, in social media, a primary problem is obtaining location data for posted photographs. Researchers who work in computer vision have struggled to create a working prototype because the majority of visual content in social media does not come with geolocation information. So they have been trying to locate the GPS coordinates from image or video content. Moreover, due to the rapid growth in using social media, some internal rules [591, 592] have been applied for using social media, and it has become more critical for information system security professionals.

5.3 Image and Video Detection and Recognition

It is necessary for photographs on social media to process and extract events instantly in real-time with an automatic image analysis method. Detecting objects is one of the most challenging tasks, and is often in the spotlight because of how widespread it is. Apart from discovering several items in the photos, another essential assignment in this sector is detecting distinct disasters in images, such as fires, floods, and earthquakes in varied settings. This section will describe several image and video object detection methods and then explain the image and video face detection and object tracking.

5.3.1 Object Detection in Images and Video Frames

To identify and analyze the items in photos or videos, we use computer vision and an object detection algorithm to locate the object. Images or videos draw us in, and we instantly figure out what we are looking at. Object detection seeks to resurrect the powers of the human mind in a computer. Object detection establishes the basis of many computer vision tasks, such as picture captioning, image segmentation, and object tracking. It is among the hardest and fundamental problems in computer vision. When looked at from a usage standpoint, the two main topics of object detection research are general object detection and the detection applications that seek to employ that object detection. To recreate human sight and recognition, the primary goal of general object detection is to examine how to detect multiple objects under a unified framework. However, the focus of detection applications is the different sorts of things detected under specific scenarios, such as human detection, face detection, and text detection. Autonomous driving, video surveillance, and robot vision have gained significant traction because of recent advances in object detection using deep learning models. In recent decades, it is evident that the development of object detection has mainly been categorized via two historical times: "traditional object detection term (before 2014)" and "deep learning-based detection term (after 2014)" [689].

5.3.1.1 Traditional Object Detectors

Hand-crafted characteristics influenced many of the initial object detection methods. Individuals have no choice but to construct sophisticated, speedy representations of features and variety to use the restricted computational resources of the period. We have included a brief explanation of several early object detection algorithms and object recognition and categorization techniques using machine learning and deep learning algorithms.

- Histogram of Oriented Gradients (HOG) Detector: HOG feature descriptor was originally introduced by Dalal et al. [150] in 2005. For many years, the HOG detector has served as a foundation for many object detectors, as well as numerous computer vision jobs. HOG is a feature descriptor widely utilized in computer vision problems for object detection and is frequently applied to image data. The shape context has to be made interesting by the scale-invariant feature transform, which HOG can do. HOG analyzes the contour of an object or its structure in a picture. HOG can even determine the edge direction. Extracting the edge orientations is feasible by finding their angle and slope. Localized sections are used to make the computations. HOG is created using homogeneous cells on a dense grid for more accurate estimates [584]. Figure 5.1 indicates a sample result of images demonstrating using mean-shift to merge windows and using enhanced HOG approach [682].

- Deformable Part-based Model (DPM) Detector: DPM is one of the most prominent conventional object detection technologies. The DPM detector was created by Felzenszwalb et al. [214] and introduced in 2009. It is a slight variation of the HOG detector. DPM trains a multi-component combination model based on Histogram of Oriented Gradients and is capable of managing demanding benchmarks with a capability for managing vast differences in appearance [31]. The DPM employs the divide and conquers concept in the detection method. For example, to detect an automobile, DPM will locate its windows, body, and wheels. One of the filters that are often used in DPM detectors is an improvement in detection accuracy.

Fig. 5.1 Some result of using enhanced HOG approach images on the INRIA dataset [682].

- Scale Invariant Feature Transform (SIFT) Detector: One of the most prominent approaches for object detection in computer vision is the SIFT introduced
  by Lowe et al. [395]. SIFT is known for its exceptional capability of working
  across several aspects such as scale, vision, and orientation. Many computer vision challenges, including stereo matching, picture matching, and motion tracking, were solved with the help of the SIFT. The SIFT extracts specific unvarying
  characteristics from images, and it is an effective tool for identifying matching
  features on objects in multiple viewpoints in an image [456]. SIFT's functionality helps organize picture points known as the local features. These essential
  features are rotation and size invariant and are hence ideal for object and scene
  detection. Using SIFT characteristics, the image can be used for the model during training. SIFT features, unlike HOG features, do not suffer from image size
  or orientation issues.
- Image Segmentation and Blob Analysis: Image segmentation techniques such
  as Fuzzy C Means, Gaussian Filter, and Snake algorithm were also introduced
  to improve automatic object detection [496]. In these techniques, object features such as size, form, and color are involved. Advantages of these techniques
  include the fact that no precise limits exist for text shape and orientation, while
  disadvantages include that it is hard to tell text lines apart when densely stacked.

5.3.1.2 Object Detection Using Machine Learning

In addition to deep learning, machine learning techniques are frequently employed
for object recognition. These techniques differ from deep learning in that they provide various methodologies. Main machine learning approaches for categorizing
objects include:

- Support Vector Machines (SVMs): SVMs are learning algorithms used to
  find patterns in data using a type of supervised learning. To achieve a non-
  probabilistic binary linear classifier, the basic SVM is given two different
  classes of data as input. SVM can be applied to a variety of different types of
  data, for classifying objects, recognizing patterns, and categorizing text. Classifying information using support vector machines has certain advantages: With
  good results even in circumstances where the number of dimensions is more
  than the number of samples, the function uses a small training subset to be
  memory efficient [330].
- Aggregate Channel Features (ACF): The ACF object detector uses training photos and ground truth locations to detect specific objects in an image. ACF operates as a kind of channel feature, extracting features in the form of pixel values
  straight out of long channels, bypassing any form of "rectangular sums" in distinct locations and scales. Even though a general channel can carry color channels like RBG and grey-scale, many more channels are used to encode specific
  types of data, depending on the complexity of the data. The employment of ACF
  can confer substantial benefits, including the better depiction of objects, faster

indication speed, and increased localization of objects inside images when combined with an improved technique of boosting [535].

- Random Forest: Random forest, a concept based on an ensemble of individual decision trees, is a method that can generate a large number of results by applying it multiple times to the same data. Every tree in the random forest assigns a class prediction and uses it to vote on the class with the most votes, which the model will predict. Pham et al. [490] utilized the random forest regressions model based on patch features for prediction relying on the majority voting. Utilizing patches of the photo has some limitations. Farhood et al. [207] used fixed sub-windows rather than using the randomly selected patches. To obtain dense SIFT features, the sub-windows are separated from the frame. Figure 5.2 illustrates a block diagram of their work.

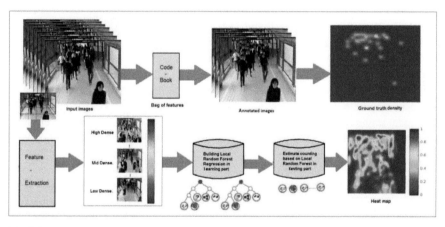

Fig. 5.2 The suggested method's structure, including the input photos, the learning process, and the testing process [207].

Applications often have two options when it comes to machine learning: starting with a pre-trained object detector or training the model from scratch using a bespoke object detector. The primary distinction is that, with machine learning, objects have to be identified by hand due to a lack of automated feature selection. In contrast, deep learning's automatic feature selection avoids that issue.

5.3.1.3 Object Detection Using Deep Learning

In object identification and recognition, the learning of feature presentations (a learning model) has led to substantial advancements thanks to the emergence of deep learning techniques [386]. Object detection, in particular, is in critical need of improvement, and it is receiving just that thanks to these techniques. Object detection is achieved using numerous approaches. The typical strategy for automatically identifying objects in photos is to use deep learning-based methods like Region-Based Convolutional Neural Networks (R-CNN) and You Only Look Once (YOLO) v2. Training and developing a bespoke object detector are the first steps. To learn the features of a given item, it is necessary to create a network architecture to train customized object detectors. It takes an extensive labeled dataset to build a Convolutional Neural Networks (CNN). In addition, this process required manually configuring the CNN model's layers and weights and also involved an extensive time commitment and training data. To ensure success, you can fine-tune it based on the application. Because the object detectors have already been trained, this approach will be more suitable to achieve the desired results. Object detection has two main types: two-stage detection and one-stage detection:

- **Two-Stage Networks**: The first step of systems like R-CNN and Spatial Pyramid Pooling (SPP) net, which includes region proposal detection, determines whether parts of the image may feature an item. A second stage involves classifying the objects that are found in the region suggestions. Object detection outcomes can be attained with the help of two-stage networks. Although they are slower than single-stage networks, they are nonetheless common. A group of an object's characteristics is extracted by performing the selective search. The RCNN approach is based on this group extraction. To do this, the deals are resized to be a standard size, and then they are sent into a computer network model trained on ImageNet to perform feature extraction. R-CNN is the earliest CNN-based two-stage object detection model, and it is the first to introduce a radically different approach. The structure of RCNN involves three main blocks as presented in Figure 5.3. The first stage involves creating class-independent region suggestions by extracting many of them from every input image's first block. A CNN with five Convolutional (Conv) layers and two Fully Connected (FC) layers has been utilized in the second block to obtain a feature vector of a given length from each region suggestion. To obtain consistent-sized input photos from region proposals of various sizes and ratios of aspect, it is necessary to apply affine image warping to every one of them. This results in one CNN extracting constant length feature vectors for every area proposal with warped images. Category-specific linear SVM classifies every region suggestion in the third block. The second and third blocks act on the second stage concurrently [585].
- **Single-Stage Networks.** A one-stage network, such as YOLO and SSD, uses anchor boxes to capture different parts of the image as they provide outputs that may be decoded to determine the final output of the network in a single pass. For situations with plenty of detail, like those with many small objects, two-stage networks provide more accuracy and can be more efficient than models of networks that run quicker. YOLO is exceptionally quick and can classify objects in a picture while simultaneously grouping them into regions. It does this while also finding the coordinates of those regions and giving a probability for each region of an object being located there. V2 is a refreshed version of the current model that improves its accuracy while remaining exceptionally fast. YOLO has dramatically increased its detection speed, but it has lost a significant amount

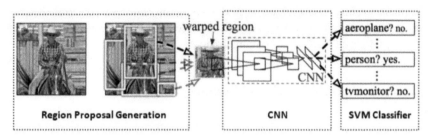

Fig. 5.3 Fast R-CNN architecture [249].

of precision with respect to localization. YOLO performs well with respect to detection, but it struggles with certain little items that other detectors do not. The Single-Shot multi-box Detection (SSD) model considers a whole image as input and passes it via several Conv layers with various sizes of filters (10×10, 5×5, and 3×3) as presented in Figure 5.4. Maps of features produced by convolutional layers in the network can be used to estimate the bounding boxes, one of which will likely be at or near the midpoint of the network. Extra feature layers create groups of bounding boxes by delivering them to the Conv layer with 3×3 filters. The parameters of the default SSD box (length, width, and height) are given by the program for Fast R-CNN. The model creates a vector of possibilities to estimate which class of object each box most likely belongs to based on the likelihood of each class's presence. To deal with the massive amount of information, SSD places constraints on the endpoints of Convolution layers. It is possible to capture things of many different sizes as the layers of Convolution all perform distinct scaling. To be both accurate and speedy, this object detector seeks a balance [585].

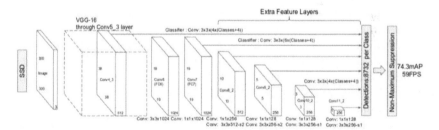

Fig. 5.4 Arcitecture of SSD [387].

5.3.1.4 Object Detection using Machine Learning vs. Deep Learning: Which One Is Better?

The method used to identify objects relies on the particular scenario and what one is aiming to achieve. It is advisable to put more weight on choosing deep learning because of the important role of a good GPU, and the many training images play. It is worth using a machine learning method if a program requires a powerful GPU and many training photos. Deep learning is more effective with more annotated images, and using GPUs cuts down the training time.

5.3.2 Face Detection and Recognition

Finding missing and displaced persons in social media, who are the target of many missing person search efforts, is one of the primary uses of face detection and recognition. An emerging interest in the exploration of picture recognition algorithms may offer exciting opportunities for exploring social media feeds of people in disaster areas, including victims of human rights violations or those who are forcibly relocated. A similar case can be made for using social media images to assist in finding missing and located individuals, which could be especially beneficial for emergency services (that are often dealing with time constraints) and those involved in urgent situations. It is also of assistance to the worried families of missing people [299].

Face detection and recognition have thus been explained in this part. The topic of facial identification and detection has recently seen a significant uptick in value, and it has garnered interest from several distinct research communities, such as the computer vision, pattern recognition, and biometrics communities. Furthermore, many different kinds of software that use facial recognition tools are found in many kinds of software, such as financial and security programs. The primary aspect of facial recognition is facial detection, which occurs in the first step of facial recognition and is executed using facial recognition software. Face identification is a complex task, as there are a wide variety of factors that influence the appearance of each face, including the subject's position (whether the face is on the front or the back of the image), occlusion, image direction, lighting conditions, and facial expression. To identify and locate faces in any picture or video and, furthermore, to identify and locate them from any angle or perspective. One significant difficulty in facial recognition is dealing with change over time, for example, adapting to a person's altered appearance due to age or posture. Because of the consequences of variable illumination circumstances, face identification remains difficult outside because even little changes in lighting can significantly alter the facial look.

People trying to avoid being seen can be difficult for surveillance cameras to handle, and camera operators often prefer cameras that their subjects cannot reach. The faces are seen through a certain degree of camera angle by positioning a camera on a tall spot. City surveillance apps often make use of quite simple operations, and this is one of them. Despite the high-profile persons openly passing by the camera without even bothering to glance at it, this is the most damning evidence. Public areas are outside the system's authority, as its ability to govern the attitudes of people is limited. In such instances, accurate recognition is nearly impossible and should be done carefully. The task of recognizing faces is difficult, as methods exist to identify specific ages, but not an all-ages approach.

The face recognition method mostly acts in three primary steps: Face Detection, Feature Extraction, and Face Recognition.

5.3.2.1 Face Detection

One of the most important aspects of facial analysis is face detection, the initial stage that involves finding the face on the image. This is an object-class detection case-specific situation. Object-Class Detection (OCD) entails recognizing the areas and sizes of all items in an image of a specific type. Face detection and face localization are closely related concepts. In recognizing faces, this part of the algorithm will pinpoint and count faces in the image.

5.3.2.2 Feature Extraction

The input data is turned into a simplified feature set, and images are broken up into patches. Image manipulation methods are most beneficial when doing picture processing, especially when dealing with image clutter and image occlusion. Feature extractions are a type of information compression, which can be used to pack, reduce, and clear out noise. After that, it was transformed into a vector with dimensions that were fixed. To be able to make a face model for the purposes of classification, feature extraction for machine learning and CNN models should use machine learning techniques. The objective of crucial importance is to figure out what feature extraction will assist picture categorization learning algorithms. Then, the model using haar similar features is helpful for multi-view face detection [674].

5.3.2.3 Face Recognition

Facial recognition software, the most basic variety of which identifies people in photographs, identifies people in footage, and can even read faces as well. Face recognition methods can be broken into three types: generic algorithms, 2D methods, and 3D approaches. Face recognition systems, such as the ones released recently, have trouble with varied stances [676]. Despite the recent popularity of 3D face recognition systems, 3D face recognition still has some significant weaknesses, namely the absence of large-scale annotated 3D data. Most research into 3D training data is performed using "one-to-many augmentation" methodologies to synthesize 3D faces [676]. Wen et al. [639] introduced a Latent Identity Analysis (LIA) layer to distinct from extracting age-invariant components, as shown in Figure 5.5, age-invariant features were acquired by subtracting age-specific effects from the representations with the help of the age estimation approach.

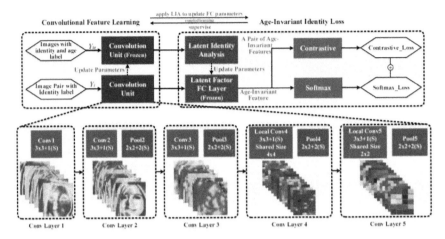

Fig. 5.5 The architecture of the proposed LF-CNNs and its training process [639].

5.4 Storytelling with Image and Video Data

5.4.1 Image and Video Captioning

Image captioning focuses on generating captions for images. Much research has been done recently in image captioning and narrative summarizing [241, 243], a field that also sees its most recent work in image-to-text translation founded on the deep learning paradigm. Social media could also be highly beneficial in capturing information at crucial times, such as during disasters or exceptional events, so that details are quickly made accessible in a concise report. An event like this is quite useful for assisting people, companies, and governments in staying up to date on the latest occurrences. Furthermore, these kinds of reports might help organize and keep photographs from social media in their records. Image captioning involves two primary components. To start, the algorithm will attempt to identify the objects, actions, and their connections in the image. To find a concise yet accurate explanation of the image, step two helps by creating an understandable description of the image [560]. For this, it relies on approaches to object recognition and natural language processing. One way to help do this is to use a deep learning approach. In the sphere of social media, however, we should modify this methodology to match the context of accidents through massive annotated datasets and transfer learning methods. One major drawback is images captured by fitness devices like FitBit and Apple Watch, which tend to be grainy and unfocused. Additionally, it depends greatly on the user's abilities and specifics of the camera [206]. In this section, we present three main approaches for image captioning, including retrieval based, template-based and deep learning-based:

- **Image Captioning Based on Retrieval**: Captioning based on retrieval is a very early method for retrieving captions from an existing caption pool. For this method, a picture that is the most similar to the original query picture is located first using image recognition. To arrange the query image in the semantic space, Markov Random Field (MRF) is employed, and for establishing the semantic distance between these images, Line similarity measure may be applied. Next, the caption next to the provided picture will be explored as the query image's caption.

- **Template-based Image Captioning**: The approach relies on algorithms that discover and align every sentence fragment. From this point, a predetermined template produces each phrase. Using templates for sentence construction frequently results in sentences. For instance, Kulkarni et al. [357], used Conditional Random Field (CRF) model to estimate labeling based on the acquired objects, attributes, and prepositions, and then produce a statement with a template by filling in slots with the majority likely labeling [662]. Using template-based approaches for image captioning necessitates the description of numerous aspects such as primary and secondary entities, as well as their connections and properties [560].

- **Deep Neural Networks-based Image Captioning**: There are some problems in generating a statement for an image using techniques such as retrieval-based and template-based image captioning. Even while deep neural network approaches deal with picture captioning, they nevertheless produce captions without regard for pre-existing captions or guesses about image content. When implemented, these methods can create pleasant, flexible, and meaning-filled phrases with improved syntax. An image caption may be generated using multi-model algorithms of neural networks trained only from the data in the image [560]. Figure 5.6 shows a sample of obtained image caption.

Fig. 5.6 An example of a machine caption is: "A soft-drink Company Pepsi is sponsoring a cricket match" [560].

5.4.2 Location Identification

Identification of the correct place is essential for getting good information via social media. Still, social media posts typically lack information regarding their location. For instance, the info in a tweet could be missing specific geolocation and picture info. Many approaches have recently been developed to address this challenge by utilizing a spatially divided deep image classification strategy that uses a deep network to choose the appropriate cell for a given picture. Jacobs et al. [620], introduced an approach to combine this method with the original Im2GPS method in which a query image is coordinated in opposition to a database of geotagged visual data, and the location is inferred from the recovered set. To find where an image is geographically located, they used kernel density estimation to assess the location of its neighboring images in the reference database. Also, in addition to the use of critical geographic places, other studies have focused on using various visual features and details about certain regions to build a system of area-level location in the city. Scene-centric pictures in an everyday setting have been shown to have image-to-location mapping capabilities. And yet, that will be difficult for natural catastrophe scenarios. Domain adaption techniques may prove beneficial to combat this issue [299].

5.5 3D Posts on Social Media

In this day and age, using social media to communicate anything from thoughts to pictures is necessary. The challenge for social networks is creating valuable, multimodal content. Then social media platforms strive to help the spread of 3D materials as 3D capabilities have long been known to encourage the spread of potentially harmful items [284]. In this section, we indicate ways to share 3D content and introduce light field technology as a novel way for 3D displays.

5.5.1 3D Content Sharing

People using mobile devices tend to share items they are interested in and things they have seen through social networks. Posting three-dimensional information and using time and space elements in it will draw the eye. Despite the steady development of 3D technology, which has started to creep into video games and entertainment, major content-sharing platforms still have trouble distributing good quality 3D material, and the job of doing so remains complex. Though sites like YouTube and Facebook provide the opportunity to publish and watch 3D material, the data is often intermingled with 2D data and is thus hard to observe [284].

Bulbul et al. [103] visualize the calculated generality on 3D virtual cities using technologies of game engine. They outlined the notion of how individuals may be linked to their settings through the popular visual content created by social media.

They are going to employ online data to automate 3D world-building to capture universalities and feelings in locales. They will help determine what locations or landmarks take up the most visual attention and should have the most photographs shot of them, as a result. They have also automatically made these landmarks that players want to be seen in a 3D world by regulating the illumination of game engines and changing the meshes' colors to make the feeling and appreciation of seeing them much more accurate. There are several uses for the extracted information in virtual environments, and the information is particularly well-suited for navigating and interacting with users Kukka et al. [356].

5.5.2 Light Field Technology

Websites and applications containing user-generated content for sharing and communicating with others are what social media is described as. The virtual world might become populated with custom avatars in real-time through social media networks. This section introduces light field technology, a system that aims to create a virtual 3D depiction of the real world by itself. We may utilize data mined from social media to help people go about in the virtual environment. A Plenoptic camera gathers information about light's brightness, coloration, and direction, and it is known as a light field camera. Traditional computer vision issues that will benefit from these cameras include depth estimation, post-capture focusing, and material estimation. These difficulties are challenging to conquer using existing approaches, which are only able to produce ordinary 2D pictures.

5.5.2.1 Description of a Light Field

Because the name makes it apparent, a light field is the representation of light as a vector field. It explains how to calculate the intensity of a ray's beam that flows in and out of every location in space [282]. A light field is seen as a way of collecting a picture from many angles to depict the same region of interest that may be represented as a collection of views. Thinking of a light field image as a collection of photographs captured by a moving camera, the camera took pictures from many distinct angles, like two views from a stereo camera. A light field adds more information about the scene's geometry, making it better for future processing. This information is more than the typical picture offers. Light field cameras most often offer unique views of the same scene, which is one of its most significant features. With this option, a spectator may see the scene's layout and distance [282]. Significant differences in perspectives and viewpoint shifts can lead to issues, such as substantial distance between them. To obtain a correct 3D reconstruction in this situation, knowledge of the scene's geometry is necessary. The construction of a 3D model is easy when many perspectives are defined.

In the 3D movie business, being able to decrease manual involvement by using passive sensors is very important since this increases the accuracy of depth measurement. Objects like shiny ones with complex material appearances are challenging to capture using a configuration of stereo or active depth sensors. Geometry data of this type can be used to enhance Virtual Reality (VR) shows by combining views or using hard or soft proxies. Besides the value of having access to a variety of points of view, light fields provide a variety of additional features, including the ability to use the known coordinates of light field rays to repeat the ray integration procedure of traditional cameras post-capture with several different parameter contexts. This feature allows users to create images that are focused at various depth levels. Light field cameras have grown more available in the last several years, and they may be used for research or commercial applications. Light-field cameras are widely available; you may find Lytro, Raytrix, and Pelican models, among others. Even though customers will recognize Lytro, they are going to like the Lytro camera the best. A light field camera, the Lytro, was created in 2005, and a year later, a version aimed at consumers was released (called the Lytro Illum). Focusing of Post-capture, estimation of the depth map, and estimates of illumination are some of the options available on light-field cameras.

The dilemma of focus is an essential topic in photography. The biggest obstacle is correctly zeroing in on the item to be captured before the image is captured [454]. If you take a picture with poor focus, it is impossible to fix the focus afterward. This gives a slow and dismal feel to the shot. One option is to utilize a digital image sensor's resolution and take light readings from every ray that contributes to the finished image to improve the focus issue. The super-sampling of the light entering a digital camera is highly flexible and gives the processing power to produce great-quality output photos. A 'light field' is the term for this visual representation in computer vision. The light field may be recorded by the use of a microlens array, which is in front of the photosensor. Every microlens covers a small photosensor pixel array and may divide light according to the angle it strikes the photosensor pixel array. A portion of a sensor array below a microlens may be thought of as a macro-element of the scene, in which each pixel has a distinct value, which can be thought of as a light ray at a certain angle. To create final 2D pictures, the previously photographed light field can be rendered using ray-tracing techniques [642]. To create a nice picture, the setup follows the photographed light rays from the optics to the plane of imaging. An array of tiny lenses directs light through the primary lens, which then reaches a sensor through an additional lens to be recorded. This ray-tracing has major implications for the situation in that it handles rays that fail to converge, which is crucial since the lack of focus should be resolved. After taking a picture, you will be able to refocus the image using this function. In addition, pictures are formed with varying depths of field. They are built by tracing the photographed light rays.

5.5.2.2 The Function of the Plenoptic

The flow of light across a particular area may be shown as a light field, which is a function that shows the quantity of light going in all directions within a region. When compared to ordinary cameras, a light field camera may record a photo not just as a 2D picture but also a value for each pixel describing how light intensity changes with the incoming light's angle [133]. In addition to the Light Field (LF) function being variable because of it being centered on a lens plane that is situated near the camera lens and a sensor plane that is situated near the sensor, the LF function is also capable of being adjusted by two arbitrarily placed parallel planes. For each pixel in the light field representation (u, v, s, t), the (u, v) location represents the lens plane, while the (s, t) position represents the sensor plane. A light ray that is in-plane (defined by the lens plane (uv plane) and the sensor plane (st plane)) is said to be aligned when it is emitted by a point that lies on a line passing through two points (u, v) and (s, t). This definition could be expressed by the function L(u, v, s, t) [645].

The sensor plane may be seen as a set of pinhole cameras where each pinhole correlates to a different point on the sensor plane. The phrase "sub-aperture image" is used to describe each of these individual views. Using the parameters (s,t) for the array of sub-aperture pictures and (u,v) for the pixels within every image, a 4D LF is denoted as L(u, v, s, t), which is a collection of views (sub-aperture images) taken by a light field camera specified by the two parallel planes, st and uv.

5.5.2.3 Applications of Light Field Cameras

The use of light field cameras has a variety of applications. There are three primary applications. At first, we should consider post-capture refocusing, depth map estimation, and 3D point cloud estimate with regard to geometry estimation. Image rendering is a prominent function in the second set of key uses, while the last major application is in categorizing material appearance [282]:

- Estimation of Geometry: There are several ways to capture 3D data on buildings and plants in the realm of environmental study. Many issues have been solved in the field of 3D modelling, determination, and monitoring, thanks to the appearance of light field cameras. Existing methods are, by and large, quite complicated and need this degree of sophistication. But light field cameras have largely put a dent in this issue. Several different remote sensing applications, such as those that are used to monitor plant development, may benefit from the ability to use light field cameras to generate 3D information [549]. Figure 5.1 demonstrates post-capture focusing in two distinct focusing planes, one of the key characteristics of light field photography [209]. Post-capture focal planes can be changed by refocusing after the image has been captured. This characteristic is critical in creating a depth map from a LF picture [208]. Within two planes, a light field is a vector function described by I(u, v, s, t) (camera plane and sensor plane) [645] as shown in Figure 5.7.

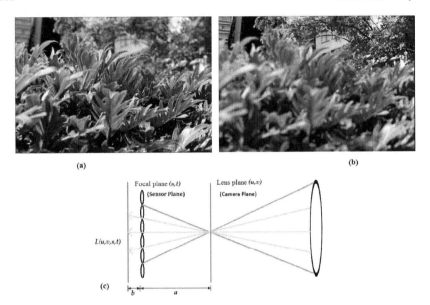

Fig. 5.7 The light field function and post-capture refocusing are illustrated. (a) In the foreground, focus, (b) In the background, focus. (c) A light field camera setup diagram denotes the distance between the lens plane and the focal plane and (b) denotes the distance between the sensor and the microlens array [209].

If a light ray starts at point (u, v) on the camera plane and continues on to point (s, t) on the sensor plane, and the camera plane and focal plane meet at (u, v), then this ray will be represented as I(u, v, s, t) [645]. Every sensor location is modeled as a pinhole camera which is located on the sensor plane at position s, t and is looking at the scene. One well-studied topic in the world of computer graphics and computer vision is how to measure the distance from two cameras (which are often placed side-by-side). A light field camera makes it feasible to get the depth map with just one snapshot, whereas multi-image correlation-based methods take several photos. A critical issue in estimating depth maps using light field pictures is occlusion, and this thesis uses an edge orientation predictor to counter this problem. Furthermore, using a light field camera is better at handling the increased difficulty of a task while calculating ill-posed depth maps. To make a 3D point cloud, utilizing a depth map to create it is essential. Matching up light points and then defocusing the light field might lead to constructing a depth map.

- Rendering of Images: Light field imaging is generally connected to the image-based rendering discipline devoted to recreating pictures by computing instead of sampling. Using light field technology, new perspectives may be created without any processing of different proxy geometry, which was previously found [282]. The calculation of the depth map, on the other hand, relies on the processing of similar rays and re-projections. Light rays may be categorized according to angle and are captured using a light field camera. After taking the photo, this option can replicate the wide range of ray angles generated by several various lens constructions. New pictures may be generated using several focus settings and varied aperture sizes from a single light field recording [301, 370].

- Material Appearance Classification: The light field and defocusing details can be utilized for another usage and might have other uses. For instance, light field's application in computer vision can help determine material appearances. It is possible to identify material aspects in the difference among light field angular patterns. The amount of data from angular samples in light fields makes this feasible. Glossy surfaces provide differing levels of illumination due to angles being perpendicular to a viewer. This variability in brightness is helpful for item recognition and extraction [401, 650]. Besides that, another benefit of the light field camera is that it gives us several views of the same thing. Reflectance, which is an issue with light field images, can be aided by this characteristic. Light fields can process a soft depth measure, which, when coupled with other light field properties, allows overcoming the challenge of disambiguating situations. It is possible to clarify the importance of an object in a scene through a detailed depth map which would normally be hard to get if the details varied with different depth planes. This is especially helpful in cases where items cannot be differentiated based on color alone. For measuring depth, the angular intensity gradients are combined with the tonal variety of places. The same might prove effective for the categorization and distinction of three-dimensional objects.

5.6 Concluding Remarks and Discussion

This chapter discussed how to detect the visual and video aspects of social media post images by way of a suitable picture content analysis. Social networking is important to day-to-day living. In addition to enabling customers to make smart decisions, it may impact consumers' behaviours and views. Images are better for doing social data research since they give valuable extra information. A picture may explain an organization or healthcare strategy in a much faster and easier way than text. Humans utilise images to figure out difficult problems they have by making a visual tool that helps them assess complicated political situations. People use images to illustrate regions' lack of data, and it makes it more challenging to analyze time-sensitive results.

We discussed modern discoveries in the realm of computer vision and machine learning and how they apply to finding and recognising objects. One of the new techniques, known as deep learning, which is still rather new, seems to be making good progress in analyzing massive data sets. We examined several kinds of approaches for locating objects in photographs and classifying everything according to its own category. It is possible to learn classifications and locations by finding objects. We demonstrated how facial recognition might benefit social media applications by finding a person's face in a picture. Besides that, the three-dimensional postings hold the viewer's interest and encourage the viewer to be active with social media. We researched how the introduction of 3D photos is one of the greatest ways to boost a company's revenue, specifically how to target younger audiences, as this has the potential to engage customers with 3D content to give more details above 2D photographs. To introduce the process of transforming from 2D to 3D pictures, we provided an entirely new segment. Light field technology describes the technique of enhancing 3D pictures.

6

Summarizing Social Data

6.1 Automatic Text Summarization: Overview

Producing a summary is a complicated text; consequently, it is even more challenging for machines. The machine is required to have the ability to understand the text and produce summaries using background knowledge [63]. Summarization approaches create the best representation of the original data, enabling efficient storage, quick browsing, and retrieval of an extensive collection of data without loss [99]. However, there is no unique definition for summarization, meaning it can be understood based on the goal of the application or user. For example, summarization is defined as any process which reduces data size or finds the essential parts of data while eliminating redundant or non-relevant data. The most general definition for summarization is the automatic mechanism of generating brief and condensed representations of the content [396]. A good summary can also be defined as short, concise, and informative, as well as grammatically correct—without redundancy [41]. Another definition for summarization is a short version of original documents, which includes essential information without human intervention [155]. Radev et al. [501] provided a more recent definition, framing summarization as 'a text that is produced from one or more texts, that conveys the critical information in the original text and usually significantly less than that'. He emphasizes three important factors, including (i) single or multiple document sources, (ii) holding important data, and (iii) reducing the size by at least 50%. Defining what is important in this definition is a challenging and subjective task. Moreover, summarization approaches are different from compression-based approaches, which focus only on the size of summaries. Section 6.1.1 compares summarization-based approaches and compression-based approaches.

6.1.1 Text Summarization v. Text Compression

While text summarization aims to discover relevant information from various sources and gather them in a concise and readable format for users, text compression seeks to reduce the amount of data needed to represent documents. Therefore, information condensation (compression) is a filtering approach for reducing an information overload. The idea behind text compression is similar to the data compression concept in information theory, such that compressed data is the original representation of data with fewer bits generated by encoding information [556]. Similarly, text compression aims to condense a sentence while maintaining the most critical aspects. Text compression has many practical applications, such as compressing micro-blogs and generating headlines for news articles. Text compression approaches are mainly categorized into two groups, including deletion-based and abstractive methods.

6.1.1.1 Deletion-based Text Compression

Deletion-based text compression approaches work based on the idea of *reducing without significant loss* [312]. Therefore, the goal is to remove as many extraneous words from a (set of) document(s) without diminishing the text's primary content or sentence transformations [406]. 'Data-intensive processing' and making data 'lean' are two main subcategories of deletion-based text compression.

Early approaches belong to the lean category since they follow an unsupervised paradigm, such as an integer linear programming (ILP)-based approach [140]. Consequently, they do not require training data since they employ a language model for finding compressed sentences instead of using training sentence–compression pairs. Conversely, the data-intensive approaches are supervised and require parallel pairs of sentences and their corresponding compression. Other proposed modelling approaches include the noisy-channel model [341, 342, 501], variational auto encoders [428] and Seq2Seq models [222]. A recent approach proposed by Zhao et al. [681] is based on a new language-model evaluator. In this approach, first, a sequence of trial-and-error deletion operations is applied. Then for obtaining the best target compression, a reinforcement learning (RL) framework is employed.

6.1.1.2 Abstractive Text Compression

In addition to the delete operation used in the previous category, abstractive models use other procedures such as insert, reorder, and reformulate to generate the condensed version of the original text [342]. A recent abstractive compression model is a tree-to-tree transduction model in which they use synchronous tree-adjoining grammars to formulate the problem as a tree-to-tree rewriting task [565] for capturing all possible ways to rewrite a sentence [142]. Other approaches include using attentive long short-term memory (LSTM) models for captioning or compressing description of scenes [648], and a Seq2Seq model [668].

6.2 Social Data Summarization: Challenges and Opportunities

Social data platforms mainly have numerous users who interact and consequently produce a tremendous amount of data, including the content publicly shared by users and other metadata such as the biographical data, location of users, and shared links. Data obtained from social media is very expressive as it reveals hidden information and actual opinions, known as 'expansiveness structure of social data' [614]. Since online communications allow users to be anonymous and keep their privacy, which is not common in personal interactions, people are more eager to honestly expose themselves in a relatively safe environment. It is even more considerable for people with stigmatized social identities or political tendencies to attend online events dedicated to that particular identity without fear and express their opinions [56]. Therefore, intimate relationships and tendencies are expressed by people more openly online. Summarizing high-volume content generated daily by users scattered globally provides valuable insights beneficial for different real-world applications. Social data are shared in different forms which includes images, videos, and text. However, text data is the most common form of shared data, such as posts, comments, or messages. Text data is required to be summarized and transformed into machine-readable forms to be utilized for practical purposes. Produced summaries are represented in different formats, including graphical forms like histograms or pie charts. While statistical representations can obtain information from extensive social data, a noise-free textual summary is preferable in most social media analyses [241, 243].

Generated text data in social platforms has various formats and structures. For instance, posts on Facebook or Tumblr, tweets from Twitter, pins on Pinterest, and check-ins on Foursquare are all different regarding their format. Nevertheless, their content values are as important as a formal document, if not more than that. The reason is that social media data is instantaneous, time-sensitive, and delicate to the world's concerns. The most significant difference among various platforms is the users' language and the length of generated text data. For instance, the language in LinkedIn, Yelp, or Reddit is more formal. Their structure is well-formed according to linguistic grammar and formality than Facebook, where user-generated content expresses emotional content. The amount of generated text data in Yelp or Reddit is also substantial compared to Twitter or Facebook. Consequently, basic natural language processing tools such as parsing, Parts of Speech Tagging (POS), and Named Entity Recognition (NER) do not perform well on most social data. Therefore, conventional summarization techniques are not applicable for social text data. A summarization approach for social data is required to work with a quick-to-change, dynamic, and large-scale data streams.

Another aspect of social data which makes it different from a formal document is the sensitivity to chronological recency. Therefore, focusing on the most chronologically significant set of social interactions is necessary for proposing a summarization technique. Scale is another aspect that affects the performance of summarization approaches. Conventional summarization techniques do not work for summarising low-scale documents such as tweets and micro-blogs [559]. For example, using term frequency as a relevancy measure in a summarization system is very common. However, the size of the input document should be large enough to be able to detect essential concepts. Instead, trending phrases specified by users, such as a hashtag, are used to define the importance of text [177]. Besides, the short-length textual social data causes sparse information space, resulting in new text classification, clustering, or information extraction challenges. Moreover, the purpose of summarizing social media has a significant impact on designing a summarization approach. For instance, event, sentiment, and opinion summarization are examples of social data summarization approaches.

This chapter categorizes approaches into two main groups. Summarization approaches for formal social data such as Reddit or LinkedIn, called 'generic' approaches, and summarization approaches for micro-blog data such as Twitter.

6.3 Social Data Summarization: Generic Approaches

Automated text summarization approaches are mainly categorized into extractive and abstractive methods. Abstractive summarization techniques generate the summary in a similar way to how humans create a summary. They use natural language generation techniques for converting the original text to internal semantic representation, conveying the same meaning. Extractive summarization approaches select a proper subset of linguistic units from the original textual corpus to present the summary of the original documents. The complexity constraints of abstractive techniques direct the research community to focus mainly on extractive methods. Automatic text summarization approaches are categorized based on the input, purpose, and output type.

We examined input documents using three criteria: (i) input size (how many text units a system can have as input), (ii) domain specificity (domains that the model can handle), and (iii) input format (the structure of documents). Input to the summarizer can be a single document or multi-document. Single-document summarization approaches process just one input document, and the first work in this category returns to 50s [59, 180, 397]. Multi-document summarizers gather many documents on the same topic as input, enabling diversification of information sources and redundancy simultaneously [419]. Input documents can be general or related to the same domain (domain-specific). However, it is more appropriate to use a summarization system specific to the domain to reduce term ambiguity, use grammar and formatting schemes, and facilitate domain knowledge by enhancing relevancy detection. An example is a medical text summarization where authors used domain-specific cue phrases joined with other standard features for measuring the relevancy of sentences [542]. Another example is LetSum, a summarization system for legal [210] and biomedical texts [506]. Input documents can take diverse forms based on their structures, scales, and mediums, from textual to multimedia documents. The structure refers to the explicit organization found in the document. Focusing on the structure is the basis of some approaches to generate summaries, as this increases the summarization performance [210].

According to the summarization goal, summarization approaches are categorized based on the audience, content, and expansiveness. Summarization is a subjective task, meaning a user may need to focus on specific aspects of a document rather than the input document's main idea. In these scenarios, the interest can be defined by a query (query-focused summarization). In a query-oriented summarization approach, a good summary is judged according to a user's query. Query-focused approaches can be built by adapting existing summarization approaches to answer a query. This strategy has been applied to various methods, including sub-modular approaches [380] and graph-based approaches [70, 498]. Besides, various other approaches are explicitly designed for answering queries [2]. In contrast to a query-based approach, a generic summarization approach tries to preserve important information presented by the author from an input document [602, 613, 616]. Summarization approaches can be indicative or informative. 'Informative summaries' include the fundamental information about the original text and help users find their interests by extracting the main idea(s). Most existing summarization approaches are informative. 'Indicative summaries' do not contain informative content. Their focus is to contain a general description of the original documents and can be helpful to decide whether to refer to the source.

According to the output summary, summarization algorithms are classified based on three measures: (i) the derivation process to generate a summary from the original document, (ii) partiality (how a summary handles the original document's opinions), and (iii) the summary's format. The derivation measure refers to the process of obtaining a summary—that is, extracting important units or understanding and generating a new summary. Abstractive summaries are made by understanding the principal concepts of documents and expressing those contents in another format using clear and natural language [57, 201]. Therefore, abstractive approaches require understanding documents deeply. However, these are challenging to design since they require semantic representation and inference. Conversely, extractive methods are more popular because of their comparative simplicity. Extractive approaches contain three steps, involving (i) representing the original documents, (ii) ranking sentence, and (iii) choosing high-scoring sentences. Concatenating selected sentences into a shorter text produces meaningful and coherent summary [424].

Produced summarization can be neutral or opinion-based. Neutral summarization algorithms produce summaries that reflect the input documents' content without judgment or evaluation, even if they are judgemental in nature. Most existing summarization works belong to this category [602, 616]. In contrast, opinion-based summarization algorithms include automatic judgments either implicitly or explicitly. An explicit judgment includes some opinion statements in summary, while the implicit one uses bias to add and/or omit material. With the growth of interest in users' opinions, this kind of summarization is more popular. For example, one approach summarizes customer opinions through Twitter by extracting the different product features and the conversation messages' polarity [468].

Produced summaries can feature in various formats, including structured in the form of a concept map [205] or unstructured in the form of some sentences using a different template [278]. Summaries may also focus on users' preferences or goals. For example, the OntoSum system [96] uses device profiles such as mobile phones and Web browsers to adjust the summary formatting and length.

Based on the input documents' language, three different categories exist for summarization: monolingual, multilingual, and cross-lingual. When the source and the target language are the same and specific, the summarization algorithm is monolingual. Multilingual summarization approaches accept documents in different languages and produce the output in the same language [307]. For example, SUMMARIST [287] is a multilingual summarizer used for various languages, including Japanese, English, Spanish, Arabic, Korean, and Indonesian. When the user can select the summary language, the summarization algorithm is called cross-lingual [227].

The main category among all mentioned categories are abstractive, extractive, hybrid, structured, and interactive and personalized approaches which is further elaborated in Section 6.3.1, Section 6.3.2, Section 6.3.3, Section 6.3.4, and Section 6.3.5 respectively. The architecture of each category is also depicted in Figure 6.1.

6.3.1 Abstractive Summarization

Abstractive summaries are created by understanding the principal concepts of documents and then expressing selected contents in another clear and natural format [57, 201]. Therefore, abstractive approaches require understanding documents deeply using semantic representation and inference. However, producing such an intelligent summary is challenging, requiring semantic representation, inference, and advanced natural language. Abstractive summarization approaches are mainly categorized into two groups: structure-based and semantic-based methods [278, 437]. The structure-based methods are based on designing a schema to describe the document. Template-based, rules-based, ontology-based, and tree-based approaches are all examples of structure-based abstractive procedures. Documents' semantic structure is used in semantic-based strategies, including linguistic data (i.e., noun and verb phrases) and semantic graph-based approaches. Joint Extractive and Compressive Summarizer (JECS) [649], Pointer-Generator Networks (PGN) [552], and Deep Communicating Agents (DCA) [117] are recent state-of-the-art abstractive methods. JECS is based on a neural network model (BLSTM as the encoder) to compress and summarize the text. The process includes selecting sentences, pruning the parsing tree for compressing chosen sentences. PGN has an encoder-decoder architecture, which is a pointer generator network.

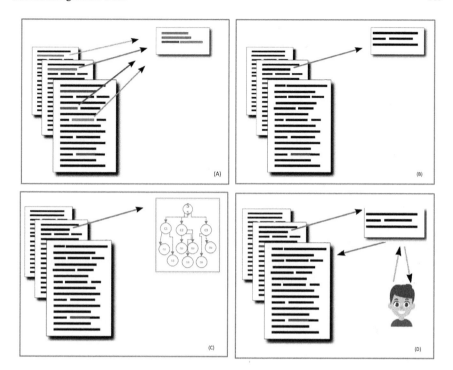

Fig. 6.1 Prototypes of different summarization categories are depicted. (A) Extractive summarization. (B) Abstractive summarization. (C) Structured summarization. (D) Interactive and personalized summarization.

6.3.2 Extractive Summarization

Extractive summarization methods choose important sentences to represent the original documents. Selected sentences are then combined to produce a coherent summary as a shorter text format [424]. Extractive summaries are mainly built based on three phases. The original document is required to be presented in a machine-readable format. A ranking system is required to score sentences. Finally, top-score sentences are required to be concatenated to make a coherent summary. These three steps are the basis of various categories of extractive approaches. For instance, there are two main representation models for capturing salient content based on representation: 'topic' representations and 'indicator' representations [32]. The indicator representation model describes each sentence as a feature (indicator) list. However, topic representation models convert the text into an intermediary model to explain the discussed topics. The complexity and representation model vary among various models. When an intermediate representation is produced, each sentence is assigned a score based on its importance. A sentence's score is computed according to the topic covered in the original documents when following a topic representation approach. Conversely, indicator representation methods aggregate the evidence from different indicators using techniques such as machine learning. Eventually, the summarizer selects the top k most essential sentences to produce a summary, where k is defined based on a size limit parameter. Some approaches work based on greedy algorithms to select representative sentences, such as converting the sentence selection into an optimization problem. In this setting, a combination of sentences is chosen to maximize overall importance and minimize redundancy.

We categorize extractive approaches as statistical approaches, graph-based approaches, knowledge-based approaches, and machine learning-based approaches.

6.3.2.1 Statistical Summarization Approaches

Early approaches used various features to score text units' relevancy to the main topic or to users' requests. Defined features are merged for score calculation; however, combining features does not necessarily improve the quality of a summary. Two significant approaches in this category are Lead-3 and the phrase-based ILP model [643]. Lead-3 chooses the three sentences which cover the most information, and the phrase-based ILP model [643] is based on a linear programming formulation using three main features, including summary lengths, coverage, and grammar constraints. Despite their simplicity, Lead-3 and phrase-based ILP demonstrate satisfactory results.

6.3.2.2 Graph-based Summarization Approaches

Graph theory facilitates representing the semantic contents of a document [621] or the document structure; therefore, it is appropriate for document summarization tasks. In graph-based methods, each text element (words or sentences) is treated as a node [155, 201, 270, 271]. Two nodes or precisely two sentences are connected if they share some similarities. Lexical and semantic graphs are commonly used to represent text. Lexical features of the text are used to generate the corresponding lexical graph. Similarly, a semantic graph employs the text's semantic properties, such as synonymy and hyponymy relations, for making the graph known as the ontological relationship. The relationship between a set of words represents the sentences' syntactic structure (dependency tree and syntactic trees). TGRAPH [477] and URANK [622] are the earlies graph-based models. Sentences' ranking scores are obtained in a unified ranking process. Further, TextRank [431] and LexRank [201] use lexical features to create a graph. The primary difference between these approaches is the similarity measure. TextRank counts the similar words among sentences as the similarity measure. LexRank employs the cosine similarity of sentences as the similarity measure [29]. Other approaches such as the cumulative sum method [271] and position weight [270] are also used for similarity measure.

6.3.2.3 Clustering-based and Frequent Term Summarization Approaches

Clustering-based approaches group together the related information retrieved from similar documents and passages. Sentences within each cluster are ranked. Senetnces' salience scores are calculated, and high-scoring sentences from each cluster are selected, which forms the final summary [271].

Frequent term approaches seek the frequent and semantically similar terms in documents [443]. Semantic similarity checks the path's length linking the terms and further measures the content difference and similarity. The summarizer then filters the most frequent sentences with which are semantically related.

6.3.2.4 Knowledge-based Summarization Approaches

Automatic text summarization approaches aim to produce summaries that are comparable to human-generated ones. However, covering all the semantically relevant aspects of data remains a challenge. Combining summarization techniques and knowledge bases is a solution to tackle this problem. Semantic-based or ontology-based summarizers such as Wikipedia, YAGO, and DBpedia can be used to incorporate the semantics of words. For example, Sankarasubramaniam et al. [540] proposed an algorithm based on a graph-based ranking technique for Wikipedia. They create a bipartite sentence–concept graph, and an iterative ranking algorithm is used to select essential sentences for the summary. Another example is the YAGO-based summarizer, leveraging YAGO ontology [582] for distinguishing critical concepts in a set of documents. Extracted concepts are employed for selecting the most representative sentences within documents.

6.3.2.5 Optimization-based Summarization Approaches

Optimization algorithms are the basis of various summarization purposes. The most applied algorithms are the Genetic Algorithm (GA) [539] and particle swarm optimization (PSO) [538]. GA algorithm simulates the evolution theory. GA is a search-based algorithm that starts with initially random solutions and optimizes over time. Simulation of natural evolution operations such as selection, mutations, and crossover are used to make the next generation of solutions. The algorithm evaluates each population member based on a defined fitness measure and estimates how close the current solution is to the preferred conditions. The algorithm then selects high-score individuals based on their fitness value. The new generation is created by merging the preferred individuals' features (crossover). This process is repeated while the latest generations achieve preferred qualifications.

Particle swarm optimization is another commonly applied bio-inspired algorithm inspired by birds' social movement [403, 494]. It starts with an initial population of particles (solutions) that are randomly selected. Individuals have random positions and velocities. The respective positions of individuals are updated through the process using their previous positions and updated velocity vectors before converging.

6.3.2.6 Fuzzy-based Summarization Approaches

The fuzzy theory has many applications in summarization methods. Numeric text representations are fed to a fuzzy system as the input, and the algorithm transforms the values to their corresponding fuzzy linguistic values (fuzzifier). Predefined fuzzy rules in the form of 'if-then' statements generate the outputs [182, 479]. The fuzzy evolutionary optimization method (FEOM) [571] is another approach in this category, which clusters the documents and selects the most important sentence in each group.

6.3.2.7 Machine Learning-based Summarization Approaches

Supervised, unsupervised, and semi-supervised approaches are broadly used for automatic text summarization. Supervised learning approaches require a large amount of labeled data as input in the training stage. These algorithms model summarization as a binary classification classified either as 'in summary' or 'not in summary'. Therefore, different machine learning algorithms used for classification tasks can also be used for this purpose. Most used supervised learning algorithms for text include support vector machines, Naive Bayes classification, regression, and decision trees [155, 263].

On the contrary, unsupervised approaches do not require any training data, making them more applicable for many applications where labeling data is expensive. Unsupervised methods discover the hidden pattern of data. Clustering and the hidden Markov model (HMM) are two commonly used techniques. The 'query, cluster and summarize' technique [178] is another system based on the HMM that computes the probability of each sentence as being appropriate for the summary set. Meanwhile, semi-supervised learning approaches require both labeled and unlabeled data for building an appropriate procedure. Conditional random field approach [562] consider the summarization task a sequence-labeling problem.

Recently, the focus has shifted to neural network-based and deep reinforcement learning methods, demonstrating outstanding outcomes. Word embedding [486] are employed to represent words in a trained feature space at the input level. This information is fed to the network to produce the summary. These models mainly have a convolutional neural network (CNN) [111], an RNN [130, 446] or a combination of the two in their cores [449, 647]. These approaches are successful in terms of performance; however, they suffer from efficiency and interpretability.

Neural network sentence extraction (NN-SE) [130] is another neural network-based model which has a hierarchical document encoder along with an attention mechanism. SummerRuNNer [446] is an RNN-based extractive document summarization approach with a hierarchical structure self-attentive model. Hierarchical Structured Self Attentive model for extractive document Summarization (HSSAS) [28] is a neural network model with complex architecture. HSSAS uses a hierarchical self-attention mechanism to generate a sentence based on document embedding. BanditSum [174] models summarization problem as a contextual bandit (CB) problem. BERT is also used in summarization approaches, called BERT-SUM, which is a pre-trained transformer for generating extractive summaries [390], achieved ground-breaking performance.

In recent years, reinforcement learning (RL) approaches have been used for both extractive and abstractive summarization [478, 482, 531]. RL-based document summarization systems use heuristic functions as the reward function and, therefore, do not require reference summaries to be trained [522, 531]. Other approaches use different Recall-Oriented Understudy for Gisting Evaluation (ROUGE) measure variants as the reward function and, therefore, require reference summaries to reward RL [354, 478, 482]. The reward quality has been recognized as the bottleneck for RL-based summarization [233].

6.3.3 Hybrid Extractive and Abstractive Summarization

Hybrid approaches combine both abstractive and extractive techniques. A hybrid approach employs an extractive phase for extracting key sentences from the input text. An abstractive approach is used to generate the final summary. Abstractive and extractive summarization approaches are complementary, and the overall summarization performance is improved. However, the research community focuses more on extractive techniques since their abstractive counterparts are highly complex. An example of a hybrid model is the approach proposed by Wang et al. [630]. They extract key sentences based on a graph model as the extractive phase. They employed an RNN-based encoder-decoder and a pointer and attention mechanisms to produce output.

SumItUp [87] is another approach that uses statistical and semantic features to generate a summary. Statistical features include sentence position and length, cue phrases, TF-IDF, noun and verb phrases, proper nouns, and cosine similarity. Redundant sentences are detected using cosine similarity and removed. A combination of WordNet, Lesk algorithm, and part-of-speech tagging is used to convert extractive summary (extracted sentences) to an abstractive summary. Their initial index is preserved to keep the original order of sentences.

6.3.4 Structured Summarization

Traditional summarization approaches cannot produce long and detailed summaries in case a user is interested since all details are omitted. Moreover, the produced summaries are unstructured and, consequently, challenging for further analysis. This prompts the need for structured summarization. Structured summaries are first introduced for Wikipedia articles and biographies [388]. We categorized structured summarization approaches into four groups, covering (i) timeline summarization approaches, (ii) document thread summarization, (iii) hierarchical summarization, and (iv) concept map summarization.

6.3.4.1 Timeline Summarization

Timeline approaches mainly produce summaries with a focus on time, for instance, dates in which news stories or collections of a news story are created. For example, partial ordering relations [343] connects all events in a narrative, annotated with temporal dependency trees. Another approach is to formalize a joint inference model for temporal representation based on time intervals [172].

Some approaches emphasize the summarization aspect for generating timelines from multiple articles. One example is to formalize the task of generating a timeline as an optimization problem that balances coherency, diversity, and summary quality [653]. Generating timelines based on inter-date and intra-date sentence dependencies is another common trend for time-based summarization [652]. Other approaches identify the most important dates and the bursts of news that surround them, and then categorize events based on the burst time [26, 131, 291, 334, 589].

6.3.4.2 Document Thread Summarization

Identifying threads of *related* documents is another category of structured summaries. Features such as time order for capturing dependencies and temporal locality of stories for event detection are fed to a supervised machine learning approach for discovering threads [445]. Combining a topic modeling and clustering approach for grouping news articles is another line of research for thread detection [22]. Statistical models have also extensively been used to detect trends, known as the sequence of events and topics, which is a group of co-occurring [598].

Identifying *coherent* document threads is another challenging task in this category. Formulating the problem as discovering articles chains and connecting specific articles is a traditional approach [553]. Gillenwater et al. [246] in the following, introduced a probabilistic model to extract distinct threads from a document collection. Shahaf et al. [554, 555] used the idea of metro maps to transform the problem of extracting coherent threads into coherent document maps where a map is a set of intersecting threads intended to express the interaction of document threads and their relation.

6.3.4.3 Hierarchical Summarization

Hierarchical summarization approaches are another structured-based summarization approaches [268, 362, 593]. The hierarchy is built based on various features such as elements of a document, including words or phrases [268, 362, 593]. A hierarchy is also defined as a structure prioritizing more general information [118, 469] or spreading the summary out across the hierarchy [624, 657]. SUMMA is a hierarchical summarization approach, producing a hierarchy of short summaries sorted according to time intervals [136].

6.3.4.4 Concept Map Summarization

Concept map approaches produce concept maps as structured summaries. A concept map that extends the mind map idea introduced by Novak and Gowin [459] is a labeled graph showing concepts as nodes and the relations between them as edges. The automatic creation of concept maps from an unstructured text has been studied in several areas and is called 'concept mapping'. Different techniques have been suggested for single documents [21, 363, 463, 617] and multiple documents [497, 502, 690, 691]. Different document models have also used concept maps, including in scientific papers [497], legal documents [691], student essays [617] and general Web pages [502].

The first step in creating a concept map is to extract the concepts and relation spans from the input documents. Extracted mentions refer to the same concept or the relations that require grouping. Concept and relation labeling and importance estimation are the final steps in creating a summarised concept map. The most recent approach in concept summarization was proposed by Falke [205]. The proposed approach has different intelligent parts, including (i) learning to identify core concepts and grouping coreferent concepts for removing redundancy, (ii) estimating concepts' importance by training a robust supervised model, and (iii) producing an optimal summary through an integer linear programming (ILP) model.

6.3.5 Interactive and Personalized Summarization

In contrast to static, non-interactive summarization approaches that provide summaries as the output to the end-user without asking their feedback, interactive summarization approaches put the human in the loop to refine their model according to their feedback, generating user-tailored summaries. Collected feedback can be in various formats including users' mouse click information [98], post-editing and rating outcomes [167, 351], defining errors [361], and selecting preferences [1] which are used for different NLP tasks.

Most existing computer-assisted summarization tools present essential parts of documents to the user using a traditional automatic summarization algorithm, asking users to adjust the output. However, they do not allow further interaction. The post-processing phase includes cutting, pasting, and reorganizing documents to produce the desired output summary [147, 450, 464]. Other works present automatically derived hierarchically ordered summaries, allowing users to navigate the hierarchy from general information to more specific one [136, 557]. Therefore, these systems are neither interactive nor user-specific since they do not update their internal summarization models based on users' feedback.

iNeATS [369] and IDS [315] are two other interactive summarization systems. These approaches allow users to tune several essential parameters in making summaries to enable customizing output such as size, redundancy, and relevancy. Avinesh and Meyer [45] proposed a more recent interactive summarization approach by using users' feedback in labeling important bigrams among a pool of candidate summaries. The proposed framework demonstrated near-optimal performance in only ten interaction rounds based on their simulation experiments. However, labeling word units among many potentially unimportant ones puts an enormous burden on users, making this approach impractical in real-world use cases.

There is increasing research interest in using preference-based feedback and RL algorithms in summarization. For example, learning a sentence ranker trained on human preferences by comparing sentence pairs is a leading approach in this category [687]. The trained ranker function is employed to evaluate summaries, giving the maximum score to summaries with the highest number of high-ranked sentences. This preference-based RL algorithm has also been used in summarization. The Structured Prediction from Partial Information (SPPI) [352, 570] is a policy-gradient RL algorithm where the rewards are defined based on the preference-based feedback. SPPI has a challenge with the high sample complexity problem.

Another recent preference RL approach is APRIL [232], which has two phases. The first stage retrieves users' ranking scores for all candidate summaries, and then a neural RL agent searches for the optimal summary. However, favoring one summary to another in both approaches places a considerable burden on users. It is worth re-mentioning that summarization aims to provide users with a summary that reduces the need to read multiple documents. However, asking users to prefer a summary to another in multiple rounds among a summary space that includes all randomly possible combinations of sentences only adds more cognitive load [58].

6.4 Micro-blog Data Summarization

Micro-blogging sites produce and distribute data at an unprecedented rate which is informative but overwhelming. The diversity of styles and formats, noise and redundancies within data, and dynamic and quick-to-change nature of produced data make social media summarization an interesting but challenging problem. Therefore, social media summarization varies according to the purpose of summarization. We discuss micro-blog summarization approaches from various aspects, including time-based, event-based, and opinion-based approaches.

6.4.1 Time-aware Summarization

Extracting meaningful information about entities such as highlighting significant activities in a given *period* from extensive and high-velocity social media data is becoming increasingly difficult for online users. Therefore, a timeline that displays a chronological list of events about the entity provides effective and efficient access to understand an entity. Consequently, automatically summarizing the timeline for social data is necessary. Generating and summarizing the timeline for news corpus is a well-defined task [291, 653]. However, timeline summarization is more challenging than standard documents. The reason is that a general timeline summarization framework requires discovering key timeline episodes about an entity, classifying them, and summarizing each episode. However, key timeline episodes are challenging to define in social data since they usually are not explicitly distinguishable. The short, informal, and noisy nature of social data makes it even more challenging, proving that building a social data timeline summarizer requires more content.

On the contrary, social media data provides distinct possibilities to detect patterns for summarizing time-aware content. For instance, given a specific entity, defining the frequency for a specified time interval can highlight the presence of a sudden spike pattern quickly [122] where time interval can be short or long. Short-term summarization of social data leads to finding the most recent trend topics, specifically integrating with the geolocation property of tweets. However, long-term summarization can detect more cause-and-effect relations, such as how opinions and sentiments on a topic have changed during a more extended period which has many applications. Besides, the unique structure of social media and available metadata such as hashtag information and users' information provides various types of signals that facilitate the timeline summarization task. Therefore, these properties require developing new algorithms for timeline summarization, proving the inefficiency of traditional algorithms.

The timeline summarization task is prevalent for news articles. Recently, personalized timeline summarization algorithms have been introduced for social media streams [372, 508]. For instance, leveraging temporal and content information using a Dirichlet-Hawkes process for event clustering is one of the approaches [176]. However, they assumed knowing the temporal gap between events, which does not fit many scenarios. In an another approach, timelines are created by optimizing temporal and event constraints simultaneously [172]. Using the Dirichlet process model to produce personal timelines [372] is another approach. Generating timelines based on a time-aware hierarchical Bayesian model and a ranking model is another promising approaches [237]. However, these frameworks do not explicitly model timeline events' temporal patterns, which is advantageous for social data.

Modeling online content according to temporal patterns are reviewd by various algorithms such as Hawkes process [413], power law distribution functions [146], infinite-state automation approach [525], and life cycle model [122]. Moreover, time series are modeled after aligning or shifting, such as Dynamic Time Warping (DTW) [503], and clustering time-series followed by shifting and scaling operations [658]. However, most mentioned methods do not consider content information. Consequently, handling dramatic event shifting and modeling life cycle patterns are not possible. In another approach, authors detect timeline episodes by focusing on defining events [121] or the use of dynamic topic models and their variations for topic tracking [93, 623].

6.4.2 Event-based Summarization

Event-based summarization approaches and time-based summarization approaches have some shared characteristics. Generally, an event is defined as a sequence of incidents or sub-events happening at different points in the event timeline, which can be ad-hoc or planned. Any event can cause tons of reports, analyses, and opinion sharing due to global attention. Besides, similar minds across the world can organize events through social activities.

Deepayan and Kunal [120] proposed an approach to extract and summarize events by segmenting event timelines. A segment is a semantically discrete part of the entire event and represents the number of tweets. They designed a Hidden Markov Model (HMM) to find the burst times among tweet streams. They used the word distribution of tweets for this purpose. Each event timeline contains tweets as representative of low activity periods and bursty periods. The idea is to consider fairness in making segments to ensure that particular bursty sub-events which produce more tweets do not dominate the summary space. On the other hand, ignoring burstiness by focusing on one-shot summarization of tweets only covers specific topics. Automatically learned language models guarantee the separation of sub-events which are not temporally far apart.

Event summarization in Twitter is also modeled as a search and summarize framework in a bootstrapping manner such that keyword-based event search integrates by time [137]. Topical relation defines the events by continuously querying tweets with a set of event-related keywords. They formalized a Decay Topic Model, which takes the temporal significance of a latent topic in the tweet as the input. An exponential decay function and conventional word co-occurrence estimations are used to evaluate the model. Each classified latent topic corresponds to sub-events. The top-rated words for topics are employed to query tweets.

The participant-based approach is another category for event summarization for micro-blog data where each participant is an entity, playing a significant role in shaping up events [561]. They used the CMU Tweet NLP tool [248] and a hierarchical clustering approach such that each cluster includes various mentions of an entity.

6.4.3 Opinion-based Summarization

Internet and, more specifically, social media have transformed the way people across the globe interact and present their ideas and opinions to a significant extent. These platforms have facilitated cultural intrusion between geographically apart communities. The massive textual data accumulating in social media due to conversations and debates happening online enable extracting insights that are useful for a large variety of purposes. Opinion summarization aims to automatically summarize various topic-related opinions, which is one of the most valued and influential NLP technologies [391]. There is an increased research interest in opinion summarization due to the critical patterns extracted from social media and its applicability in different domains, making it commercially valuable. To give some examples, summarizing thousands of reviews on Amazon can help users settle on a choice. It can also help predict the political tendency among different users. Moreover, politicians can review their public image from social users' perspectives. However, the large volume of data causes extraordinary challenges on the summarization system and puts a need for building automatic opinion summarization systems [427].

Mass opinions about an entity are required to contain different aspects of the entity. An ideal opinion summary provides a fine-grained representation of prevailing opinions on various aspects of an entity. A crucial phase in opinion summarization, especially on micro-blog platforms, is the feature extraction phase [65]. Feature extraction reduces the feature space result in facilitating the classification task [241]. In addition to features used commonly for text summarization, symbol-based features such as Twitter-specific notions such as hashtags and other indicative punctuation are also used. Noise filtering is another step that helps to remove irrelevant and low-quality information for summarization, including spam, slang, and sarcasms [476]. A content-based and compression-based text classifiers are often employed for filtering noisy or spam tweets.

Based on the process and the output format, different methods for opinion summarization exist, including non-textual, abstractive, aspect-based, and query-focused opinion summarization approaches. Non-textual opinion summarization approaches provide different visualizations or statistics aids to present summaries using tools such as Google Chart API to visualize the data in a user-friendly manner [67, 337]. In another work [381], authors proposed a structural retweeting approach for a Website very similar to Twitter in China, called Weibo[1]. The system demonstrates sentiment dispersion through an opinion summarization chart. Using a graph-based summary and time series in the opinion tracking system is another approach for finding opinions' trends from numerous data sources [69, 355]. There is also another trend of non-textual summaries focusing on statistics. For instance, OSVS [319] is a statistic-based approach that generates bar and pie charts using Google Chart API using a graphical structure. Topic modeling approaches are also widely have been used for comments analysis and visualization on non-textual summaries [504] where topics are represented as graphs or clouds. Generally, visualization-based approaches facilitate quick analysis of data and give a concise representation of data.

Abstractive opinion summarization approaches are similar to general abstractive methods discussed in Section 6.3.1. They are categorized as semantic-based, graph-based, data-driven, machine learning, and neural networks approach. In graph-based approaches, one solution is to use extractive summarization initially to extract main sentences. Extracted sentences are compressed and merged based on word graphs [392]. Opinosis [229] is a graph-based summarization approach that produces a textual graph. It constructs abstract summaries of most redundant opinions.

Semantic-based approaches incorporate various analytic tasks to discover semantically related sentences. Employed procedures include sentence simplification and

---

[1] https://weibo.com/us.

regeneration, and summarization followed by sentence selection techniques [391]. Another work in this category uses semantic role labeling and grouping semantically similar predicate-argument structures. Besides, they employ a genetic algorithm to score the predicate-argument structures [336].

Using unsupervised learning is a general technique in machine learning-based approaches. The main approach in this category aims to find a concise and unique set of readable phrases [230]. Facebook AI Research proposed an entirely data-driven summarization approach called NAMAS. NAMAS is an abstractive sentence summarization approach based on a neural attention-based model [530]. A standard feed-forward Neural Network Language Model (NNLM) is designed to measure the next word's contextual probability with a contextual input encoder.

An aspect-based summarization is designed to summarize documents according to various target aspects or features [441]. Optimizing the sentence selection process through minimizing redundancy and maximizing coverage are examples of an approach in this category [686]. Another trend of work in this category is the entity and topic-based opinion summarization framework by incorporating weakly supervised information into topic modeling algorithms [427].

Query-focused or search-based summarization approaches focus on retrieving summaries according to a query. Different frameworks are proposed by focusing on three metrics, including relevance, coverage, and novelty [628, 629]. Using sentence compression approaches [398], probabilistic-modeling relevance, and greedy topic balance algorithm [629] are among common approaches. Two other popular frameworks in this category are TweetMotif [462] and QOS [310]. TweetMotif is designed for exploratory search and topic summarization of Twitter by assembling messages based on frequent significant terms. Then a set of subjects are extracted to cluster and summarize messages. QOS [310] is another query-specific opinion summarization approach. QOS is optimized to make summaries by considering the relevancy to the query and the represented sentiment. The process includes employing a lexicon-based method for determining the sentence's opinion orientation and defining a diversity penalty for redundancy removal. Sentences are scored according to a given query.

6.5 Evaluation Techniques

Different approaches for social data summarization exist to solve key drawbacks of traditional general methods. However, evaluating summarization approaches is challenging due to the subjectivity aspect of the task. One approach to evaluate produced summaries is by comparing the generated summary and the reference summary. Comparing summaries to the original text helps to understand the measures, including information loss. Conversely, comparison to a reference summary will quantify the quality of summaries against humans. In both situations, the evaluation strategy is deemed 'intrinsic' in nature since it is compared against itself as a content evaluation method or to verify linguistic aspects of the output summary, including the grammar, coherence, and reference clarity coherence [576]. To comprehensively evaluate the proposed approach, we categorized evaluation as 'automatic evaluation' and 'human evaluation'. Automatic summarization approaches are used to perform other tasks such as information retrieval, translation, or question answering. Therefore, one strategy is to evaluate the summarization approach towards a specific task, known as an 'extrinsic method'.

There are some conferences with a primary role in designing evaluation standards for automatic scoring of summaries and human evaluation [470]. Recall-Oriented Understudy for Gisting Evaluation (ROUGE) [377] is the most commonly accepted metric for evaluating summaries, which automatically determines the summary quality by comparing it to human (reference) summaries. It computes the common units (n-grams) mentioned in summary produced by the model and the reference summary. ROUGE-N is a recall-based measure and is based on a comparison of n-grams. Equation 6.1 describes how ROUGE-N is calculated.

$$ROUGE_n = \frac{\sum_{S \in \{ReferenceSummaries\}} \sum_{gram_n \in S} Count_{match}(gram_n)}{\sum_{S \in \{ReferenceSummaries\}} \sum_{gram_n \in S} Count(gram_n)},$$

$$(6.1)$$

where n is the n-gram size, $Count_{match}(gram_n)$ is the number of common n-grams in the candidate and the reference summaries, and $Count(gram_n)$ is the number of n-grams in the reference summary. ROUGE-L use to find the longest common sequence between two summaries. The idea behind ROUGE-L is that the longer the common sequence is, the more similar summaries are. Although ROUGE is a flexible metric, it suffers from a critical drawback. ROUGE discovers consecutive sequences to compares the n-gram units, ignoring the semantic similarity [202]. Therefore, one other category of evaluation is human-centric evaluation techniques. Crowd-based platforms such as Amazon Mechanical Turk (MTurk)[2] facilitates the process.

6.6 Concluding Remarks and Discussion

The ubiquitous availability of computing devices and the widespread use of the internet have continuously generated a large amount of data. For example, the amount of available data on any social network could be far beyond humans' processing capacity to properly process, causing what is known as 'information overload'. Navigating through all social data to extract insights for decision-making is a challenging task. Blogs and social media data are noisy and unstructured without any defined rule, including a casual dialect structure containing sarcasm, emoticons, and non-dictionary-standard words [591, 592]. They also contain spelling, grammar, punctuation, and capitalization mistakes. Besides, different social media platforms have

---

[2] https://www.mturk.com/.

specific structures. Therefore, traditional text summarization approaches do not perform well on social data.

In this chapter, we reviewed the social data summarization problem from different perspectives. A summary is expected to represent the original documents and convey the contained information. We categorized social data summarization based on their data types into two main groups of micro-blog data and generic data. We explained and provided both the challenges and state-of-the-art approaches in each category. We also discussed evaluation metrics for social data summarization approaches. There are still many challenges that need to be addressed in this domain. Specific information about users and their interests must be extracted to generate insightful summaries tailored to users' interests. An ideal summary requires to summarize various aspects of social data, including interactions in a user-activity network and other attributes such as geographical location, age, batch mates in college, or people with similar tastes and interests. However, people are instinctively endowed with their privacy settings, making the problem more challenging.

7

Storytelling with Social Data

7.1 Storytelling with Social Data: Overview

In modern enterprises, businesses accumulate massive amounts of data from various sources, including social, private, and open data. To interpret customers' and stakeholders' activities, businesses may need to analyze the large hybrid collections of heterogeneous and partially unstructured social data. The social data increasingly comes to show all typical properties of the *big data*: wide physical distribution, diversity of formats, independently-managed and heterogeneous semantics. The discovery and communication of meaningful stories from social data can help understand and discover hidden insight and knowledge [63, 65].

To understand social data in the context of social data analytics, we need to represent information items (e.g., users, posts, and activities such as comments and likes), understand their relationships, and enable the analysis of those relationships from various perspectives. In this context, narratives are perhaps the most effective way to understand the story and the account of events: narratives have to do with sequences of events and may have a hierarchical structure.

Discovery and analysis of social data narratives by building formal models is an essential step toward understanding how analysts might reason about the impact of internal and external events and tasks/actions. To achieve this, different dimensions of a narrative should be taken into account. Such dimensions may include: event structure (narratives are about something happening), the purpose of a narrative (narratives about actors and artifacts), and the role of the listener (narratives are subjective and depend on the perspective of the process analyst). Also, it is vital to emphasize the importance of time: narratives may have different meanings over time. In this chapter, we aim to highlight the vital role of storytelling with social data. A storytelling system can be considered as an alternative to querying and analysis techniques. The storytelling system would be able to isolate the analyst from the process of explicitly linking a story's content. Instead, the system should be able to use interactive story generation to select and sequence narratives dynamically.

7.1.1 Challenges and Opportunities

Social Data can change the way we do everything; however, it is essential to understand stories that communicate what is happening in social networks and what needs to be done: actionable insights. Furthermore, since the generation of social data over computer networks has brought with it an exponential increase in the type and frequency of cyber-attacks, storytelling with data can be a great asset for security analytics, i.e., the application of social data analytics techniques to cybersecurity. For example, in Law Enforcement, storytelling can help with understanding complex investigations as a simple process journey and assist police investigators in the discovery and understanding of vulnerabilities and towards improving risk-based decision-making by understanding and analyzing social data [548].

Storytelling with social data deals with the curation (covered in Chapter 3), summarization (covered in Chapter 6), and the presentation of large amounts of data in a concise and consumable manner to business users. In this context, storytelling is considered an appropriate metaphor because it can capture and represent the temporal/sequential order of key events about an activity performed on social data. Moreover, a story can be told at multiple levels, i.e., a very abstracted story versus a detailed story. To enhance storytelling with more comprehensive insights, it is possible to use data mining tools (e.g., Rapid Miner[1], Oracle Data Mining[2], IBM SPSS Modeler[3], Knime[4], and Python[5]) and techniques.

A recent report from Tableau[6] stated the need for modern data visualization techniques for storytelling with data and how data stories can be used to communicate with decision-makers. Data visualization is defined as the graphical representation of data, aiming to understand patterns and outliers through visual summaries such as diagrams, charts, and maps that will support better decisions. Data visualization techniques are mainly categorized into two groups, including exploratory and explanatory methods. Exploratory analysis aims to understand the data by answering questions such as what, when, why, and how and highlighting the main points. For instance, how a specific parameter is changed over time? Or when a parameter is expected to be decreased? In contrast, explanatory analysis, known as informative visuals, is typically used to display distinct aspects of the story. A compelling story

---

[1] https://rapidminer.com/.

[2] https://www.oracle.com/database/technologies/.

[3] https://www.ibm.com/products/spss-modeler.

[4] https://www.knime.com/.

[5] https://www.python.org/.

[6] https://help.tableau.com/current/pro/desktop/en-us/stories.htm.

through visualization enables making intelligent decisions. Effective visualization helps audiences avoid being lost in the data, leading to prolonged decision-making.

IBM[7] highlights the need for storytelling with data and how stories help organizations to know their audience and improve the business processes. Ginni Rometty, who served as executive chairman of IBM after stepping down as CEO in April 2020, highlighted that data analytics would revolutionize decision-making. Google's Chief Economist Hal Ronald Varian stated, "The ability to take data to be able to understand it, process it, extract value from it, visualize it, and communicate it is going to be a hugely important skill in the next decades".

It is expected that, as a result of the move towards combining narratives and analytics with data, a vast amount of analysis produced in the form of stories, i.e., a set of related narratives presenting different perspectives of what happens in the enterprise, will feed and impact the business, creating a more pervasive analytics-driven environment, while at the same time supporting the data scientists who can shift their focus onto the more complex analysis. To achieve this goal, it is vital to consider time-aware dimensions of a narrative, including event structure, the purpose of a narrative, and the role of the listener. In particular, discovery and analysis of narratives (i.e., set of related summaries) will be an important step toward understanding how analysts might reason with the impact of related features [66, 241, 243]. Accordingly, a story will combine data with narratives to reduce the ambiguity of social data, connect this data with the context, and describe a specific interpretation.

The main challenges in storytelling include: building the foundation for organizing the raw data, contextualizing the raw data, enhancing the summarization and discovery of connected events and entities and finally presenting the data to the end-user in an interactive manner. In Chapter 2, we presented techniques for organizing the large amount of data generated on social data islands and introduced technologies from relational to NoSQL database management systems. We also introduced the notion of Data Lakes as a modern technology that facilitates storing raw data and lets the data analyst decide how to curate them later. In Chapter 4, we presented techniques for curating social data and introduced curation tasks including cleaning, integration, transformation, and adding value. We also discussed modern technologies, including the Knowledge Lake, i.e., a contextualized Data Lake, that facilitates turning the raw data (stored in Data Lakes) into contextualized data and knowledge. In Chapter 6, we provided an overview of summarization techniques and discussed how social data summarization could help gather related information and collect it into a shorter format that enables answering complicated questions, gaining new insight, and discovering conceptual boundaries. We also discussed modern topics, including time-aware, opinion-based, and event-based summarization of social data. The next section of this chapter focuses on data-driven storytelling via data visualization techniques.

---

[7] https://www.ibm.com/analytics/data-visualization.

7.2 Data-driven Storytelling via Visualization

In the modern world, a vast amount of data is available with hidden interesting patterns which are required to be discovered. Facilitating access to data helps decision-makers develop personalized insights. However, raw data does not provide any actionable insights. Therefore, it is required to be transformed into an understandable format. Moreover, a compelling story should be made out of data to support claims and highlight the values of a product or service. An interactive consolidation of visuals supported by an available data set, known as the dashboard, is the best setting for engaging end-users.

Data storytelling is the general term used to leverage information to make compelling data-driven stories. A compelling narrative allows the audience to view and draw insights and find patterns and correlations to form their customized story. A good story assigns meaning and context to data and facilitates understanding data and conveying the main points. However, tailoring summaries to specific audiences generates the least cognitive load [58]. Consequently, it is easier for the audience' to grasp the idea without requiring mental energy. Data visualization is fundamental for this purpose by engaging the audience and inspiring action. It helps decision-makers make intelligent and informed decisions that might not be possible with textual data. Storytelling through visualization has many advantages summarized below.

- Mixing narrative and visual elements using techniques such as interactive data visualization engage audiences. Therefore, they can be guided to examine data and draw a conclusion based on their observation. Consequently, decision-making is more straightforward after assigning meaning and context to data.
- Using numbers and visualization aids based on facts increases content credibility and builds trust with the audience [239].
- Data-driven stories are versatile. Data-driven stories can be used for various purposes, such as brochures, annual reports, Website content, and social media posts. They are valuable for various professionals such as government, finance, marketing, service industries, and education.

Data storytelling is not simply data visualization or analytics reporting. Value is required to be identified from data. Data storytelling processes turn raw data into a story by highlighting valuable information and supporting ideas and facts [74]. Storytelling and data visualization techniques together make an indispensable tool for expanding internal and external communications and adding credibility to the content while engaging audiences. However, some factors need to be considered to augment data-driven storytelling with effective visualization discussed in the following.

7.2.1 Defining Objectives and Knowing the Audience

Defining the purpose of data visualization is the first step to creating a compelling story. Identifying trends, focusing on a specific part of data, categorizing data, supporting a claim, or highlighting a product value are examples of different storytelling needs. Besides, various stories can be built based on the same data set for different audiences and purposes. Moreover, the audiences' prior knowledge affects how to tell the story. For instance, convincing mobile app users compared to researchers requires different forms of stories. Visual and narrative elements are needed to convey the intended purpose and obtain the desired actions.

7.2.2 Identifying a Compelling Narrative

A narrative should guide audiences to understand the story and ends with concluding. The content and context affect the narrative structure. For instance, describing a time series requires different tools compared to emphasizing profit growth. However, there are five main trends for defining a narrative, including (i) trends: describing the rise and fall in a given period, (ii) comparison: comparing features and analyzing their changes in a period, (iii) ran over: making a hierarchy to analyze various factors, (iv) statistical relationships: exploring and predicting the effect of different features, and (v) counterintuitive data: capturing audiences' attention and engaging them.

7.2.3 Incorporating Key Elements

Any narrative has some key elements required to be designed carefully to make a compelling story. The *story plot* should be selected to help follow the story easily and make a conclusion efficiently. The *setting* impacts the way audiences interpret data. *Character* is another element that addresses audiences' priorities. The last element is *end* which helps users to conclude as it is the intention of the story.

7.2.4 Transparency

Data visualization should be selected such that they present insights in an unbiased way. Even unintentional biases increase the risk of reducing credibility and trust for audiences. Proper labeling, matching dimensions, presenting the actual values without manipulation are examples of transparency in visualizing data.

7.2.5 Visualization Method

The goal of visualization techniques is to help users understand the main idea and reduce their cognitive load. Therefore, regardless of the selected approach, simplicity and clarity are two main factors. For instance, white space guides the readers' attention. Bold colors are used to highlight a fact. Being consistent throughout the story and using standard visualization methods helps audiences better follow the information. We discuss various visualization techniques in Section 7.3.

7.3 Visualization Techniques

Data visualization employs visual aids to facilitate understanding the significance of data. Selecting the proper method among various visualization methods depends on the target customer and the story's complexity. We categorize visualization into three groups, including static, interactive, and adaptive visualization.

Static data visualization techniques do not incorporate any interaction capabilities. They present the story from a single viewpoint, and therefore, are not adjustable. However, one static representation is not sufficient to make a compelling story in many cases. Static visualization is mainly used for presenting the relationships between features in less complex stories and giving a concise overview of the whole story to encourage exploration. Interactive visualization techniques allow users to interact with data and create their customized story, proper for complex stories. In general, building static designs are significantly less expensive. However, interactive visualizations reduce humans' cognitive load. In addition to static and interactive visualization, adaptive or personalized visualization has emerged recently, incorporating users' interest in making their data stories.

7.3.1 Static Data Visualization

Static visualization techniques focus on a single view in a single-page layout. This section introduces the main static visualization techniques, including text, chart, table, and plot. Examples of static data visualization are depicted in Figure 7.1.

Text: The text as a visualization technique aims to convey the main message, reduce ambiguity, and have specific usage. For instance, when there are only some numbers to present, such as the growing percentage of a factor, a few supporting words explain the purpose more clearly.

Charts: Charts are used to present the relationship between different features. Different variations of charts exist for several purposes, such as bar chart, line chart, and pie chart. Bar and line charts demonstrate a relationship, such as a correlation between two features. A line chart mainly presents trends or linear relations among continuous data. A bar chart is used for visualizing and comparing categorical data and categorized as horizontal, vertical, and stacked. Bar charts are required to have

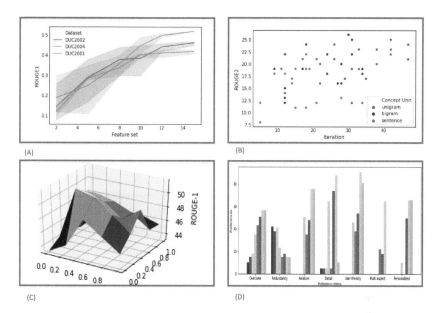

Fig. 7.1 Examples of static data visualization. (A) A line chart to present the relations of two features and their fluctuations. (B) A scatter plot to demonstrate the relations of various features. (C) A 3D plot to demonstrate the relations of three parameters. (D) A bar chart to compare categorical data.

a zero baseline to avoid biases. Pie charts are used to present different proportions of a feature compared to the entire element.

Tables: Tables are used for communicating to a mixed audience with particular interests. It can be useful for displaying several categories simultaneously. Besides, describing multiple different measure units using a table is more convenient. However, using a table in a live presentation distracts users, especially if heavy borders are used.

Plot: Point-based plots such as scatter plots are used to reveal a hidden pattern such as correlation in a large data set. A dependent and an independent variable are paired to present a relationship, and a line that is fitted on data highlights the trend. Scatter plots are primarily used in scientific fields to analyze the cause and effect relations.

7.3.2 Interactive Data Visualization

An interactive data visualization technique is the ideal solution for complex data stories to engage users with minimal technical knowledge to manipulate and explore graphical representations of data directly. Interactive visualization techniques have various advantages summarized in the following. An example of interactive visualization technique is also depicted in Figure 7.2.

- Faster analysis of trends: graphical representation of data, with direct manipulation ability, makes pattern extraction faster and easier.
- Efficient relation extraction: the ability to interact with data and narrow it to the desired detailed level helps detect cause-and-effect relationships efficiently.
- Complex data stories: an interactive environment with the ability to group, filter, and zoom help manage data and deliver a better understanding of data by demonstrating multiple viewpoints.

Data visualization tools can be in various forms, such as workflow-centric, spreadsheet-focused, or code-based. Among various visualization techniques, tools that focus on visualizations are more popular since they empower users to explore the data interactively. The most popular interactive data visualization techniques are introduced in the following.

Fig. 7.2 An example of interactive visualization using Google Data Studio.

Google Data Studio:[8] Google Data Studio was created by Google in 2016 and integrated with Google Analytics. Google Data Studio is a cloud-based powerful data visualization and reporting tool that allows the creation of fully customizable dashboards and reports. Conventionally, all visual elements are divided into three groups: (i) visualization elements, (ii) design elements, and (iii) filtering elements. Besides, there are many pre-built templates in Data Studio, allowing the creation of beautiful dashboards full of charts quickly and easily. Data Studio is also more straightforward compared to the alternatives. However, Google Data Studio is only a visualization tool, therefore requires collected data.

Microsoft Power BI:[9] Microsoft Power BI is a business intelligence, and data visualization tool which converts data from various sources such as Excel spreadsheets or cloud-based and on-premises hybrid data warehouses to interactive dashboards and BI reports. Power BI has a collection of applications, software services, and connectors, working together with various advantages summarized in the following.

- Connecting data: data can be collected from various sources such as Excel or cloud-based sources, Salesforce, Azure SQL DB, and SharePoint.
- Preparing data: ingesting, transforming, integrating, and enriching data in Power BI is more manageable with data modeling tools.
- Providing advanced analytics: it can find patterns that lead to actionable insights by using grouping, forecasting, and clustering features.
- AI-driven augmented analytics: with the AI capabilities, Power BI users can discover hidden patterns required for strategic prediction of business outcomes.
- Creating customized business reports: it provides various modern data visuals to create interactive dashboards.

Tableau:[10] Tableau is an interactive data visualization software focused on business intelligence. collects data from various locations and services, including spreadsheet, Google Cloud SQL, amazon Webs services, and Microsoft Azure SQL. The most significant advantage of Tableau is providing end-users a better experience by allowing non-technical users to design customized dashboards. Other specific features include (i) data blending, (ii) real-time analysis, (iii) data collaboration, (iv) query translation, and (v) extensive datasets management.

OpenRefine:[11] OpenRefine, previously known as GoogleRefine, is a powerful and open-source software that goes beyond data visualization. OpenRefine looks like a spreadsheet but operates like a database, enabling cleaning and transforming data and enlarging it with external data and Web services, which increases discovery capabilities.

Qlik:[12] Qlik is a data visualization software for building business intelligence products, supporting visual data discovery, and developing data dashboards. Two

---

[8] https://marketingplatform.google.com/.

[9] https://powerbi.microsoft.com/.

[10] https://www.tableau.com/.

[11] https://openrefine.org/.

[12] https://www.qlik.com/.

primary services are QlikView and Data Market. QlikView is used for data analysis and visualization without the need for programming skills. Manipulating dashboards is possible through a drag-and-drop interface, reducing the risk of data governance problems. Data Market provides QlikView users access to a pool of curated datasets such as business filing, financial, and census data.

Most of the related works [46, 200, 212] in data-driven storytelling presented interactive visualizations to convey data-driven discoveries. While interactive visualization is an important step in storytelling with data, data storytelling is much more than a sophisticated way to present data visually. A recent work, iStory [67], presented an intelligent pipeline for storytelling with social data. The pipeline starts with leveraging Data Lakes [61] to organize social data, then feed the raw data into Knowledge Lakes [62] to automatically contextualize the raw data and prepare it for analytics. The next phase in the pipeline focuses on summarizing the large contextualized social data and feeding it into an interactive digital dashboard to enable intelligent narrative construction based on the important features (extracted and ranked automatically) and enable storytelling at multiple levels and from different views. The proposed approach enables feature engineering in social data analytics to enhance the discovery of connected events and entities and present the data and insight to the end-user in an interactive manner. Figure 7.3 illustrates the storytelling engine proposed in iStory [67], which is responsible for organizing the raw data in Data Lake, transforming the raw data into contextualized data and knowledge to build a Knowledge Lake, summarizing the contextualized data to construct the Story Knowledge Graph [70]; and a screenshot of the interactive digital dashboard.

7.3.3 Adaptive Data Visualization

Interactive data visualization techniques help humans reduce their cognitive load in the process of making a decision by providing interactive aids. One-size-fits-all data visualization models, known as traditional approaches, are ubiquitous. However, they do not consider individual users' preferences, abilities, or context. Recently, adaptive data visualization techniques have emerged, proving that individual user characteristics impact visualization effectiveness, and therefore, should be incorporated in the visualization framework. Several related research have focused on showing the effect of users' characteristics on their processing mechanism of visual information [415]. Proposing an adaptive data visualization technique required of defining two phases: (i) extracting particular characteristics and interests which impact users' interaction with the system and (ii) designing proper methods to facilitate interaction based on characteristics and interests [575].

Recommending alternative visualizations based on users' preferences is a common interaction and adaptation technique used in data visualization [69, 255]. For instance, Kong et al. [344] proposed a system that dynamically selected overlays to be added to visualization for a better understanding of charts. Their proposed overlays include a reference structure for grids, highlight bars in a bar chart, us-

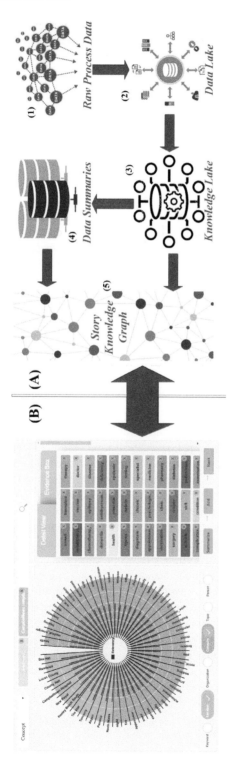

Fig. 7.3 The storytelling engine presented in iStory [67]: (A) which is responsible for organizing the raw data (A.1) in Data Lake (A.2), transform the raw data into contextualized data and knowledge in Knowledge Lake (A.3), summarize the contextualized data (A.4) and construct the Story Knowledge Graph (A.5); and a screenshot of the digital interactive dashboard (B).

ing summary statistics, and annotation to provide comments. However, they did not examine the effect of each overlay according to users' preferences. Later, Carenini et al. [113] proposed a personalized data visualization techniques instead of recommending alternative visualizations. They proposed to highlight a specific part of data related to users' tasks. However, the system is required to know the users' tasks for emphasizing users' interests. In the following, a recent work [575] focused on adding visualization aids without considering the exact data point that the user is interested in making the task more independent and applicable for various scenarios. Besides, they examined the impact of cognitive style on aid preference and usage.

Adaptive context-aware strategies have also been examined for user interfaces (UIs). A collection of reusable UI elements such as templates or services can be recommended using a rule-based system [591, 592]. A knowledge base is used to keep different rules for the UI layout and the composition of UI components for further usage. However, rules are automatically created based on the modification history [340]. Improving the UI development for Web services is also analyzed in this work, which is required to be adapted by the contexts. However, adjusting UI code to a specific context is very resource-intensive, complex, and time-consuming. Besides, UI development techniques are behind humans' ability to deploy new services since they demand manual programming to develop UI components. Therefore, more advanced techniques are required for designing practical context-aware UI components.

7.4 Concluding Remarks and Discussion

Discovery and analysis of social data narratives by building formal models is an important step toward understanding how analysts might reason about the impact of internal and external events and activities. Understanding the activities performed on social data, and perceiving their execution through discovery and exploration of stories from social data will help the end-users and analysts better understand the increasing complexity of interrelated information items in social data. Accordingly, a story will be able to combine data with narratives to reduce the ambiguity of data, to connect data with the context, and to describe a specific interpretation.

Current state-of-the-art in storytelling with social data does not provide sufficient techniques for the discovery and understanding of hidden insight from social data. In particular, the goal of social data analytics should be to identify opportunities for insight discovery and process improvement. This chapter, focused on advancing the scientific understanding of storytelling with social data. We introduced storytelling as an incremental and interactive process that enables analysts to turn insights into actions. We discussed the related work in this domain and highlighted the importance of enabling analysts to communicate analysis findings, supporting evidence and evaluate the quality of the social data stories.

8

Social Data and Recommender Systems: The Future of Personalization

8.1 Introduction

Over the past few years, the rapid growth of social networks has resulted in the production of a substantially big amount of social data and is posing challenges due to the high *volume, variety*, and *velocity* (3V) of social data [238]. While having such big data can be beneficial when learning the behaviors and preferences of online users in social environments, it can at the same time create undesired effects to users when browsing the social networks to obtain their desired content [69, 276, 651]. As an example, it has been reported that *YouTube*, as one of the largest social networks, owns the records of more than a billion active users, consuming around billions of video content every single day[1]. The 3Vs of the social data has caused the users to feel desperate when searching the content suitable for their needs from a large catalog of items and making them nearly fail to find what they need [276].

Social Recommender Systems are decision support tools that can tackle this challenge by helping the users when making choices on which content to consume [9, 16, 394, 520]. Social recommender systems utilize advanced Machine Learning algorithms to build models on top of the users' particular preferences mined from their social behaviors and generate personalized suggestions for them based on the models. Such suggestions, hence, support users to find the right content that better suits their personal needs and constraints [58, 65, 107, 303, 521].

---

[1] https://www.omnicoreagency.com/youtube-statistics.

8.1.1 Overview of Recommendation Approaches

A wide range of recommendation approaches has been proposed by the community [9, 518, 580]. In this section, we briefly review the common approaches found in the literature.

- *Content-based approaches*: are a class of approaches that generate recommendation according to the associated features of the item content. For example, news recommender systems model the news articles according to the terms as features and suggest to the user news articles with terms similar to the ones the user has liked in the past [51, 484].
- *Demographic approaches*: find the users who are similar to each other according to their demographics (e.g., age, gender, or geo-location). Then the recommendation is generated according to these similarities. Hence, the demographic approaches attempt to classify the users based on some form of personal attributes and make recommendations considering the identified user classes [483, 636].
- *Utility-based approaches*: compute the potential links between the needs of the users and a set of items (as available choices to choose from). Hence, the recommendations are built by computing and using the utility score of each item for a target user [265, 297].
- *Knowledge-based approaches*: suggest items that are inferred - with a particular reasoning process - from the personal needs and constraints of every user. Knowledge-based approaches are identified by their knowledge on how a specific item meets criteria made according to a user's needs. Hence, they can reason on the particular relationship among users, their constraints, and the potential recommendation [63, 105, 213].
- *Collaborative Filtering approaches*: predict the ratings of a user utilizing the ratings of the other users who are part of a connected network in order build a rating prediction model. The recommendations are generated accordingly by adopting the model and filtering the items that have been assigned with the highest predicted ratings [169, 347].
- *Hybrid approaches*: combine several individual recommendation approaches, to deal with the potential limitations of single approaches, among those listed above [141, 373].
- *Cognitive Recommender System* [69], are a new type of data-driven, knowledge-driven, and cognition-driven Recommender Systems. Such Recommender Systems, may benefit from learning algorithms such as, Personality2Vec [66] to enable the analysis of customers personality, behaviour, and attitude to facilitate the understanding of user's preferences, detect changes in user preferences over time, and predict the user's unknown favorites. They also enable exploring adaptive mechanisms to enable intelligent actions within the compound and changing environments.

Despite the wide range of the introduced recommendation approaches, the most popular approaches are either Collaborative Filtering or Content-based Filtering approaches, discussed in more details in the next section.

8.1.2 Collaborative Filtering Approaches

Collaborative Filtering (CF) approaches adopt the ratings provided by a network of users to predict the future ratings of users for items that have not been rated by them yet, and suggest the items with the highest predicted ratings. And recommend those items that a target user may be interested in [169, 347]. The classical *K-Nearest Neighbors (K-NN)* methods are examples of the collaborative filtering approaches that assess the user-to-user or item-to-item similarities based on the co-rating patterns. The users are considered similar provided that they similarly co-rate items. Analogously, the items are considered similar provided that a network of users have similarly rated them. The recommendations are generated for a target user by considering the items that received a high rating from a set of users similar to the target user. This is typically referred to as *user-based* collaborative filtering. The *item-based* collaborative filtering, on the other hand, computes the similar items if their ratings are analogous to those who have been rated by the target user in the past, and considers them candidate items for suggestion to her.

Matrix Factorization (MF) approaches are also among common techniques of collaborative filtering [347]. Matrix Factorization models the users and items with a vector of latent factors computed by "learning" the rating patterns from the data collected from a network of users. Matrix Factorization goes beyond the users-to-users and items-to-items similarities by using Machine Learning algorithms to model the user and items and their relationships with vectors of hidden factors. The computed relationships between users and items are then utilized to build relevant recommendations for the target users.

In the following section, we provide more technical details on neighborhood-based and matrix factorization approaches.

8.1.2.1 Neighbourhood-based Approaches

Neighborhood-based techniques use two sets of data for making a rating prediction: (i) the rating data (as user preferences data) provided by a target user for the items, and, (ii) the rating data elicited from the users similar to that user (i.e., the neighbors). Hence, a neighborhood-based recommender system computes the rating prediction according to the process that starts with identifying the users who co-rated items similar to a target user. Then, the rating $\hat{r}_{u,i}$ for the user u and the item i is predicted in the following way:

$$\hat{r}_{u,i} = \bar{r}_u + \frac{\sum_{u' \in N_{i(u)}} sim(u, u')(r_{u',i} - \bar{r}_{u'})}{\sum_{u' \in N_{i(u)}} |sim(u, u')|} \tag{8.1}$$

where $\bar{r}_u$ is the *mean* rating computed for the user u, $sim(u, u')$ is a similarity measure between two users u and u', and $N_{i(u)}$ is a set of like-minded users, identified to be similar to user u (neighbours) based on their rating provided for the item i. The similarity among users can be computed using different similarity measurements, for instance, the *Pearson Correlation* [514]:

$$sim(u, u') = \frac{\sum_{i \in I_{u,u'}} (r_{u,i} - \bar{r}_u)(r_{u',i} - \bar{r}_{u'})}{\sqrt{\sum_{i \in I_{u,u'}} (r_{u,i} - \bar{r}_u)^2 \sum_{i \in I_{u,u'}} (r_{u',i} - \bar{r}_{u'})^2}} \tag{8.2}$$

where $I_{u,u'}$ denotes the set of items co-rated by both users u and u'.

8.1.2.2 Matrix Factorization Approaches

Matrix factorization approaches, are also referred to as *Latent Factor* models, and follow a different methodology for predicting the ratings [345, 346, 347, 349, 399]. Matrix factorization computes vectors that describe the users and items with a form of latent factors. Those vectors have a similar length and are inferred from the rating of the users. Every value within these vectors indicates the extent to which the item represents a specific latent aspect. In the movie domain, as an example, the factors can be an indication of the genres of the movie (e.g., the level of comedy score of the movie). User factor vectors can analogously reflect the taste of the user for each factor. Accordingly, the task of the factorization is to divide the matrix of ratings R into two matrices S and M in such a way that:

$$R \approx SM^T \tag{8.3}$$

where S is $|U| \times F$ matrix, and M is $|I| \times F$ matrix. F reflects the number of factors to be computed.

The prediction of the ratings is made according to the following formula:

$$\hat{r}_{ui} = \sum_{f=1..F} s_{uf} m_{if} \tag{8.4}$$

where s_{uf} denotes to what extend the user u prefers the factor f and m_{if} denotes the level of the factor f potentially been reflected within the content of item i. The factor matrices are estimated by minimizing the sum of error [345, 347, 349, 399]:

$$e_{ui} = r_{ui} - \hat{r}_{ui} \tag{8.5}$$

$$s_{uf} = s_{uf} + \gamma \times (e_{ui} \times m_{if} - \lambda s_{uf}) \tag{8.6}$$

$$m_{uf} = m_{uf} + \gamma \times (e_{ui} \times s_{if} - \lambda m_{uf}) \tag{8.7}$$

When the factors are computed, the predicted rating is usually mapped to the range from 1 to 5.

8.1.2.3 Improvement of Collaborative Filtering

Collaborative filtering may suffer from several challenges and limitations. *Cold Start* problem is an example that occurs when the recommender system has insufficient data to operate properly [188, 199]. In real-world situations, the cold start problem is caused when there are users that have provided no rating to any item, or items have received no rating. There are various solutions that can mitigate the cold start problem. A potential solution can be to utilize a *hybrid* recommendation approach, i.e., combining the collaborative filtering and content-based approaches, that can help to avoid the limitations of collaborative systems [9, 107, 190, 458]. Another potential solution is to extend the existing rating dataset by exploiting some domain knowledge on items. In the food domain, the knowledge on food items, e.g., ingredients, or cuisines, may be beneficial in collaborative filtering-based food recommender system [9, 105, 236, 521].

In addition, a potential solution is to adopt extra information about the user, e.g., *Personality* traits of the users, to deal with severe cases of cold start problems. Personality traits are stable factors that constitute human behaviors [66]. In psychology, the personality of a human is defined as a "consistent behavior pattern and interpersonal processes originating within the individual" [74, 104]. Indeed, it accounts for the specific differences of individuals in the emotional, experiential, and motivational styles [313]. It has been found that personality can influence human choices and tastes [512]. Accordingly, there exists a direct relation between personality and interests of people [512]. Hence, people with similar personality traits often share similar interests.

Prior studies support the possibility of utilizing personality traits in collaborative filtering-based recommender systems [292, 294, 604]. As an instance, psychological studies [512] have found that extravert individuals are likely to enjoy upbeat and conventional songs. As a result, the personality-based music recommendation approach can better predict the songs that are more relevant to the extravert people [293]. Another example is to adopt the personality traits to calculate the similarities among users and hence find like-minded users [604]. The similarity scores can be, then, adopted by a collaborative filtering recommender system so that more relevant recommendations are made for users.

8.1.3 Content-Based Approaches

Classical methods utilized in the early times of recommendation and personalization have been primarily based on the *Content-based Filtering approaches (CBF)*. These approaches can model users by computing their preferences with the item content [163, 186, 193, 275, 303, 402, 509]. The user preferences can be of diverse characteristics and can be collected *explicitly* [89], or *implicitly* [332]. The item content can be described with different semantic features, e.g., the category or description of the item. The recommender systems can exploit these features to establish a *Vector Space Model* [484]. Then, the item is modeled by a vector associated with its content. This enables the recommender systems to measure how relevant the preferences are in terms of the item features [394, 618]. As an example, in the movie domain, a content-based recommender system can exploit the genre, description, producer, and cast as content features [442].

Over the many years, different content-based approaches have been proposed. A common approach adopts the methods based on *K-Nearest Neighbors (K-NN)* to compute the similarity patterns among items based on their content features and then suggest, to a target user, the items highly similar to those they enjoyed before. The similarity among items is typically computed based on *Cosine* similarity metric [394, 484]. More precisely, given a list of users $u \in U$ and items $i \in I$, the rating r_{ui} provided by a user u to an item i has been elicited. Each item $i \in I$ is described by a set of features $\boldsymbol{f_i}$. For every pair of items i and j, the similarity metric s_{ij} is measured and exploited to predict the ratings, according to the following formula:

$$s_{ij} = \frac{\boldsymbol{f_i}^T \boldsymbol{f_j}}{\boldsymbol{f_i f_j}} \qquad \hat{r}_{ui} = \frac{\sum_{j \in NN_i, r_{uj} > 0} r_{uj} s_{ij}}{\sum_{j \in NN_i, r_{uj} > 0} s_{ij}} \tag{8.8}$$

where NN_i represents the neighbourhood items, similar to the item i. Other content-based approaches use techniques based on *Relevance Feedback* [23] and *Probabilistic Models*, such as *Bayesian Models* [438]. For example, by computing the item features and user ratings, the probability that a target user is interested in a particular item is measured. Then, items with the highest probabilities are suggested to a user. Furthermore, other forms of content features can be adopted by recommendation and personalization systems ranging from classical *semantic* features to recent *visual* features [67]. The former type is more *high-level* and it is extracted from traditional sources, such as databases, online taxonomies, review forums, or social web applications [23, 90, 110, 430, 438, 442]. The latter type, is more *low-level* and it is extracted by directly analyzing the movies [164, 165]. The majority of prior research works on content-based approaches primarily focused on utilizing the traditional high-level features, while limited works have studied the potential power behind the low-level visual features. These features are more descriptive of the production style, and hence they may empower the recommender systems to become more of a *style-aware* personalization tools [109, 366, 656, 680].

8.2 Social Recommendation and Personalization

The exponential growth of social networks has made opportunities for recommendation and personalization systems to elicit a substantial amount of invaluable social data and incorporate them when building personalized experiences through the recommendation. In a single moment of every day, a large network of active users provides such social data in various forms and volumes. They provide their personal data when opening their accounts, enter information about their social ties when connecting to their friends, provide their topics of interest when joining communities, enter their feedback when posting comments or giving ratings, and provide their annotations when adding tags to the digital resources [566]. This empowers recommendation and personalization systems to build enhanced user profiles that range from age and gender to the hobbies and relationships. Recommender systems can analyze the communities that every user joined and build group-based profiles for the users. Such data enables recommendation and personalization systems to build advanced predictive models that can learn complex relationships among users who share similarities in terms of their tastes and preferences. Based on such models, different forms of recommendations can be provided for users, namely, friend recommendation and content recommendation. This makes the recommender systems an essential part of any modern social network [566].

In the next section, we further discuss social data from a recommender system's point of view.

8.2.1 Social Data

There are different types of social data recorded by social networks and exploited by recommender systems. These types of data can be categorized into *explicit feedback* and *implicit feedback* [189]. Explicit feedback is generally a more informative form of data, and it refers to the assessments of the users collected from them in social networks, e.g., *likes* provided by users in Instagram posts [13, 348, 577]. While beneficial, the explicit feedback needs substantial efforts from the users, which makes such data expensive to collect [198, 453]. Another type of social data is the implicit feedback that contains the *actions* taken by the users through interacting with the social networks, e.g., watching an Instagram video [264, 296, 461]. While implicit feedback is easier to obtain from the users, it is less valuable than explicit feedback. For instance, the *watch* history of a user on Instagram can be exploited by the recommender system to predict the preferences of the user and ultimately build relevant recommendations for them. An example can be a user who frequently reads a blogger's posts on Instagram. They will likely be interested in that blogger and eventually will follow them.

Despite the benefits of implicit feedback, exploiting this type of social data has limitations. For instance, it is easier to infer "positive" feedback from a user action than a "negative" one. Furthermore, the social network can only estimate the user preferences from the online behavior of a user. Indeed, watching a video may not necessarily mean that the user has been satisfied with it, since there is the possibility that she regrets watching that video later on [296]. Social data can be also categorized into *absolute* or *relative* feedback [189]. The former category of data is a more popular one and can be collected in the form of absolute assessments in a predefined scale, e.g., the five-star ratings in YouTube [348, 383, 544]. On the other hand, this type of social data is limited due to its characteristics. For example, a user who really likes two items but prefers one over the other item can be inclined to assess them similarly, or to penalize one due to the limited number of points in the rating scale [189]. This may be dealt with through elicitation of the relative feedback, i.e., pairwise comparisons: *"I prefer Titanic to Inception"*. One can also provide to what

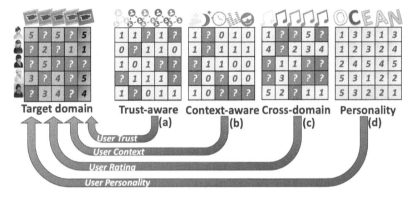

Fig. 8.1 Schematic view of different types of social data that can be utilized for personalization and recommendation, e.g., user ratings, trust relationships, user context, cross-domain ratings, and user personality traits.

extent an item is desired compared to another item, hence, building pair scores (positive or negative). The bigger the score, the more one item is preferred to the other item in the pair [92, 314, 318, 510].

The social data, as discussed above, can be used by recommender algorithms and adopted to generate different recommendation forms [566]. In this process, there are essential factors that are taken into account when developing a recommendation. Examples of such factors are trust, context, or temporal dynamics. Figure 8.1 illustrates a schematic view of different forms of personalization and recommendation generated based on different types of social data. In the next section, we discuss how social recommender systems can take these factors into account when generating recommendation.

8.2.2 Trust-aware Recommendation

Trust is an essential factor in social networks and can be effectively employed by social recommender systems. Trust corresponds to the social relationship according to the social ties among users of a social network. The trusted connections within the community of users in a social network creates a *trust network* [115, 239]. Trust relationships among users can be mined based on the social data, observed in social networks, and exploited further to build trust-aware recommendations (see Figure 8.1-a) [194]. For instance, trust relationships can be adopted to compute the *confidence score* for the ratings provided by the users resulting in different types of relationships among users. Such relationships can be incorporated to enhance the quality of the recommender systems [563].

An example of social recommender systems adopting trust factor is called TrustMF, a model that can be viewed as an extension of matrix factorization that incorporates the trust data [654]. Another example of a social recommender system that adopts trust data is called dTrust, a model that extends *Deep Neural Networks* to exploit trust-user-item network for recommendation [152]. There have been plenty of other prior research works who proposes similar methods for recommendation.

In a notable work, the authors proposed a trust-ware algorithm to be utilized in the recommendation process utilizing either direct or indirect trust relationships among users [603]. In another research a trust-aware algorithm has been developed for video recommendation in social networks [149]. Furthermore, the authors have designed a combined discovery model for users and videos. The user discovery model is adopted to measure the similarity level among a target user and the most influential users, based on their estimated trust link according to users' interaction and friendship data. The video discovery model is adopted, on the other hand, to measure the video trust based on the activities and ratings for users.

8.2.3 Context-aware Recommendation

Context-awareness is another factor that has been taken into account by social recommender systems. Context can be defined as "any information about the user and the environment that can be used to enhance the user experience" [170]. Context can correspond to the condition a user might be experiencing, namely, the *social*, *physical*, or *emotional* conditions. Utilizing context enables the social recommender systems to extend the user profile with additional data and hence gain more informative knowledge about users (see Figure 8.1-b) [473]. Various contextual factors can play a crucial role when generating recommendation in social media. Examples of such factors are the geo-location of the users, the time that the user is active in the social network, or even the mood of the user [566]. Incorporating such contextual factors into the recommendation process can effectively improve the relevancy of the generated recommendation to make it a better match the specific needs of the users at the right moment and the right place [566]. While adoption of contextual factors into recommendation can be beneficial, it is still challenging how and which contextual factors should be used in different recommendation scenarios [10].

One of the most important contextual factors in social networks is the geo-location data collected from the users [566]. The geo-location data contained in social networks can be a rich source to be used to establish the user-to-user, the user-to-place, and place-to-place connections in the data to be potentially used for recommendation purposes [54]. Modern social networks have implemented functionalities that enable the users to add location-based reviews and ratings that are eventually be exploited to generate a recommendation of Point-of-Interests (POIs) for users [384, 663]. As an example, [384] proposes a POI recommendation technique based on probabilistic factor analysis to be used to mine patterns from check-ins of the users. The factors that have been analyzed include user mobility behavior, geographical influence, and user preferences. In a more recent work [374], the authors developed a POI recommendation approach using tensor factorization using the location of the users shared in social networks. Accordingly, check-in data has been split into multiple time segments and then fused to create a user-topic-time tensor. More advanced techniques devise a hybrid technique for the recommendation. For instance, in a notable work, the authors developed a technique called GeoSRS, combining collaborative filtering with content-based filtering approaches to exploit geographical preferences as well as reviews to generate a location-aware recommendation [112].

8.2.4 Temporal Recommendation

Another important dimension of the social data is time. A user who would like to watch a movie today may change her opinion the other day and prefer to watch another movie. The social connection of users is another example that can change over time. Users establish some new social relationships and end some old relationships. Such dynamics in the social data are an important aspect to be taken into account when generating recommendations based on social data [566]. Disregarding such characteristics can harm the quality of social recommender systems and cause negative influence on their output [159].

Prior works have investigated the impact of the time factor on the social recommendation [231, 489]. The main focus of these works have been the development of different types of context-aware recommendation by incorporating the temporal characteristics of the data [231]. Accordingly, in some of the works, the authors have commonly studied the potential characteristics of the social data and reported the nonuniformity and consecutiveness as important properties that correlate with the observed check-in time and preferences of users. Nonuniformity explains the tendency of a user to have different check-in preferences at different points in time, and consecutiveness explains the tendency of a user to express similar check-in preferences consecutively in time. The developed approaches typically exploit such properties to generate an enhanced location-aware recommendation. In some other works, the authors focused on utilizing the Spatio-temporal structure to model user-sessions-locations relationships [70, 331]. The proposed structures include bipartite graphs (user-time, location-time, and user-location) and unipartite graphs (user-user, location-location, and session-session). The proposed structures have been exploited to generate location and friend recommendations. In a different approach, the authors employed a decay function together with the social relations to build friend recommendations in a popular social network called Weibo. Two recommendation techniques have been developed, one adopting social relations and another adopting a time-sequenced topic [677].

8.2.5 Cross-Domain Recommendation

A different type of social recommender systems focus investigating the cross-domain aspects of social media, hence, adopting the user data from one domain (e.g., microblogging domain) and using them to generate recommendation in another domain (e.g., fashion domain). In such a scenario, the former domain is referred to as *auxiliary* domain and the latter called *target* domain (see Figure 8.1-c) [148]. Cross-domain approaches can be categories in the following: (i) approaches that extend the knowledge from several auxiliary domains to generate recommendations of items in a target domain, and (ii) approaches that primarily focus on transferring knowledge between domains to support recommendations [189]. In a remarkable example of the former approaches, the authors propose different aggregation techniques: (i) centralized prediction, i.e., the aggregated knowledge containing the preferences of users, (ii) distributed peer identification, i.e., the aggregated knowledge contains the similarities among users, and (ii) distributed neighborhood formation, i.e., the aggregated knowledge contains the user neighborhoods, and (iiii) distributed prediction, i.e., the aggregated knowledge contains only the single-domain recommendations. The results of the experiments revealed that the proposed method can boost the performance of the recommendation in the target domain [85].

In an example of the latter approaches, the authors proposed different cross-domain models, i.e., *UserItemTags, UserItemRelTags* and *ItemRelTags*. Accordingly, the knowledge obtained from social tags provided by users through their interaction and exploited to improve the quality prediction model. The assumption here is that the social data in an auxiliary domain can be exploited to boost the quality of recommendation in a different target domain, if an overlap exists in the data collected in two domains [199]. The primary differences among the proposed models are related to different methods adopted to incorporate the social tags collected for rating prediction. While UserItemTags and UserItemRelTags can predict the preferences of a target user by utilizing only her social tags, ItemRelTags considers the tags even assigned by other users to predict preferences of the target user. To evaluate the quality of these models, a series of offline experiments have been conducted using public datasets. The results have shown the benefit of using social tags and the proposed models.

8.2.6 Group Recommendation

Group recommendation is a novel category of recommendation and personalization systems that have emerged lately. Group recommendation in social media plays a central role, making it highly relevant research to the social recommender system. In contrast to individual recommendations, group recommendation aims to generate recommendations that can suit a group of individuals. Indeed there are scenarios where recommendations shall be adapted to the group scenario. For example, watching an on-demand TV is a social activity rather than an individual activity and is typically done by a group of people (e.g., a family). Another example can be a group of friends planning to go out together for a drink or dinner and would like to use a restaurant recommender to choose the right place to go [266].

So far, many research studies have been conducted on group recommenders systems and many different approaches have been proposed. These approaches could be categorized into two main classes, i.e., (i) approaches based on profile aggregation, and, (ii) approaches based on recommendation aggregation [411]. In the former case, the profile of group members are aggregated to create a group model and exploit the model to generate a group recommendation. Examples of this type of group recommender systems can be *INTRIGUE [40]* and *POLYLENS* [471], where the individual preferences are elicited and merged to build recommendations based on collaborative filtering.

In the latter case, the recommendations are first generated for individual group members and then aggregated to form the recommendation for the entire group. As an example, a prior work proposed a hybrid technique to aggregate the recommendations [84]. In a different example of works, the recommendations are generated for individuals and then combined together to build up the group recommendation [160].

There might be numerous strategies employed when aggregating the preferences of group members. Perhaps the simplest strategy is the *averages* strategy which simply computes the mean of the individual ratings and uses them for the recommendation. Another simple strategy is the *maximum pleasure* which considers the maximum of the ratings given by individuals to an item to build group preference for an item. Another similar strategy can be *average without misery* which computes the mean of the individual ratings, while eliminating the items that have received the lowest ratings (i.e., the most hated items). There exist strategies that take into account the *fairness* by ranking the items based on the choice of group members in turn so that each member will have a chance to choose. Other strategies are opposite and take into account only the choice of the most respected person and form a *dictatorship* where the rating of the dictators of the group is used for recommendation [411].

Many studies have focused on the mechanisms that result in group formation and how the recommendation can play a role in that process. In a notable study, the authors proposed a mechanism based on combining user-based affinities and trust-awareness. User-based affinities have been utilized to estimate similar neighbors' preferences, and trust-awareness is utilized to form the trusted neighbours. Such neighborhood information has been used to compute the factors responsible for motivating the members to join groups. One of the findings of this research was that users with either a high active degree and a low active degree could be willing to join the groups. Another finding was that new users might be willing to initially join groups of their interests, while later on, they may prefer to join the groups where their followees joined [260].

8.3 Bias in Social Recommendation

Bias in the data collected in social networks is an important research topic that has drawn attention in recent years [48, 194]. Several prior works have studied what can potentially be the type and the amount of bias in data and how such bias can affect the output of recommender systems. The bias originated from the popular content being viewed more by users of social networks and subsequently being recommended more to the users and can be an example of such biases [3, 195]. While most types of biases are inherited from the data, the algorithms adopted by recommendation and personalization systems can also play a role in the reinforcement of the bias [185]. A potential root cause for that can be the algorithmic approach exploited by recommendation and personalization systems to build suggestions for the users. Another potential root cause can be the particularities of the user data recorded from the observed user behaviors and utilized by the recommender approach [125, 126]. In case the algorithmic approach adopted for the recommendation avoids exploration of new data and focuses on the exploitation of the previous data, the users may primarily receive the recommendation of items they would like to see. As a consequence, the users will be kept within a closed space typically referred to as the *Filters Bubble* . Such a limited space will not allow the users to be exposed to the novel and different recommendations, which can still be interesting to the users [633].

The bias in the recommendation may come from the bias inherited from the original data. The bias can eventually be increased by the recommendation and personalization systems according to which algorithmic approach adopted the initial level of bias in the elicited user data. This phenomenon can be further increased since users interact with the suggestions generated by the system and presented to them. Several prior works have investigated this undesired effect and found the more complicated process. In Mansoury et al. [404], for instance, the feedback loop effect and its consequences on the bias amplification in recommendation and personalization systems has been studied. Accordingly, a set of recommendation algorithms have been analyzed in a set of experiments to understand whether they increase or decrease the level of bias found in the input data. The outcome showed that different recommendation algorithms could influence the level of bias differently. The study has been extended to analyze and compare the male and female users in terms of the level of bias in their recommendations. The results have shown that the bias has been more increased for female users as well as other minority groups, perhaps due to the size of the population.

Some of the prior works have also shown that user ratings can be heavily biased toward automated recommendations and personalization. As an example, in work presented by Adomavicius et al. [7], the authors computed the bias originated from the display context believed to be the primary difference among conclusions of individuals when large and small values of ratings are presented. In this work, various display designs have been compared when utilized within different recommender systems to present the generated recommendations to the end-user. The results have shown a significant level of bias and noted that none of the rating displays could comprehensively mitigate the observed biases that originated from the system. They reported that some interface displays were more advantageous than others for reducing biases. In fact, a certain form of display utilized for graphical recommendation presentation could lead to a considerably lower level of biases in the post-consumption ratings of the individuals in comparison to their equivalent numerical forms.

An example of known bias in recommendation and personalization systems is the *Popularity Bias* which naturally originates from the input data. The data typically includes a tiny set of popular items (known as *short head*) and a bigger number of less-popular items (known as the *long tail*) [97]. Since the short head items are already popular (e.g., most-watched movies), the recommender systems may further promote these unpopular items and increase their popularity. Despite the problems, there might also be benefits for the users, e.g., navigating attractive items that might be niche and offering benefits for service providers (e.g., Netflix). Moreover, it has been shown that even the user ratings can be strongly influenced by the recommendations presented to them by the system. Although popular items are overall *good* recommendations, they are also likely to be familiar for the users. Delivering only popular items will not necessarily improve the discovery of new items and can eventually ignore users' interests with niche tastes [4, 5].

8.4 Application Domains

8.4.1 Video Domain

Video streaming and sharing have always been one of the most important activities performed within social networks. Due to the rich nature of social data, social recommender systems could exploit various features (attributes) describing the content of video items or the profiles of users. The content adopted by social recommender systems could be of different forms, ranging from classical *semantic* attributes to novel *visual* features. The semantic attributes provide a more of *high-level* representation of videos [23, 110] while the visual features depict a more *low-level* representation of the video files [164, 165, 186].

Despite the importance of both types of video features, the majority of the research works have mainly focused on the high-level features [90, 430, 438, 442]. However, there have been several recent works that investigated the potential of the low-level features and showed that these features could be more representative of the production style of the videos [109, 276, 366, 656, 680]. Some of these approaches have also considered the scenarios where low-level features are exploited and additional features to improve the quality of recommendations.

8.4.2 Music Domain

Music recommendation is another important application domain of recommendation and personalization systems operating in the social networks that have received considerable attention from academia and industry [547]. Music recommender systems typically adopt abundant data collected in social streaming platforms, learn the users' specific musical preferences, and build their profiles accordingly. The users' musical preferences are typically dependent on various factors learned from their interactions with musical items. In addition to the user interaction, other factors are also taken into account when generating the recommendation, describing the particular characteristics of the users and the situation where the music is consumed by the users [8]. The emotional state of the user [221, 511] and the activity, performed while listening to the music, are examples of such factors that shall significantly influence the musical preferences of the users [247, 632]. The social context or the location where the music is played can be other examples of important factors [8, 320]. Recent works have also investigated the significant importance of the composition of the playlist as well as the listening session in music recommendation task [418, 683].

Generating recommendations in the music domain has several specific characteristics that differ this domain from the other application domain systems [546]. In traditional recommendation domains (e.g., movie domain), the common duration of items is 90 minutes or more. In the music domain, however, the normal duration of items is 3 to 5 minutes, making these items more disposable [547]. Another uniqueness of the music domain can be related to the sequentially of the consumption. This can result in challenges relevant to identifying the right arrangement of items in a recommendation list. Moreover, in the music domain, recommending the same item again can be appreciated by the user in contrast to other domains such as the movie domain.

8.4.3 Fashion Domain

These days, social media is full of fashion bloggers who introduce and promote fashion products and brands. Checking the related literature, the definition of fashion is not all clear. In general, fashion can be described as *"The cultural construction of the embodied identity"*[2]. Fashion is commonly referred to as the prevailing form of clothing, and it can be described by the notion of *change*. Fashion consists of different forms of self-fashioning, such as styles in the street to the other calls of *high* fashion made by designers. [95, 488].

One of the biggest issues in the fashion domain is the exploding diversity of fashion products and services. This is perhaps a phenomenon that can result in a choice overload for consumers following fashion trends in social media. This is not necessarily bad, as the more choices, the better the opportunity for the consumers to find the desired product. However, this phenomenon can lead to difficulty in choosing a vast number of options [36]. Recommendation and personalization systems can mitigate this challenge by learning from social data and generating personalized suggestions of products matching the particular needs of fashion consumers. Social recommender systems utilize advanced filtering methods to shrink the range of choices by ignoring the irrelevant products and building a shortlist of interesting recommendations. They can deeply analyze the social data and learn the specific fashion tastes of users from the data produced by users. As an example, Instagram

---

[2] Editorial policy of Fashion Theory: The Journal of Dress, Body & Culture.

can look into users' interaction history when online in this social network and create predictive models that can ultimately be exploited to build relevant recommendations for the user. Hence, the core machine learning algorithms adopted by the recommender system can actively understand from the users' behaviors based on the collected social data and learn the user tastes, and individual needs of every user [505, 528, 580].

8.4.4 Tourism Domain

Another popular application domain of the social recommender systems is tourism. The majority of modern social networks enable users to include geo-location to the data (e.g., images or videos) uploaded in these networks. Such a large amount of data allows these networks to generate recommendations of POIs personalized to the users' needs. In addition to personalization, the tourism domain heavily benefits from *contextualization* defined as the process of incorporating contextual factors in the recommendation process. Examples of contextual factors are weather conditions, expenditure budget, travel goals, and transportation mean [53, 272]. The primary goal is to create recommendations from different forms of social data as well as using the specific *situation* based on the recorded contextual factors [11, 124]. For instance, in bad weather, a group of tourists is more likely to visit the indoor attractions (e.g., museums), while in good weather, they may likely opt for an outdoor activity (e.g., hiking). Context-aware Recommender Systems (CARS) can utilize such contextual factors and use them effectively [226, 321, 451].

8.4.5 Food Domain

One of the main categories of content produced in social networks is food. Many bloggers and influencers review food items and generate content for their followers. Hence, the food domain is one of the important applications of social recommender systems.

There is a range of techniques used for the recommendation of food items based on social media [409, 607, 640]. In one of the prior works, the authors proposed a model that exploits the user interaction data and creates a user preference matrix to make personalized suggestions of food items. Their proposed, converts the preferences of the users for recipes into preferences for ingredients and then merges these converted preferences to form user suggestions [225]. In another work, the authors proposed a different approach for food recommendation, which can merge the predictions for food items along with different aspects of social data. The proposed approach could also utilize the nutrition data and the ingredients to measure a score for a target food item [192]. The primary goal is to utilize factors that can influence the user's food choices to make a more beneficial list of recommendations [600]. In general, users' food preferences collected in social media can represent long-term affinities or short-term affinities. While collecting both forms of such data that express different parts of the user profile is essential, many research works in this domain do not distinguish the differences between these forms of data. Indeed, limited research works have taken such differences into account [516].

8.5 Concluding Remarks and Discussion

The ever-growing number of social networks has resulted in production of a massive amount and diversity of social data generated in every single day. This has caused the online users to feel desperate when navigating social networks and making choices among a large number of options. This chapter focused on this problem and introduced a novel set of digital tools to address this problem, i.e., Social Recommender Systems. Such tools can be utilized to effectively mitigate the problem through building personalization in social environments by exploiting social data indicative of user preferences. This chapter further provided an overview of different types of social recommender systems, commonly integrated within social networks, and can operate in various application domains, including video and music, fashion, tourism, and food.

Due to the importance of these systems, they have become an inevitable component of social networks as they can provide personalized suggestions to the users matching their specific needs and preferences. This can be conducted by deeply analyzing the social data collected from users and building predictive models utilizing advanced machine learning algorithms that can learn from user interactions in social networks and their personal tastes and preferences. Such models can then be adapted to generate personalized recommendations for the users satisfying their needs and constraints.

Social Data Analytics Applications

9.1 Social Data and Trust

Social data can be viewed as a rich resource to be used when building knowledge in various domains and with a variety of applications. As an example, the connections among social media members can potentially build up an extensive network expressing the trust links among the members. Such trust links create a network that facilitates the spread of opinions and ideas among the connected users, referred to as *social contagion* [135, 239]. When a user on Facebook makes a friendship or when a user on Twitter follows other users, they implicitly express their trusted group [595].

Extracting trust links requires heavy processing of the raw data collected from social networks. In this context, one of the primary challenges is modeling and organizing a large amount of user data and harnessing them for the extraction of trust links. This is where AI techniques can effectively be utilized. This further allows modern social networks to establish a trusted network among their users.

Many prior research works have focused on trust networks within social communities with all interconnected trust links among individual users. Such works have studied how to take advantage of social trust networks while investigating their potential impacts on the personal behaviors of the individual users [66, 515]. This impact and its potential side-effects have been commonly referred to as *Homophily* [420]. In one of the prior works, the authors have conducted an analysis of this effect in social communities and shown that users tend to be strongly influenced by their social connections. They have further reported that relationships among users can even cause strong effects on changing personal characteristics [655]. Hence, analyzing the social data collected from users can be beneficial to form a comprehensive picture of user behaviors in social communities, and consequently, help researchers better understand the actions taken by users.

Some of the notable research works have also focused on building knowledge from the trust networks obtained from social data in various application domains. The social recommendation is one of the notable applications [69, 234, 302, 407, 408, 651, 670]. Most notably, exploiting the knowledge from trust networks can be utilized when generating social recommendation and personalization with their subsequent benefits [400]. As an example of such benefits, a trust-based recommendation can be made in addressing data sparsity and scarcity as a known problem in social networks. Trust knowledge can effectively mitigate this problem originated from the characteristics of the social data [65, 669].

As a notable example, in a previous study, the authors proposed a trust-based recommendation technique called *TrustSVD* [262]. TrustSVD builds a matrix of user-user and user-item interactions and generates recommendations for users accordingly [262]. *TrustMF* is another model to formulate the social behavior of the users based on their ratings and their trust links [655]. TrustMF is constructed by exploiting two independent models, i.e., $Truster$ and $Trustee$, and combining them to predict the future behaviors of the users. *Moletrust* is another technique to process and utilize the social data and form a local trust measure, used to compute the similarity matrix among users of the social networks [408]. The trust information has also been adopted in a popular recommendation approach called Collaborative Filtering [134]. Accordingly, the ratings provided by trusted users (trusted neighbors) are provided to the approach to incorporate in the recommendation process. In a similar work [261], a technique has been adopted for merging the preferences of the trusted users to compute the similarity score between different users. Such similarity scores have been used as a base to generate a personalized recommendation for the users.

9.2 Bias in Social Data

Investigation of *bias* in social data collected from social networks have been the topic of recent research works while it is rooted back in earlier research in disciplines that ranges from Data Science to Social Science. Bias in social data can be viewed and investigated from a diverse set of perspectives. Generally, bias is described as a *deviation from a standard*, indicating the existence of any statistical pattern in the social data [153, 218]. This is a generic and rather simplified definition for a complicated phenomenon, and there might be other definitions depending on the particularity of the research field.

In general, bias within social networks is commonly believed to originate from the way the data is collected from the users while interacting within such networks. However, there might be other sources for bias, not necessarily originating from these environments. In a recent publication, the authors have focused on this and reviewed different forms of existing biases in social data. They further classified different forms of biases through two classes, (i) data bias and (ii) algorithmic bias [423].

For instance, a well-known form of bias can originate from the imbalanced data collected within social media from different groups of individuals. In one of the seminal studies, a considerable amount of bias has been found in the Internet links, indexed by search engines [49]. In a follow-up work [50], the authors have reported a significant activity bias in user-generated content online. Some of the examples of the findings are very surprising: only 2% of Twitter users have produced more than 50% of tweets in 2009; Users have produced only 1.1% of the tweets with very few followers; As low as 4% of Amazon users have provided 50% of the written reviews; And only 0.04% of Wikipedia editors generated 50% of the English entries. These examples clearly indicate a high level of bias potentially generated within the social communities.

In a different analysis, the authors investigated the mechanism of *following*, i.e., when a user is followed by the other users on the network of Twitter [646]. The results have shown that 0.05% of the top popular users may attract nearly 50% of the followers, meaning that almost half of the Twitter users follow a tiny portion of top celebrities. In a similar work, the data collected from Facebook has been analyzed. The results showed that 7% of the users within this social network generates more than 50% of all posted content [48]. The bias in the social data has severe consequences. For instance, plenty of intelligent algorithms are implemented in modern social networks for various purposes, such as recommendation and personalization. Recommendation algorithms operating in social networks exploit the collected social data and build advanced machine learning models on top of the data.

Having a significant level of bias in the data causes algorithms to be affected, and subsequently, re-produce biased output. This can further be replicated, hence, reinforcing the preexisting biases [181]. As another notable instance, considering a revealed fact, nearly 70% of Twitter users are expected to be male and 30% to be female [599]. The integrated algorithms in Twitter may unintentionally learn from such an imbalance in the data and disproportionately generate a recommendation of more male users to follow. When the algorithms are biased, more undesired issues can be made. For instance, it has been found that the number of friends for a Facebook user does not necessarily indicate the popularity of that user, while it can represent the bias of the recommendation algorithm operational in Facebook [611]. This can conclude that the algorithms trained on biased social data may substantially reinforce the original bias.

9.3 Personality Detection from Social Data

Personality characteristics of people are a predictable part of their *existence* and have a significant and steady influence on their preferences and actions. In the psychology literature, personality is defined as a "constant behavior pattern, and interpersonal processes originating within the individual" [104]. People's emotional, interpersonal, cognitive, behavioral, and incentive styles are all accounted for under this theory [58, 313]. Personality has been demonstrated to influence human judgment and desires [512]. As a result, it has been commonly believed that personality and preferences/interests are inextricably linked [512]. This means that individuals with comparable personality traits tend to have similar hobbies.

Previous research on the users' personalities supports the use of this data in various application domains, including recommendation and personalization [292, 294, 604]. Psychological research has demonstrated that extroverts enjoy cheerful and traditional music [512]. As a result, tools for personality-based music recommendation can take advantage of this research finding and improve their prediction for the affinities of extrovert users [293].

Personality information could be used in different ways, such as estimating user similarity and recognizing others with common interests [604]. A neighborhood-based collaborative filtering method can use the similarity values to generate more relevant, personalized recommendations for users.

Users' personalities may generally be elicited either directly, i.e., requiring the user to undertake a questionnaire form via one of the personality assessment inventories, or implicitly, i.e., by monitoring how the user behaves in different situations [350]. However, according to previous research, explicit personality acquisition interfaces lead to higher user pleasure, usability, and accuracy in the predictions [179]. Personality traits can also be extracted from social media platforms. Several works have proposed techniques to extract personality traits from social profiles [47, 250, 254, 499]. In one study, authors found a relationship between personality traits and the visual features extracted from users' Instagram photos [67, 220]. The impact of the users' social behavior on their personality traits has also been studied [253]. The authors assessed the personality traits from self-reported Facebook usage and correlated it with the public profile. In another work, a prediction method has been proposed capable of identifying the personality traits from Facebook profiles based on linguistic or social network features [250]. Examples of the utilized features were word count and friends' number. It has also been reported that shyness has a correlation with the time spent online and the number of friends [527]. The correlation between the personality traits of the users and their Facebook usage has also been found [587]. In addition, a correlation has been found between the posts' content and the emotional signal. Moreover, they have shown that openness has a correlation with the words expressing emotions.

Personality traits extracted from social profiles are adapted for various applications. In a study [605], the authors computed different similarity metrics among users to generate recommendations, i.e., rating-based similarity and personality-based similarity. The results of the experiments have revealed that recommendations by using personality-based similarity perform better compared to recommendations using the rating-based similarity. In another work, the author investigated the usage of personality data according to IPIP-NEO model in comparison to the Big Five factors model [460]. The results showed that a fine-grained personality model leads to a superior recommendation quality. Utilizing the correlations among personality traits, tastes, and preferences of the users for musical items are also incorporated in the recommendation model [292, 294]. Accordingly, the similarity scores among users are computed according to Pearson's correlation metric. The generated hybrid recommendations based on personality traits and ratings have revealed substantial improvements compared to the baseline based on ratings. Last but not least, [526] proposed a technique that computes the five factors profiles by analyzing the reviews written by users for hotels. The computed personality traits have been incorporated into a KNN model to generate personalized recommendations for users.

9.4 Sentiment Analysis of Social Data

Sentiment Analysis applied on social data has recently gained considerable attention from both research and industry communities. Sentiment analysis is commonly referred to the process of exploiting Natural Language Processing (NLP) techniques to extract the potential sentiments encapsulated within the written opinions. Sentiment analysis is an automated process heavily relying on Artificial Intelligence enabled methods capable of understanding the polarity within the textual data provided by users. Such polarity can be rooted behind the positive or negative sentiment extracted from the user data. As an example, the comments written by users on social media can reveal the user's opinion about a particular product. Analyzing such statements can inform the relevant businesses to figure out hidden cues, potential strengths, or weaknesses of certain products. For instance, a user's posts about movies or music can reveal personal preferences and tastes. Such information can be precious for the business to address the users' particular needs and constraints, hence gaining higher customer satisfaction.

Different tools are proposed to incorporate sentiment within services and processes, such as Lexicon-based tools and AI-based tools [88]. Lexicon-based classify the extracted sentiment based on a dictionary of terms, e.g., SentiWordNet and WordNet [551]. Then a positive or negative orientation is attributed to a set of determining terms, and the sentiment is computed according to the average orientation of the terms. The sentiment orientation can be computed according to the context, e.g., in corpus-based semantic analysis [472]. On the other hand, AI-based tools exploit AI algorithms, are trained on a big corpus, and are applied to many different contextual conditions.

Sentiment analyses are performed in various levels, i.e., term, sentence, and document. Word-level analysis can be seen as an approach similar to the lexicon-based approach since it focuses on the sentiment orientation of a term (or a phrase) [322]. The sentence-level analysis considers the document of "subjective" sentences hence applicable as a basis to evaluate the sentiment polarity. The document-level analysis takes into account the overall polarity within a sentence. Therefore, it merges each sentiment orientation computed for the sentences [157, 289]. Other combinations of these analyses are also possible depending on the overall formation of the written text. For instance, in a study [157], authors propose a different analysis in the phrase level, where the goal is to extract the sentiment polarity of features expressed by users according to their attitude towards a particular feature of the product.

Sentiment information can be exploited in various application domains. Sentiment information may correlate with users' online behavior, such as purchasing decisions. Therefore, it can be effectively utilized to build recommendations according to the users' preferences, showing a wide range of benefits [183, 193, 638]. Sentiment information can be combined with other types of user data (e.g., clicks) and be exploited to generate a hybrid recommendation [151]. Sentiment can be used to evaluate the quality of the recommendation output according to the written feedback of the users [493]. In addition, sentiment is used as a side-information either for users, i.e., by extending the user profiles with sentiment information, or for items, i.e., by enriching the content describing the items [12, 368, 534]. Furthermore, sentiment information is used for generating contextual recommendations describing the particular context that users have been experiencing [274, 465]. Sentiment information is also used to generate explanations to the recommendation, improving user control over the system. A set of explicit attributes are required to be extracted, describing the feedback provided by users on the items obtained through analysis of the written reviews [678].

Up to the present, a range of different techniques has been proposed to build a recommender system incorporating sentiment information. For example, many prior works have exploited sentiment information as part of user feedback (e.g., semi rating). In one work [367], the authors have proposed a technique that aggregates different pieces of sentiment information, namely, the sentiment similarity among users, interpersonal sentiment, and reputation similarity, which enhance the accuracy of the recommendation. Different types of user feedback have been combined, including reviews and ratings, to build recommendations for TV programs [485]. In another work, authors have proposed leveraging a physiological signal correlated with the sentiment and received from the users to infer the contextual condition of them and use it to generate a higher quality of recommendation [30]. In a recent work [635], the authors developed a recommendation framework adopting a hybrid model based on sentiment analysis. Sentiment-aware frameworks have been shown to be superior compared to traditional baselines. In another study [367], the authors exploited phrase-level sentiment analysis and generated personalized recommendations for users by computing a reputation score for items.

9.5 Personalization with Social Data

In the age of fast-growing social networks, personalization tools have been found crucial when creating customization for the e-commerce industry [492]. Due to rapid expansion in the number of products and services available in online stores, the choice of what to consume can become unbelievably difficult without personalization [326]. In addressing this problem, personalization tools significantly contribute to the customization of the consumer experience in purchasing the products through various mechanisms such as presenting the product description, summarizing the customer feedback, and offering a fair comparison with the potential items.

Personalization tools typically utilize advanced AI-based algorithms to deeply analyze the social data for learning the personal preferences of users and generate recommendations accordingly [17]. Personalization tools have been heavily implemented in social networks to improve the user experience. They commonly profile the users based on a large set of features extracted according to the social characteristics of the user. Examples of such features can be connection numbers or the popularity of posted content. Consequently, the quality of such models, and their output, directly depend on the quantity and quality of the social data collected from the users and used as the input data.

The presence of the personalization tools is not just limited to modern social networks and is used in any popular e-commerce application such as Netflix, Apple App Store, and Amazon. In the former Web application, the movies are organized according to their genre, popularity, or the watch history of the users. App Store adopts a similar approach to guide users to find relevant iOS apps to download. Amazon has also been one of the key players who offered personalization to enhance the customers' shopping experience [195, 487].

On another side of the story, the development of personalization in Ad-targeting, which serves different consumers differently, can offer a wide range of golden opportunities to any e-commerce to obtain a piece of the massive market within the advertisement industry. Personalization techniques adopted by big players of the industry, such as search engines or advertising companies, empower them to construct targeted ads that are presented on the navigation screen of users adapted to their personal behavior. In addition to that, discount coupons automatically generated and offered to the user significantly promote the products and increase the sale of the relevant businesses. Therefore, big tech industries such as Google [154], Amazon [382] are actively pursuing the development of sophisticated personalization approaches enabling them to achieve several goals [82]:

- Conversing visitors into purchaser: users' preferences are learned by exploiting social data (e.g., views and clicks). Therefore, potential products that might purchase by users can be predicted. Consequently, top products are recommended to the users while dynamically adjusting the cost-to-quality ratio. As a result, the chance of the products being purchased by the target user is increased.
- Enhancing the cross-sell: by utilizing users' shopping history and the current shopping cart, a set of additional products with high similarity to the existing products in the cart are generated. Top products are then selected and recommended to the target user.
- Increasing customer loyalty: the purchase history of the users according to the given supplier is analyzed. A value-added relationship between the e-commerce shop and the customer is created, commonly referred to as *loyalty*. Such a relationship will be utilized to obtain more information on the particular needs and preferences of the target user, and hence to generate a personalized set of recommendations [545].

9.6 Sales and Marketing: Creating Successful Campaigns with Social Media Marketing Analytics

In recent years, social media data analytics have drawn considerable attention from academic researchers and industry practitioners. The findings coming from such analytics and the effective usage of the outcomes have been the focus of many prior studies. In general, social media data analytics aims to support business players to understand their customers' values and behaviors better. Indeed, understanding customers' beliefs and behaviors are essential for any modern and successful business. The knowledge gained in this process can certainly impact the business in various tasks towards succeeding in their data-oriented vision and mission. Instances of such tasks can be outsourcing, acquiring, and renewing information resources [81].

There might be a wide range of approaches towards achieving the above-mentioned business goals and objectives. As an example, the objectives can be realized through the implementation of several different measures, e.g., assessing the quality of online marketing strategies and employing it to enhance the branding and retention of a business. Increasing market speed, engagement levels, supply chain adaptability, and enhancing marketing campaign efficacy are among the other measures.

Social platforms, with their unlimited capacities, can be beneficial in this regard. Some of the platforms, launched recently, have facilitated several functionalities that might not have been feasible a few years ago. Enabling commercial transactions directly on the platform is among those functionalities, which can result in a new generation of online businesses fully operational on social platforms. More particularly, this has enabled the active businesses on these social platforms to take advantage of a modern and vital marketplace for selling a range of products and providing various services. This can be translated into forming the new building blocks of the *"4Ps"* of business, i.e., *Product, Price, Place,* and *Promotion* [305].

Accordingly, a wide range of benefits has been reported from conducting social media analytics for business organizations, e.g., increasing customer profitability, reducing operating costs, enhancing brand recognition, understanding market trends, and improving success rates from marketing efforts [81]. Latest reports have revealed that the total investment of online marketing, operating in social media platforms, already exceeded the limits and reached billions of dollars in capital [204].

The findings of a study conducted by the *Economist Intelligence Unit*[1] in 2014, have reported more benefits for the business organizations that effectively leverage and analyze user data obtained from their pages on social platforms. The study further recommends such organizations uncover their users' interests and affinities, projected into the social data. This is, in return, expected to ultimately lead to a superior business value perceived by the customers. The study further notes that the modern form of data analytics, must be followed by proper digital marketing strategies, to achieve the distinct noted advantages for the business.

---

[1] https://www.eiu.com/n/.

Many works have studied the real-world impacts of data analytics, focusing on different tasks, namely, successful campaign creation or digital marketing on the Web. Bristol Myers[2], has been an example reported in one of these studies, an active company in the medical domain with a success story to reveal. According to a report, the company has managed to utilize the outcome of the analytics conducted on the user data obtained from the Website to increase the number of registered clients through online campaigns [204]. Digital networking companies can be other notable examples, which reshaped the marketing strategies through the invention of novel methods to interact with, learn from, and promote target products to customers [360].

In summary, to persuade the business goals, firms and companies of the 21 century need to devise strategies to take advantage of social media marketing. To analyze the efficiency of social media marketing efforts, firms and companies need to define *Key Performance Indicators (KPI)* to assess and determine crucial variables towards a company's online success [81, 204].

9.7 Influence Maximization: Identify Influencers for Brands and Industries

One of the important areas that have drawn considerable attention in academia and industry is the identification of influential members within social media networks. There might be different objectives for researching this area, e.g., maximization of the speed and coverage of information or spread of the influence in the social networks. This process is commonly referred to as *Influence Maximization* [586], and marketing based on this process, is known as lead generation.

Several approaches have been proposed so far taking advantage of popular Sociological and Psychological theories, foundations, and frameworks. For instance, metaphor of a directed graph can be used to model social networks, for which the users are nodes, and the connections (or relationships) are edges [70]. Utilizing the model, an influence score can be calculated for all nodes and the most influential nodes can be identified. When computing the influence scores, it is important to focus on increasing the overall impact of the network by taking into account the overall distribution of influence scores for popular nodes [439]. While the findings are interesting, however, a considerable number of research works primarily focused on conducting simulation experiments.

In real-world scenarios, on the other hand, business players and companies typically aim to find *Influencers*, not in generic definition, but those social media members who are in contextual congruence with the company brand. According to the related literature, defining an influencer member of a social media network is not straightforward. Based on a common definition, a member who evaluates new products with the aim or ability to influence other members might be considered an influencer. Hence, social media influencers are those individuals in the social net-

---

[2] https://www.bms.com/.

work who can affect the potential purchase choices of customers by influencing their opinions and beliefs. Examples can be social media bloggers identifying a target group and publishing content to persuade them to buy a product or use a service. The objective is to get as many people as possible to obtain the provided information and take action appropriately [439]. It is worth noting that, normally, the influencer is not associated with the company.

So far, a varity of prior works have studied this process, e.g., by analyzing the social graph structure. Goyal et al. [256] is an example of such works which developed a model known as credit distribution, which utilizes the various propagation channels to assess influence spread. Furthermore, they proposed an innovative technique that incorporates knowledge on new levels of influenceability and the spatial correlation of influence. The study by Teng et al. [601] examines the relationship between user interest intensity and dynamic influence to understand information dissemination strategies that best accomplish user goals. Some other works focused on finding influential individuals on social networks, which is a challenging task [586].

The social impact of influential customers over other customers has been found to be more complicated than expected. Hence, there are scenarios where customers are loyal to a particular brand due to different factors, e.g., trust. Moreover, the above-discussed research focuses on more of a positive impact, made by influential customers, while these social influencers might also make a negative impact.

As an example, there might be cases where customers decide to discontinue a well-known brand altogether and switch to an alternative brand since their socially connected people (e.g., friends) have recommended it. Hence, on a large scale, there might be situations where the sale is actually lowered due to negative feedback socially spread by customers who have posted critical comments on social networks. This explains the high dynamism of the information flow in social networks. Business owners consistently exploit such dynamics in social networks to make decisions, e.g., when selling a new product [586].

9.8 Situational Awareness: Discover Trending Topics

In recent times, social networks have become an important and primary source for finding trendy topics and factual evidence of recent events [63]. The process of obtaining such information can be viewed from positive or negative eyes. However, regardless of the particular judgment, this can create a substantial impact on the lives of the individuals (at a *micro* scale) and the societies (at a *macro* scale). Example consequences of such impact can be the generation of *Situational Awareness*. The vast quantity of data accessible from such networks, coupled with a broad user base can intensify this. Such an impact can be further monitored and summarized to identify trending topics [241, 243]. While a big part of the effect comes from social networks, the mainstream media can still create a similar impact.

Situational awareness refers to all existing evidence that may be incorporated into a cohesive picture to evaluate and deal with a circumstance. Ensuring the highest level of accurate and up-to-date information is a top consideration in situational awareness. Natural disasters, as examples of crisis, are typically temporary situations while still creating tremendous economic, ecological, and social costs over a long period. Situational awareness and the various processes are critical for confronting a natural disaster. People have an instinct to go online in the wake of a natural disaster to seek or exchange intelligence to keep themselves and others safe. Real-time big data used to generate high levels of situational awareness assist disaster risk management [325]. A holistic situational awareness to assist emergency response in natural disasters is difficult due to factors such as the unpredictability of catastrophic events. In the time of a natural catastrophe or after that, media activists tend to obtain public opinions, e.g., based on traditional opinion polls as a classical technique. However, this can be a costly and complicated process with potential limitations. Social media allows researchers to obtain alternate data on such issues. Social media members can hence be enabled to openly express their thoughts on what is an ongoing and relevant issue, hence transparently shaping the general public opinion [325].

Many prior studies have investigated such impacts by conducting extensive online analyses on social media networks and performing offline simulations. Kelly et al. [333] designed a scheme for factual retrieval of knowledge using text and image material in tweets. The framework has been applied in a particular application domain, i.e., to support emergency response to extract spatial-temporal data streams through social media posts for a geographical location of floods disasters [333]. In this particular application of situation awareness, the focus is on crisis management, e.g., in difficult situations such as the disaster or search and rescue conditions, and the goal is to enable the decision-makers to make better decisions in such situations [665].

To continuously extract helpful information from Internet sources, data should be monitored in real-time. A topic-level, sentient representation of the social linked list can be constructed by identifying subjects addressed by the crowd. Topic object recognition has been accomplished in the previous for fixed record corpora. However, social media contexts are dynamic, fragmented, and noisy, making topic extraction challenging [24]. Combining a message's time information with its geographic location is used to locate discussions on floods on Twitter in Ireland. It helps emergency responders stay up to date with ongoing incidents [333]. Feature-pivot approaches are connected to topic models in natural language processing for mathematical analyses such as topic models. Trial pipelines were previously evaluated on Twitter for topic recognition (for example, Twitter Topic Detection). However, it includes key criteria and URLs, as well as geographical terms, to enhance the discovered topics [24].

While methodologies and variables for such data acquisition and processing may widely vary, the overall quality of outcomes of such opinion mining depends on many factors [24]. For instance, the type and quality of the data describing the media user and media content plays an important role. Prior studies have proposed efficient and consistent analytical methods beneficial in this regard. They have further shown the outcome of the analysis of the data coming from geographical and time-related profiles of social media users. Textual and image content of the communications has been also studied as popular forms of media content. Devising representative modeling approaches to profile users and media content can improve situational awareness based on social media networks. Further summarizing and visualizations can also be beneficial [333].

9.9 Social Media Information Discovery: From Topic Trends to Sentiment Ratio

Many modern social media applications have been developed over the past few years, ranging from video sharing platforms (e.g., Youtube) to online broadcasting mediums (e.g., Twitter). These platforms offer many different functionalities that enable their users to upload, share, videos, or even stream their media content in different formats. The shared content can be accessed through different devices on the user side, ranging from tiny mobile phones and large TV screens.

Despite the diversity of social applications and the differences among users, growing demand can be observed for approaches and tools to analyze the massive amount of data obtained from users interacting with these applications with different devices. Such analytics will empower business owners or decision-makers to carefully observe the online activities of their customers to obtain insights into their thoughts and feelings.

The idea is to build up unified predictive models that can be applied for a range of potential tasks. Examples of such tasks include topic trend identification and sentiment analysis. Such tasks are typically conducted with a focus on a specific social media platform. Among the popular platforms, conducting analytical experiments on Twitter has been observed to be of high interest to big business players. Many research works have published many reports on experiments, with different approaches, e.g., popularity analysis of the trendy tweets, and the analysis of the sentiment in tweets [27]. In the former case, the tweets are analyzed, through tracking models, to understand which popular products received the largest number of *mentions* or *hashtags*. It allows business owners to constantly monitor social media and alert them when online users include the brand within the tweets. In the latter case, the predictive models are applied to estimate the sentiment scores computed for the content of the tweets.

Such analyses are performed to understand the market reaction to certain online marketing strategies. The primary goal is to make machines able to locate information rapidly, such as what the news-press or Websites are stating about the business or a product. An example of analysis has been reported by Nguyen et al. [457] which employed a popular predictive model, i.e., *Support Vector Machine (SVM)*, capable of handling social data with its high-dimensionality for the task of sentiment analysis. A technique based on combined sentiment or topic analysis is referred to as a topic or aspect method. The prominent role of social media is to facilitate the posting of comments on financial topics such as earnings and dividends. Objective measurements of "interestingness" might be used to anticipate future rates of interest terms frequency. There is a major concern to understand social media's hottest subjects before they gain momentum inside the mainstream media [251]. It is worth noting that, due to the massive volume and velocity of the generated content within this platform and the extremely costly and repetitive process of analysis, either of the cases cannot be done manually by human resources and instead are performed through a fully automated process [251]. The automated service navigates through millions of social media pages and carefully checks to find the desired matches of the input keywords (e.g., the brand of a company) [27].

While a large body of prior research focused on the above-discussed tasks, however, the analytics of social media can go beyond them and include other tasks of interest, e.g., the estimation of the stock market through analysis of the attitudes predicted for the social media users [457], or election monitoring with applications in the e-governance [27].

9.10 Linking Social Media Performance to Business and Revenue Growth

Social media platforms have gone beyond the content sharing applications and have been popularly employed by their users for various social tasks, e.g., group formation, social advisory, community building, and collaboration. Many firms and companies have well studied these characteristics in searching for new advantages, such as utilizing these platforms for novel business opportunities. Despite that goal, the concrete link between such characteristics of social platforms and the success factors of activities performed by firms and companies need a more comprehensive investigation.

While businesses can benefit from the new social media opportunities for social marketing, enhanced sales, economics advisory, and client services, there might be challenges for businesses. For example, there has been a revolution in the methods employed for online marketing, and traditional methods may no longer be effective. The fast pace and high dynamics of social environments require brand-new strategies for marketing and enhancing sales. Such particularities within social platforms are important factors that need to be studied as they play a pivotal role in improving the potential capacities of the businesses in these platforms.

In addition to the above-described potentials, social media platforms can support the firms and companies to better understand the needs and constraints of their customers through customer data analysis. This can enable them to design more effective strategies utilizing personal data from customers and develop a targeted method for marketing, e.g., sending personal messages, employing social influencers, or adopting approaches based on behavioral contagion [258]. Advanced techniques for analyzing customer data can be exploited. The outcomes can be adapted to provide personalized services and products that match customers' needs, contributing to sales growth.

Social media networks can potentially impact business performance in various ways, e.g., through financial resources, disclosed values, and social marketing. Each of these may utilize several social media assets and link them into the performance measures of a business [475]. Companies may get important information about brands and prominent individuals and topics by tracking conversations that pertain to their brands that are occurring on social networks. Companies identify influential individuals and utilize the information to increase the company's reach [358].

In addition to marketing, tools enhances income by improving the customers' prominence. However, the new marketing techniques do not provide an obvious Return On Investment (ROI) compared to classic source node advertising. For instance, television commercials that run during the Super Bowl have an immediate and measurable influence on the company [475]. Companies should identify shared interests and behaviors in the applicants based on these shared characteristics. Gathering personal profiles provide businesses with the required materials to find and encourage all influential peers to discuss goods or services. Previously, social media platforms have shown three key aspects of engagement: (i) spread of message (the number of times a text is posted, with or without alteration, by those who will be receiving);(ii) influence (the amount of times receivers post the text to their buddies); and (iii) social impact (the degree to which the message reaches a significant audience of people, and if the message has any tangible social impact) [358].

A complete understanding of social media's effects on business performance is available in the disclosed preferences channel. The value of the company of traded businesses is one of the most fundamental and objective measures of financial success. However, the majority of organizations are still figuring out their approach to social media accounts and their ability to measure social influence and customers' influence with metrics such as Hokey Pokey's customer. The increased effectiveness of social media campaigns necessitated determining the economic importance of each customer's influence in a system. Consequently, it is required to measure the importance of customers' impact in a network for Hokey Pokey marketers to maximize the effectiveness of their online marketing strategy. Kumar et al. [358] measured Hokey Pokey's revenue (based on ice-cream sales) produced via Facebook and Twitter in comparison to the revenue increase, ROI, number of positive and negative dialogues, and amount of multiple trips from the three prior years. They report 49% in brand recognition, 83% in ROI, and 40% pace of rising in sales revenue [358].

9.11 Performance Analysis of the Industry

Digital Marketing based on social media has become one of the popular multidisciplinary fields, involving researchers from Data Science, business, and economics. Experts in digital marketing heavily utilize modern social media platforms in building up effective engagement techniques when interacting with consumers [309]. Such techniques are applied to uncover opportunities in a variety of ways, including broadening the network of potential consumers or even suppliers. Furthermore, they analyze the outcome of these techniques and provide fruitful insights from the market performance to the managers and ultimately support them when making decisions [644].

Various factors obtained from different forms of analysis can be indicative of the market performance. The history of the stock market behavior is generally known to be a good factor when measuring market performance. Stock market behavior, in turn, can also be impacted by many different sources, including social media. Prior studies have reported a significant impact on stock market performance caused by social media. As an example, it has been reported that the larger the number of posts about a brand published on social the greater influence is made on the stock of that brand. Such impact may not necessarily be positive and may include undesired impacts such as price volatility, or poor investment. Furthermore, the reaction of the audience to such social posts and their sentiment can either mitigate or reinforce such impact. Such factors can be well utilized to build a form of prediction mechanisms for an estimate of the future and interpretability of certain stocks [309]. Hence they can be seen as influential impacts concerning the market performance.

There might be notable examples of such influential impacts. It is commonly believed that the stocks of the green industry (and consequently the sales) can decrease during catastrophic situations, perhaps due to the drops in housing values or homeownership. They may indeed be caused by the lowered demand for decorative crops, yard and garden goods, as well as support services. This itself can create further negative impacts such as a recession. As a response, marketing further types of analysis have been conducted in this business sector, e.g., the research on user acceptance and social marketing.

Checking the literature, surprisingly, many prior researches tend to undermine the immense impact of the crises on social media, and consequently, how it can influence the markets (e.g., stock market). A crisis might impact social media participation; when there is a crisis, people may be interested in the hot issues that participants are closely watching. A significant societal effect can occur in a very short period after a catastrophe, resulting in a flood of new knowledge. A good illustration of this would be that starting in 2008, the Great Recession and the resulting debt crisis drove the American banking system into failure. The impact of this issue was quite widespread, affecting many stock and forum-related online sites in the banking industry. During a crisis, people first notice macroeconomic factors and stock market activity [309]. Social media financial capabilities and benefit chain store retailers per the resource-based approach and social media marketing strategy. Service quality is favorably influenced by implementing a social media campaign, organizational culture, management planning, organizational learning, social network, and performance outcomes. The findings show that a resource-based variable is found to affect the success of the organization in a straightforward additive manner [644].

It is worth noting that, the field of assessing the performance of the market (e.g., stock market) is a highly complex and multi-stakeholder discipline of research [644]. Hence, it might be beneficial to consider the roles of different stakeholders when conducting studies in this discipline. Notable stakeholders can be consumers, employees, investors, and policymakers. Each of these stakeholders may potentially have certain degrees of influence on the stock performance, with or without a necessary connection to social media. However, further investigation of such a role can be an interesting research topic for future works [309].

Finally, the evaluation of the marketing strategies applied in social media, and their impact on the market performance can be conducted in various forms, and while offering different benefits, each of them may hold certain limitations. Hence, it is important to take into account that none of the evaluation metrics alone may provide a full and comprehensive viewpoint related to any performance analysis [661].

9.12 Concluding Remarks and Discussion

Understanding and identifying novel applications of social data analytics is essential as the world, and the businesses that run it, are becoming increasingly social. Over the last few years, governments started to extract knowledge and derive insights from vastly growing social data to personalize the advertisements in elections, improve government services, predict intelligence activities, unravel human trafficking activities, understand the impact of news on stock markets, analysis of financial risks; accelerate scientific discovery, as well as to improve national security and public health. Novel applications focus on a combination of data, social, and cognitive analytics to understand, analyze, measure, and interpret topics and ideas posted on online social media and the relationships among social users on such networks.

Social data is useless unless processed in analytical tasks from which humans or downstream applications can derive insights. This chapter focused on various aspects of social data by discussing topics such as trust, sentiment analysis, and bias within the social data. In addition to that, a wide range of potential applications for social data is provided, namely, personalization and information discovery with social data, opportunities of using social data for business growth by increasing sales, and enhancing marketing. Such discussions with all the provided details can be a valuable resource for academic researchers and industry practitioners within the relevant research fields.

References

[1] Adam: A method for stochastic optimization. *arXiv preprint arXiv:1412.6980*, 2014.

[2] Asad Abdi, Siti Mariyam Shamsuddin and Ramiz M. Aliguliyev. Qmos: Query-based multi-documents opinion-oriented summarization. *Information Processing & Management*, 54(2): 318–338, 2018.

[3] Himan Abdollahpouri, Gediminas Adomavicius, Robin Burke, Ido Guy, Dietmar Jannach, Toshihiro Kamishima, Jan Krasnodebski and Luiz Pizzato. Multistakeholder recommendation: Survey and research directions. *User Modeling and User-Adapted Interaction*, 30(1): 127–158, 2020.

[4] Himan Abdollahpouri, Robin Burke and Bamshad Mobasher. Controlling popularity bias in learning-to-rank recommendation. In *Proceedings of the Eleventh ACM Conference on Recommender Systems*, RecSys'17, pp. 42–46, 2017.

[5] Himan Abdollahpouri, Robin Burke and Bamshad Mobasher. Managing popularity bias in recommender systems with personalized re-ranking. In *Proceedings of the Thirty-Second International Florida Artificial Intelligence Research Society Conference (FLAIRS'19)*, pp. 413–418, 2019.

[6] Albaraa Abuobieda, Naomie Salim, Ameer Tawfik Albaham, Ahmed Hamza Osman and Yogan Jaya Kumar. Text summarization features selection method using pseudo genetic-based model. In *2012 International Conference on Information Retrieval & Knowledge Management*, pp. 193–197. IEEE, 2012.

[7] Gediminas Adomavicius, Jesse C. Bockstedt, Shawn P. Curley and Jingjing Zhang. Reducing recommender system biases: An investigation of rating display designs. *MIS Quarterly*, 43(5): 1321–1341, 2019.

[8] Gediminas Adomavicius, Bamshad Mobasher, Francesco Ricci and Alexander Tuzhilin. Context-aware recommender systems. *AI Magazine*, 32: 67–80, 2011.

[9] Gediminas Adomavicius and Alexander Tuzhilin. Toward the next generation of recommender systems: A survey of the state-of-the-art and possible extensions. *Knowledge and Data Engineering, IEEE Transactions on*, 17(6): 734–749, June 2005.

[10] Gediminas Adomavicius and Alexander Tuzhilin. Toward the next generation of recommender systems: A survey of the state-of-the-art and possible extensions. *IEEE Transactions on Knowledge and Data Engineering*, 17(6): 734–749, 2005.

[11] Gediminas Adomavicius and Alexander Tuzhilin. Context-aware recommender systems. In *Recommender Systems Handbook*, pp. 217–253. Springer, 2011.

[12] Basant Agarwal, Namita Mittal, Pooja Bansal and Sonal Garg. Sentiment analysis using common-sense and context information. *Computational Intelligence and Neuroscience*, 2015, 2015.

[13] Deepak Agarwal and Bee-Chung Chen. Regression-based latent factor models. In *Proceedings of the 15th ACM SIGKDD International Conference on Knowledge Discovery and Data Mining*, KDD'09, pp. 19–28, New York, NY, USA, 2009. ACM, ACM.

[14] Charu C. Aggarwal and Haixun Wang. *Managing and Mining Graph Data*. Springer Publishing Company, Incorporated, 2010.

[15] Charu C. Aggarwal. An introduction to social network data analytics. In *Social Network Data Analytics*, pp. 1–15, 2011.

[16] Charu C. Aggarwal. An introduction to recommender systems. In *Recommender Systems*, pp. 1–28. Springer, 2016.

[17] Charu C. Aggarwal. *Recommender Systems*. Springer International Publishing, 2016.

[18] Charu C. Aggarwal and Nan Li. On node classification in dynamic content-based networks. In *Proceedings of the 2011 SIAM International Conference on Data Mining*, pp. 355–366. SIAM, 2011.

[19] Charu C. Aggarwal and Haixun Wang. Text mining in social networks. In *Social Network Data Analytics*, pp. 353–378. Springer, 2011.

[20] Eugene Agichtein, Carlos Castillo, Debora Donato, Aristides Gionis and Gilad Mishne. Finding high-quality content in social media. In *Proceedings*

of the 2008 International Conference on Web Search and Data Mining, pp. 183–194, 2008.

[21] Camila Z. Aguiar, Davidson Cury and Amal Zouaq. Automatic construction of concept maps from texts. In *Conference on Concept Mapping-CMC. Tallinn. Retrieved from http://cmc. ihmc. us/cmc2016papers/cmc2016-p90. pdf.[GS SEARCH]*, 2016.

[22] Amr Ahmed and Qirong Ho. Unified analysis of streaming news. In *WWW*, pp. 267–276, 2011.

[23] Jae-wook Ahn, Peter Brusilovsky, Jonathan Grady, Daqing He and Sue Yeon Syn. Open user profiles for adaptive news systems: Help or harm? In *Proceedings of the 16th International Conference on World Wide Web*, pp. 11–20. ACM, 2007.

[24] Luca Maria Aiello, Georgios Petkos, Carlos Martin, David Corney, Symeon Papadopoulos, Ryan Skraba, Ayse Göker, Ioannis Kompatsiaris and Alejandro Jaimes. Sensing trending topics in twitter. *IEEE Transactions on Multimedia*, 15(6): 1268–1282, 2013.

[25] Akiko Aizawa. An information-theoretic perspective of tf–idf measures. *Information Processing & Management*, 39(1): 45–65, 2003.

[26] Cuneyt Gurcan Akcora, Murat Ali Bayir, Murat Demirbas and Hakan Ferhatosmanoglu. Identifying breakpoints in public opinion. In *Proceedings of the First Workshop on Social Media Analytics*, pp. 62–66, 2010.

[27] Ali Al-Laith and Muhammad Shahbaz. Tracking sentiment towards news entities from arabic news on social media. *Future Generation Computer Systems*, 118: 467–484, 2021.

[28] Kamal Al-Sabahi, Zhang Zuping and Mohammed Nadher. A hierarchical structured self-attentive model for extractive document summarization (hssas). *IEEE Access*, 6: 24205–24212, 2018.

[29] Nabil Alami, Mohammed Meknassi and Noureddine En-nahnahi. Enhancing unsupervised neural networks based text summarization with word embedding and ensemble learning. *Expert Systems with Applications*, 123: 195–211, 2019.

[30] Mohammed F. Alhamid, Majdi Rawashdeh, Hussein Al Osman, M. Shamim Hossain and Abdulmotaleb El Saddik. Towards context-

sensitive collaborative media recommender system. *Multimedia Tools and Applications*, 74(24): 11399–11428, 2015.

[31] Alaa Ali and Magdy A. Bayoumi. Towards real-time dpm object detector for driver assistance. In *2016 IEEE International Conference on Image Processing (ICIP)*, pp. 3842–3846. IEEE, 2016.

[32] Mehdi Allahyari, Seyedamin Pouriyeh, Mehdi Assefi, Saeid Safaei, Elizabeth D. Trippe, Juan B. Gutierrez and Krys Kochut. Text summarization techniques: A brief survey. *arXiv preprint arXiv:1707.02268*, 2017.

[33] Mehdi Allahyari, Seyedamin Pouriyeh, Mehdi Assefi, Saied Safaei, Elizabeth D. Trippe, Juan B. Gutierrez and Krys Kochut. A brief survey of text mining: Classification, clustering and extraction techniques. *arXiv preprint arXiv:1707.02919*, 2017.

[34] Sattam Almatarneh and Pablo Gamallo. Comparing supervised machine learning strategies and linguistic features to search for very negative opinions. *Information*, 10(1): 16, 2019.

[35] G. Alonso, F. Casati, H.A. Kuno and V. Machiraju. *Web Services-Concepts, Architectures and Applications*. Data-Centric Systems and Applications. Springer, 2004.

[36] Chris Anderson. *The Long Tail*. Random House Business, 2006.

[37] Michael R. Anderson, Dolan Antenucci, Victor Bittorf, Matthew Burgess, Michael J. Cafarella, Arun Kumar, Feng Niu et al. Brainwash: A data system for feature engineering. In *CIDR*, 2013.

[38] Ralitsa Angelova and Gerhard Weikum. Graph-based text classification: Learn from your neighbors. In *Proceedings of the 29th Annual International ACM SIGIR Conference on Research and Development in Information Retrieval*, pp. 485–492, 2006.

[39] Peter G. Anick and Shivakumar Vaithyanathan. Exploiting clustering and phrases for context-based information retrieval. In *Proceedings of the 20th Annual International ACM SIGIR Conference on Research and Development in Information Retrieval*, pp. 314–323, 1997.

[40] Liliana Ardissono, Anna Goy, Giovanna Petrone, Marino Segnan and Pietro Torasso. Tailoring the recommendation of tourist information to heterogeneous user groups. In *Workshop on Adaptive Hypermedia*, pp. 280–295. Springer, 2001.

[41] Abdelkrime Aries, Walid Khaled Hidouci et al. Automatic text summarization: What has been done and what has to be done. *arXiv preprint arXiv:1904.00688*, 2019.

[42] Jari Arkko and Pekka Nikander. Weak authentication: How to authenticate unknown principals without trusted parties. In *International Workshop on Security Protocols*, pp. 5–19. Springer, 2002.

[43] Patricia C. Arocena, Boris Glavic, Giansalvatore Mecca, Renée J. Miller, Paolo Papotti and Donatello Santoro. Benchmarking data curation systems. *IEEE Data Eng. Bull.*, 39(2): 47–62, 2016.

[44] Malcolm P. Atkinson, Peter J. Bailey, Ken J. Chisholm, W. Paul Cockshott and Ron Morrison. Ps-algol: A language for persistent programming. In *Proc. 10th Australian National Computer Conference, Melbourne, Australia*, pp. 70–79, 1983.

[45] P.V.S. Avinesh and Christian M. Meyer. Joint optimization of user-desired content in multi-document summaries by learning from user feedback. In *Proceedings of the 55th Annual Meeting of the Association for Computational Linguistics (Volume 1: Long Papers)*, pp. 1353–1363, 2017.

[46] Benjamin Bach, Moritz Stefaner, Jeremy Boy et al. Narrative design patterns for data-driven storytelling. In *Data-Driven Storytelling*, pp. 125–152. AK Peters/CRC Press, 2018.

[47] Mitja D. Back, Juliane M. Stopfer, Simine Vazire, Sam Gaddis, Stefan C. Schmukle, Boris Egloff and Samuel D. Gosling. Facebook profiles reflect actual personality, not self-idealization. *Psychological Science*, 21(3): 372–374, 2010.

[48] Ricardo Baeza-Yates. Bias on the web. *Communications of the ACM*, 61(6): 54–61, 2018.

[49] Ricardo Baeza-Yates, Carlos Castillo Ocaranza and Vicente López Martínez. Characteristics of the web of spain. 2005.

[50] Ricardo Baeza-Yates and Diego Saez-Trumper. Wisdom of the crowd or wisdom of a few? *Proceedings of the 26th ACM Conference on Hypertext & Social Media - HT'15*, 2015.

[51] Marko Balabanović and Yoav Shoham. Fab: Content-based, collaborative recommendation. *Commun. ACM*, 40(3): 66–72, March 1997.

[52] Alexandra Balahur. Sentiment analysis in social media texts. In *Proceedings of the 4th Workshop on Computational Approaches to Subjectivity, Sentiment and Social Media Analysis*, pp. 120–128, 2013.

[53] Linas Baltrunas, Bernd Ludwig, Stefan Peer and Francesco Ricci. Context relevance assessment and exploitation in mobile recommender systems. *Personal Ubiquitous Comput.*, 16(5): 507–526, June 2012.

[54] Jie Bao, Yu Zheng, David Wilkie and Mohamed Mokbel. Recommendations in location-based social networks: A survey. *GeoInformatica*, 19(3): 525–565, 2015.

[55] Geoffrey Barbier and Huan Liu. Information provenance in social media. In *International Conference on Social Computing, Behavioral-Cultural Modeling, and Prediction*, pp. 276–283. Springer, 2011.

[56] John A. Bargh and Katelyn Y.A. McKenna. The internet and social life. Annu. Rev. Psychol., 55: 573–590, 2004.

[57] Cristina Barros, Elena Lloret, Estela Saquete and Borja Navarro-Colorado. Natsum: Narrative abstractive summarization through cross-document timeline generation. *Information Processing & Management*, 56(5): 1775–1793, 2019.

[58] Moshe Chai Barukh, Shayan Zamanirad, Marcos Báez, Amin Beheshti, Boualem Benatallah, Fabio Casati, Lina Yao, Quan Z. Sheng and Francesco Schiliro. Cognitive augmentation in processes. In *Next-Gen Digital Services. A Retrospective and Roadmap for Service Computing of the Future—Essays Dedicated to Michael Papazoglou on the Occasion of His 65th Birthday and His Retirement*, volume 12521 of *Lecture Notes in Computer Science*, pp. 123–137. Springer, 2021.

[59] Phyllis B. Baxendale. Machine-made index for technical literature—an experiment. *IBM Journal of Research and Development*, 2(4): 354–361, 1958.

[60] Amin Beheshti, Boualem Benatallah, Hamid Reza Motahari-Nezhad, Samira Ghodratnama and Farhad Amouzgar. A query language for summarizing and analyzing business process data. *arXiv preprint arXiv:2105.10911*, 2021.

[61] Amin Beheshti, Boualem Benatallah, Reza Nouri, Van Munin Chhieng, Huang Tao Xiong and Xu Zhao. Coredb: A data lake service. In *Proceedings of the 2017 ACM on Conference on Information and*

Knowledge Management, CIKM 2017, Singapore, November 06–10, 2017, pp. 2451–2454. ACM, 2017.

[62] Amin Beheshti, Boualem Benatallah, Reza Nouri and Alireza Tabebordbar. Corekg: A knowledge lake service. *Proc. VLDB Endow.*, 11(12): 1942–1945, 2018.

[63] Amin Beheshti, Boualem Benatallah, Quan Z. Sheng and Francesco Schiliro. Intelligent knowledge lakes: The age of artificial intelligence and big data. In Leong Hou U., Jian Yang, Yi Cai, Kamalakar Karlapalem, An Liu and Xin Huang (eds.). *Web Information Systems Engineering— WISE 2019 Workshop, Demo, and Tutorial, Hong Kong and Macau, China, January 19–22, 2020, Revised Selected Papers*, volume 1155 of *Communications in Computer and Information Science*, pp. 24–34. Springer, 2019.

[64] Amin Beheshti, Boualem Benatallah, Quan Z. Sheng and Francesco Schiliro. Intelligent knowledge lakes: The age of artificial intelligence and big data. In *International Conference on Web Information Systems Engineering*, pp. 24–34. Springer, 2020.

[65] Amin Beheshti, Boualem Benatallah, Alireza Tabebordbar, Hamid Reza Motahari-Nezhad, Moshe Chai Barukh and Reza Nouri. Datasynapse: A social data curation foundry. *Distributed Parallel Databases*, 37(3): 351–384, 2019.

[66] Amin Beheshti, Vahid Moraveji Hashemi, Shahpar Yakhchi, Hamid Reza Motahari-Nezhad, Seyed Mohssen Ghafari and Jian Yang. personality2vec: Enabling the analysis of behavioral disorders in social networks. In James Caverlee, Xia (Ben) Hu, Mounia Lalmas, and Wei Wang (eds.). *WSDM'20: The Thirteenth ACM International Conference on Web Search and Data Mining, Houston, TX, USA, February 3–7, 2020*, pp. 825–828. ACM, 2020.

[67] Amin Beheshti, Alireza Tabebordbar and Boualem Benatallah. istory: Intelligent storytelling with social data. In *Companion of the 2020 Web Conference 2020, Taipei, Taiwan, April 20–24, 2020*, pp. 253–256. ACM/IW3C2, 2020.

[68] Amin Beheshti, Kushal Vaghani, Boualem Benatallah and Alireza Tabebordbar. Crowdcorrect: A curation pipeline for social data cleansing and curation. In *International Conference on Advanced Information Systems Engineering*, pp. 24–38. Springer, 2018.

[69] Amin Beheshti, Shahpar Yakhchi, Salman Mousaeirad, Seyed Mohssen Ghafari, Srinivasa Reddy Goluguri and Mohammad Amin Edrisi. Towards cognitive recommender systems. *Algorithms*, 13(8): 176, 2020.

[70] Seyed-Mehdi-Reza Beheshti, Boualem Benatallah and Hamid Reza Motahari-Nezhad. Scalable graph-based OLAP analytics over process execution data. *Distributed Parallel Databases*, 34(3): 379–423, 2016.

[71] Seyed-Mehdi-Reza Beheshti, Boualem Benatallah and Hamid Reza Motahari-Nezhad. Scalable graph-based OLAP analytics over process execution data. *Distributed Parallel Databases*, 34(3): 379–423, 2016.

[72] Seyed-Mehdi-Reza Beheshti, Boualem Benatallah and Hamid R. Motahari Nezhad. Enabling the analysis of cross-cutting aspects in ad-hoc processes. In Camille Salinesi, Moira C. Norrie and Oscar Pastor (eds.). *Advanced Information Systems Engineering—25th International Conference, CAiSE 2013, Valencia, Spain, June 17–21, 2013. Proceedings*, volume 7908 of *Lecture Notes in Computer Science*, pp. 51–67. Springer, 2013.

[73] Seyed-Mehdi-Reza Beheshti, Boualem Benatallah, Hamid R. Motahari Nezhad and Mohammad Allahbakhsh. A framework and a language for on-line analytical processing on graphs. In Xiaoyang Sean Wang, Isabel F. Cruz, Alex Delis and Guangyan Huang (eds.). *Web Information Systems Engineering—WISE 2012—13th International Conference, Paphos, Cyprus, November 28–30, 2012. Proceedings*, volume 7651 of *Lecture Notes in Computer Science*, pp. 213–227. Springer, 2012.

[74] Seyed-Mehdi-Reza Beheshti, Boualem Benatallah, Sherif Sakr, Daniela Grigori, Hamid Reza Motahari-Nezhad, Moshe Chai Barukh, Ahmed Gater and Seung Hwan Ryu. *Process Analytics—Concepts and Techniques for Querying and Analyzing Process Data*. Springer, 2016.

[75] Seyed-Mehdi-Reza Beheshti, Boualem Benatallah, Sherif Sakr, Daniela Grigori, Hamid Reza Motahari-Nezhad, Moshe Chai Barukh, Ahmed Gater and Seung Hwan Ryu. *Process Analytics—Concepts and Techniques for Querying and Analyzing Process Data*. Springer, 2016.

[76] Seyed-Mehdi-Reza Beheshti, Boualem Benatallah, Srikumar Venugopal, Seung Hwan Ryu, Hamid Reza Motahari-Nezhad and Wei Wang. A systematic review and comparative analysis of cross-document coreference resolution methods and tools. *Computing*, 99(4): 313–349, 2017.

[77] Seyed-Mehdi-Reza Beheshti, Hamid Reza Motahari-Nezhad and Boualem Benatallah. Temporal provenance model (TPM): Model and query language. *arXiv preprint arXiv:1211.5009*, 2012.

[78] Seyed-Mehdi-Reza Beheshti, Hamid R. Motahari Nezhad and Boualem Benatallah. Temporal provenance model (TPM): Model and query language. *CoRR*, abs/1211.5009, 2012.

[79] Seyed-Mehdi-Reza Beheshti, Hamid R. Motahari Nezhad and Boualem Benatallah. Temporal provenance model (TPM): Model and query language. *CoRR*, abs/1211.5009, 2012.

[80] Seyed-Mehdi-Reza Beheshti, Sherif Sakr, Boualem Benatallah and Hamid R. Motahari Nezhad. Extending SPARQL to support entity grouping and path queries. *CoRR*, abs/1211.5817, 2012.

[81] Nargiza Bekmamedova and Graeme Shanks. Social media analytics and business value: A theoretical framework and case study. In *2014 47th Hawaii International Conference on System Sciences*, pp. 3728–3737. IEEE, 2014.

[82] J. Ben Schafer, J.A. Konstan and J. Ried. E-commerce recommendation applications. *Data Mining and Knowledge Discovery*, pp. 115–153, 2001.

[83] Yoshua Bengio, Réjean Ducharme, Pascal Vincent and Christian Janvin. A neural probabilistic language model. *The Journal of Machine Learning Research*, 3: 1137–1155, 2003.

[84] Shlomo Berkovsky and Jill Freyne. Group-based recipe recommendations: Analysis of data aggregation strategies. In *Proceedings of the Fourth ACM Conference on Recommender Systems*, pp. 111–118, 2010.

[85] Shlomo Berkovsky, Tsvi Kuflik and Francesco Ricci. Distributed collaborative filtering with domain specialization. In *Proceedings of the 2007 ACM Conference on Recommender Systems*, pp. 33–40. ACM, 2007.

[86] Dmitriy Bespalov, Bing Bai, Yanjun Qi and Ali Shokoufandeh. Sentiment classification based on supervised latent n-gram analysis. In *Proceedings of the 20th ACM International Conference on Information and Knowledge Management*, pp. 375–382, 2011.

[87] Iram Khurshid Bhat, Mudasir Mohd and Rana Hashmy. Sumitup: A hybrid single-document text summarizer. In *Soft Computing: Theories and Applications*, pp. 619–634. Springer, 2018.

[88] B.K. Bhavitha, Anisha P. Rodrigues and Niranjan N. Chiplunkar. Comparative study of machine learning techniques in sentimental analysis. In *International Conference on Inventive Communication and Computational Technologies*, pp. 216–221, 2017.

[89] Daniel Billsus and Michael J. Pazzani. *A Hybrid User Model for News Story Classification*. Springer, 1999.

[90] Daniel Billsus and Michael J. Pazzani. User modeling for adaptive news access. *User Modeling and User-Adapted Interaction*, 10(2-3): 147–180, 2000.

[91] Christian Bizer, Tom Heath and Tim Berners-Lee. Linked data: The story so far. In *Semantic Services, Interoperability and Web Applications: Emerging Concepts*, pp. 205–227. IGI Global, 2011.

[92] Laura Blédaité and Francesco Ricci. Pairwise preferences elicitation and exploitation for conversational collaborative filtering. In *Proceedings of the 26th ACM Conference on Hypertext & Social Media*, HT'15, pp. 231–236, New York, NY, USA, 2015. ACM.

[93] David M. Blei and John D. Lafferty. Dynamic topic models. In *Proceedings of the 23rd International Conference on Machine Learning*, pp. 113–120, 2006.

[94] David M. Blei, Andrew Y. Ng and Michael I. Jordan. Latent dirichlet allocation. *The Journal of Machine Learning Research*, 3: 993–1022, 2003.

[95] Dirk Bollen, Bart P. Knijnenburg, Martijn C. Willemsen and Mark Graus. Understanding choice overload in recommender systems. In *Proceedings of the Fourth ACM Conference on Recommender Systems*, pp. 63–70. ACM, 2010.

[96] Kalina Bontcheva. Generating tailored textual summaries from ontologies. In *European Semantic Web Conference*, pp. 531–545. Springer, 2005.

[97] Ludovico Boratto, Gianni Fenu and Mirko Marras. Connecting user and item perspectives in popularity debiasing for collaborative recommendation. *Information Processing & Management*, 58(1): 102387, 2021.

[98] Alexey Borisov, Martijn Wardenaar, Ilya Markov and Maarten de Rijke. A click sequence model for web search. In *The 41st International ACM SIGIR Conference on Research & Development in Information Retrieval*, pp. 45–54, 2018.

[99] Harold Borko and Charles L. Bernier. Abstracting concepts and methods. 1975.

[100] Michael Franklin Bosu and Stephen G. MacDonell. A taxonomy of data quality challenges in empirical software engineering. In *2013 22nd Australian Software Engineering Conference*, pp. 97–106. IEEE, 2013.

[101] Paul S. Bradley and Usama M. Fayyad. Refining initial points for k-means clustering. In *ICML*, 98: 91–99. Citeseer, 1998.

[102] Matthias Braunhofer, Mehdi Elahi and Francesco Ricci. Techniques for cold-starting context-aware mobile recommender systems for tourism. *Intelligenza Artificiale*, 8(2): 129–143, 2014.

[103] Abdullah Bulbul and Rozenn Dahyot. Social media based 3d visual popularity. *Computers & Graphics*, 63: 28–36, 2017.

[104] Jerry M. Burger. *Personality*. Wadsworth Publishing, Belmont, CA., USA, 2010.

[105] Robin Burke. Knowledge-based recommender systems, 2000.

[106] Robin Burke. Hybrid recommender systems: Survey and experiments. *User Modeling and User-Adapted Interaction*, 12(4): 331–370, 2002.

[107] Robin Burke. Hybrid recommender systems: Survey and experiments. *User Modeling and User-Adapted Interaction*, 12(4):331–370, 2002.

[108] Paul Suganthan G.C., Chong Sun, Krishna Gayatri K., Haojun Zhang, Frank Yang, Narasimhan Rampalli, Shishir Prasad, Esteban Arcaute, Ganesh Krishnan, Rohit Deep, Vijay Raghavendra and AnHai Doan. Why big data industrial systems need rules and what we can do about it. In *Proceedings of the 2015 ACM SIGMOD International Conference on Management of Data, Melbourne, Victoria, Australia, May 31–June 4, 2015*, pp. 265–276, 2015.

[109] Luca Canini, Sergio Benini and Riccardo Leonardi. Affective recommendation of movies based on selected connotative features. *Circuits and Systems for Video Technology, IEEE Transactions on*, 23(4): 636–647, 2013.

[110] Iván Cantador, Martin Szomszor, Harith Alani, Miriam Fernández and Pablo Castells. Enriching ontological user profiles with tagging history for multidomain recommendations. 2008.

[111] Ziqiang Cao, Furu Wei, Sujian Li, Wenjie Li, Ming Zhou and Wang Houfeng. Learning summary prior representation for extractive summarization. In *Proceedings of the 53rd Annual Meeting of the Association for Computational Linguistics*, 2: 829–833, 2015.

[112] Joan Capdevila, Marta Arias and Argimiro Arratia. Geosrs: A hybrid social recommender system for geolocated data. *Information Systems*, 57:111–128, 2016.

[113] Giuseppe Carenini, Cristina Conati, Enamul Hoque, Ben Steichen, Dereck Toker and James Enns. Highlighting interventions and user differences: Informing adaptive information visualization support. In *Proceedings of the SIGCHI Conference on Human Factors in Computing Systems*, pp. 1835–1844, 2014.

[114] Michael J. Carey, Nicola Onose and Michalis Petropoulos. Data services. *Commun. ACM*, 55(6): 86–97, 2012.

[115] Alberto Lumbreras Carrasco et al. *Towards Trust-aware Recommendations in Social Networks*. PhD thesis, Universitat Politècnica de Catalunya. Facultat d'Informàtica de Barcelona, 2012.

[116] Elise Rose Carrotte, Ivanka Prichard and Megan Su Cheng Lim. fitspiration on social media: A content analysis of gendered images. *Journal of Medical Internet Research*, 19(3): e95, 2017.

[117] Asli Celikyilmaz, Antoine Bosselut, Xiaodong He and Yejin Choi. Deep communicating agents for abstractive summarization. In *Proceedings of the 2018 Conference of the North American Chapter of the Association for Computational Linguistics: Human Language Technologies, Volume 1 (Long Papers)*, pp. 1662–1675, 2018.

[118] Asli Celikyilmaz and Dilek Hakkani-Tur. A hybrid hierarchical model for multi-document summarization. In *48th Annual Meeting of the Association for Computational Linguistics*, 2010.

[119] Xiaoyong Chai, Omkar Deshpande, Nikesh Garera, Abhishek Gattani, Wang Lam, Digvijay S. Lamba, Lu Liu, Mitul Tiwari, Michel Tourn, Zoheb Vacheri, STS Prasad, Sri Subramaniam, Venky Harinarayan, Anand Rajaraman, Adel Ardalan, Sanjib Das, Paul Suganthan G.C. and AnHai Doan. Social media analytics: The kosmix story. *IEEE Data Eng. Bull.*, 36(3): 4–12, 2013.

[120] Deepayan Chakrabarti and Kunal Punera. Event summarization using tweets. In *Proceedings of the International AAAI Conference on Web and Social Media*, volume 5, 2011.

[121] Yi Chang, Jiliang Tang, Dawei Yin, Makoto Yamada and Yan Liu. Timeline summarization from social media with life cycle models. In *IJCAI*, pp. 3698–3704, 2016.

[122] Yi Chang, Makoto Yamada, Antonio Ortega and Yan Liu. Ups and downs in buzzes: Life cycle modeling for temporal pattern discovery. In *2014 IEEE International Conference on Data Mining*, pp. 749–754. IEEE, 2014.

[123] Artem Chebotko, Shiyong Lu, Xubo Fei and Farshad Fotouhi. Rdfprov: A relational rdf store for querying and managing scientific workflow provenance. *Data Knowl. Eng.*, 69(8): 836–865, 2010.

[124] Guanliang Chen and Li Chen. Recommendation based on contextual opinions. In *User Modeling, Adaptation, and Personalization*, pp. 61–73. Springer, 2014.

[125] Jiawei Chen, Hande Dong, Xiang Wang, Fuli Feng, Meng Wang and Xiangnan He. Bias and debias in recommender system: A survey and future directions. *CoRR*, abs/2010.03240, 2020.

[126] Jiawei Chen, Yan Feng, Martin Ester, Sheng Zhou, Chun Chen and Can Wang. Modeling users' exposure with social knowledge influence and consumption influence for recommendation. In *Proceedings of the 27th ACM International Conference on Information and Knowledge Management (CIKM'18)*, pp. 953–962, 2018.

[127] Ling Chen and Abhishek Roy. Event detection from flickr data through wavelet-based spatial analysis. In *Proceedings of the 18th ACM Conference on Information and Knowledge Management*, pp. 523–532, 2009.

[128] Tao Chen and Mark Dredze. Vaccine images on twitter: Analysis of what images are shared. *Journal of Medical Internet Research*, 20(4): e130, 2018.

[129] James Cheney, Laura Chiticariu and Wang-Chiew Tan. Provenance in databases: Why, how, and where. *Found. Trends Databases*, 1: 379–474, April 2009.

[130] Jianpeng Cheng and Mirella Lapata. Neural summarization by extracting sentences and words. In *Proceedings of the 54th Annual Meeting of the*

Association for Computational Linguistics (Volume 1: Long Papers), pp. 484–494, 2016.

[131] Hai Leong Chieu and Yoong Keok Lee. Query based event extraction along a timeline. In *Proceedings of the 27th Annual International ACM SIGIR Conference on Research and Development in Information Retrieval*, pp. 425–432, 2004.

[132] Nivet Chirawichitchai, Parinya Sa-nguansat and Phayung Meesad. A comparative study on feature weight in thai document categorization framework. In *IICS*, pp. 257–266. Citeseer, 2010.

[133] Donghyeon Cho, Minhaeng Lee, Sunyeong Kim and Yu-Wing Tai. Modeling the calibration pipeline of the lytro camera for high quality light-field image reconstruction. In *Proceedings of the IEEE International Conference on Computer Vision*, pp. 3280–3287, 2013.

[134] Maria Chowdhury, Alex Thomo and Bill Wadge. Trust-based infinitesimals for enhanced collaborative filtering. In *15th International Conference on Management of Data*, Mysore, 2009.

[135] Nicholas A. Christakis and James H. Fowler. Social contagion theory: Examining dynamic social networks and human behavior. *Statistics in Medicine*, 32(4): 556–577, 2013.

[136] Janara Christensen, Stephen Soderland, Gagan Bansal et al. Hierarchical summarization: Scaling up multi-document summarization. In *Proceedings of the 52nd annual meeting of the association for computational linguistics (volume 1: Long papers)*, pp. 902–912, 2014.

[137] Freddy Chong Tat Chua and Sitaram Asur. Automatic summarization of events from social media. In *Seventh International AAAI Conference on Weblogs and Social Media*, 2013.

[138] Kenneth Church and William Gale. Inverse document frequency (idf): A measure of deviations from poisson. In *Natural Language Processing using very Large Corpora*, pp. 283–295. Springer, 1999.

[139] Charles L. Clarke, Nick Craswell and Ian Soboroff. Overview of the trec 2009 web track. Technical report, WATERLOO UNIV (ONTARIO), 2009.

[140] James Clarke and Mirella Lapata. Modelling compression with discourse constraints. In *Proceedings of the 2007 Joint Conference on Empirical Methods in Natural Language Processing and Computational Natural Language Learning (EMNLP-CoNLL)*, pp. 1–11, 2007.

[141] Mark Claypool, Anuja Gokhale, Tim Miranda, Pavel Murnikov, Dmitry Netes and Matthew Sartin. Combining content-based and collaborative filters in an online newspaper. In *Proceedings of the ACM SIGIR'99 Workshop on Recommender Systems: Algorithms and Evaluation*, Berkeley, California, 1999. ACM.

[142] Trevor Anthony Cohn and Mirella Lapata. Sentence compression as tree transduction. *Journal of Artificial Intelligence Research*, 34: 637–674, 2009.

[143] Paul Compton and Byeong Ho Kang. *Ripple-down Rules: The Alternative to Machine Learning*. CRC Press, 2021.

[144] Carlos Coronel and Steven Morris. *Database Systems: Design, Implementation, & Management*. Cengage Learning, 2016.

[145] David Camilo Corrales, Juan Carlos Corrales and Agapito Ledezma. How to address the data quality issues in regression models: A guided process for data cleaning. *Symmetry*, 10(4): 99, 2018.

[146] Riley Crane and Didier Sornette. Robust dynamic classes revealed by measuring the response function of a social system. *Proceedings of the National Academy of Sciences*, 105(41): 15649–15653, 2008.

[147] Timothy C. Craven. Abstracts produced using computer assistance. *Journal of the American Society for Information Science*, 51(8): 745–756, 2000.

[148] Paolo Cremonesi, Antonio Tripodi and Roberto Turrin. Cross-domain recommender systems. In *Data Mining Workshops (ICDMW), 2011 IEEE 11th International Conference on*, pp. 496–503. IEEE, 2011.

[149] Laizhong Cui, Lili Sun, Xianghua Fu, Nan Lu and Guanjing Zhang. Exploring a trust based recommendation approach for videos in online social network. *Journal of Signal Processing Systems*, 86(2-3): 207–219, 2017.

[150] Navneet Dalal and Bill Triggs. Histograms of oriented gradients for human detection. In *2005 IEEE Computer Society Conference on Computer Vision and Pattern Recognition (CVPR'05)*, 1: 886–893. IEEE, 2005.

[151] Cach Nhan Dang, María N. Moreno and Fernando De la Prieta. An approach to integrating sentiment analysis into recommender systems. *Preprints* (*www.preprints.org*), 2021.

[152] Quang-Vinh Dang and Claudia-Lavinia Ignat. dtrust: A simple deep learning approach for social recommendation. In *2017 IEEE 3rd International Conference on Collaboration and Internet Computing (CIC)*, pp. 209–218. IEEE, 2017.

[153] David Danks and Alex John London. Algorithmic bias in autonomous systems. In *Proceedings International Joint Conference on Artificial Intelligence (IJCAI'17)*, 17: 4691–4697, 2017.

[154] A.S. Das, M. Datar, A. Garg and S. Rajaram. Proceedings of the kdd cup and workshop, san jose, ca, usa. In *Proceedings of the 16th International Conference on World Wide Web, Banff, AB, Canada*, pp. 271–280, 2007.

[155] Dipanjan Das and André FT Martins. A survey on automatic text summarization. *Literature Survey for the Language and Statistics II course at CMU*, 4(192-195): 57, 2007.

[156] Ali Daud. Using time topic modeling for semantics-based dynamic research interest finding. *Knowledge-Based Systems*, 26: 154–163, 2012.

[157] K. Dave, S. Lawrence and D.M. Pennock. Mining the peanut gallery: Opinion extraction and semantic classification of product reviews. In *Proceedings of 12th International World Wide Web Conference*, pp. 519–528, 2003.

[158] Kushal Dave, Steve Lawrence and David M. Pennock. Mining the peanut gallery: Opinion extraction and semantic classification of product reviews. In *Proceedings of the 12th International Conference on World Wide Web*, pp. 519–528, 2003.

[159] Toon De Pessemier, Simon Dooms, Tom Deryckere and Luc Martens. Time dependency of data quality for collaborative filtering algorithms. In *Proceedings of the Fourth ACM Conference on Recommender Systems*, pp. 281–284, 2010.

[160] Toon De Pessemier, Simon Dooms and Luc Martens. Comparison of group recommendation algorithms. *Multimedia Tools and Applications*, 72(3): 2497–2541, 2014.

[161] Jeffrey Dean and Sanjay Ghemawat. MapReduce: Simplified data processing on large clusters. *Commun. ACM*, 51(1): 107–113, 2008.

[162] Scott Deerwester, Susan T. Dumais, George W. Furnas, Thomas K. Landauer and Richard Harshman. Indexing by latent semantic

analysis. *Journal of the American Society for Information Science*, 41(6): 391–407, 1990.

[163] Marco Degemmis, Pasquale Lops and Giovanni Semeraro. A content-collaborative recommender that exploits wordnet-based user profiles for neighborhood formation. *User Modeling and User-Adapted Interaction*, 17(3): 217–255, July 2007.

[164] Yashar Deldjoo, Mehdi Elahi, Massimo Quadrana and Paolo Cremonesi. Toward building a content-based video recommendation system based on low-level features. In Dietmar Stuckenschmidt and Heinerand Jannach (eds.). *E-Commerce and Web Technologies*, pp. 45–56. Springer, 2015.

[165] Yashar Deldjoo, Mehdi Elahi, Massimo Quadrana and Paolo Cremonesi. Toward building a content-based video recommendation system based on low-level features. In *International Conference on Electronic Commerce and Web Technologies*, pp. 45–56. Springer, 2015.

[166] Yashar Deldjoo, Mehdi Elahi, Massimo Quadrana and Paolo Cremonesi. Using visual features based on mpeg-7 and deep learning for movie recommendation. *International Journal of Multimedia Information Retrieval*, 7(4): 207–219, 2018.

[167] Michael Denkowski, Chris Dyer and Alon Lavie. Learning from post-editing: Online model adaptation for statistical machine translation. In *Proceedings of the 14th Conference of the European Chapter of the Association for Computational Linguistics*, pp. 395–404, 2014.

[168] Mukund Deshpande, Dhruva Ray, Sameer Dixit and Avadhoot Agasti. Shareinsights: An unified approach to full-stack data processing. In *Proceedings of the 2015 ACM SIGMOD International Conference on Management of Data, Melbourne, Victoria, Australia, May 31–June 4, 2015*, pp. 1925–1940, 2015.

[169] Christian Desrosiers and George Karypis. A comprehensive survey of neighborhood-based recommendation methods. In Francesco Ricci, Lior Rokach, Bracha Shapira and Paul B. Kantor (eds.). *Recommender Systems Handbook*, pp. 107–144. Springer, 2011.

[170] Anind K. Dey, Gregory D. Abowd and Andrew Wood. Cyberdesk: A framework for providing self-integrating context-aware services. *Knowledge-based Systems*, 11(1): 3–13, 1998.

[171] Xenofontas Dimitropoulos, Dmitri Krioukov, Amin Vahdat and George Riley. Graph annotations in modeling complex network topologies. *ACM Transactions on Modeling and Computer Simulation (TOMACS)*, 19(4): 1–29, 2009.

[172] Quang Do, Wei Lu and Dan Roth. Joint inference for event timeline construction. In *Proceedings of the 2012 Joint Conference on Empirical Methods in Natural Language Processing and Computational Natural Language Learning*, pp. 677–687, 2012.

[173] AnHai Doan, Alon Halevy and Zachary Ives. *Principles of Data Integration*. Elsevier, 2012.

[174] Yue Dong, Yikang Shen, Eric Crawford, Herke van Hoof and Jackie Chi Kit Cheung. Banditsum: Extractive summarization as a contextual bandit. In *EMNLP*, pp. 3739–3748, 2018.

[175] Harris Drucker, Donghui Wu and Vladimir N. Vapnik. Support vector machines for spam categorization. *IEEE Transactions on Neural Networks*, 10(5): 1048–1054, 1999.

[176] Nan Du, Mehrdad Farajtabar, Amr Ahmed, Alexander J. Smola and Le Song. Dirichlet-hawkes processes with applications to clustering continuous-time document streams. In *Proceedings of the 21th ACM SIGKDD International Conference on Knowledge Discovery and Data Mining*, pp. 219–228, 2015.

[177] Yajuan Duan, Zhumin Chen, Furu Wei, Ming Zhou and Heung Yeung Shum. Twitter topic summarization by ranking tweets using social influence and content quality. In *Proceedings of COLING 2012*, pp. 763–780, 2012.

[178] Daniel M. Dunlavy, Dianne P. O'Leary, John M. Conroy and Judith D. Schlesinger. Qcs: A system for querying, clustering and summarizing documents. *Information Processing & Management*, 43(6): 1588–1605, 2007.

[179] Greg Dunn, Jurgen Wiersema, Jaap Ham and Lora Aroyo. Evaluating interface variants on personality acquisition for recommender systems. In *Proceedings of the 17th International Conference on User Modeling, Adaptation, and Personalization: Formerly UM and AH*, UMAP'09, pp. 259–270, Berlin, Heidelberg, 2009. Springer-Verlag.

[180] Harold P Edmundson. New methods in automatic extracting. *Journal of the ACM (JACM)*, 16(2): 264–285, 1969.

[181] Michael D. Ekstrand and Daniel Kluver. Exploring author gender in book rating and recommendation. *User Modeling and User-Adapted Interaction*, forthcoming, 2021.

[182] Wafaa S. El-Kassas, Cherif R. Salama, Ahmed A. Rafea and Hoda K. Mohamed. Automatic text summarization: A comprehensive survey. *Expert Systems with Applications*, pp. 113679, 2020.

[183] Bakhshandegan Moghaddam, Farshad and Elahi, Mehdi. Cold start solutions for recommendation systems. Big Data Recommender Systems: Recent Trends and Advances, IET Publication, 2019.

[184] Mehdi Elahi. *Empirical Evaluation of Active Learning Strategies in Collaborative Filtering*. Ph.D. Thesis, Ph.D. Dissertation. Free University of Bozen-Bolzano, 2014.

[185] Mehdi Elahi, Himan Abdollahpouri, Masoud Mansoury and Helma Torkamaan. Beyond algorithmic fairness in recommender systems. In *Adjunct Proceedings of the ACM Conference on User Modeling, Adaptation and Personalization (UMAP'21)*, 2021.

[186] Mehdi Elahi, Farshad Bakhshandegan Moghaddam, Reza Hosseini, Mohammad Hossein Rimaz, Nabil El Ioini, Marko Tkalcic, Christoph Trattner and Tammam Tillo. Recommending videos in cold start with automatic visual tags. In *Adjunct Proceedings of the 29th ACM Conference on User Modeling, Adaptation and Personalization*, pp. 54–60, 2021.

[187] Mehdi Elahi, Amin Beheshti and Srinivasa Reddy Goluguri. Recommender systems: Challenges and opportunities in the age of big data and artificial intelligence. In *Data Science and its Applications*, pp. 15–39. Chapman and Hall/CRC, 2021.

[188] Mehdi Elahi, Matthias Braunhofer, Tural Gurbanov and Francesco Ricci. *User Preference Elicitation, Rating Sparsity and Cold Start*, Chapter 8, pp. 253–294. 2018.

[189] Mehdi Elahi, Matthias Braunhofer, Tural Gurbanov and Francesco Ricci. User preference elicitation, rating sparsity and cold start, 2018.

[190] Mehdi Elahi, Matthias Braunhofer, Francesco Ricci and Marko Tkalcic. Personality-based active learning for collaborative filtering recommender systems. In *Proceedings of the 13th International Conference of the Italian Association for Artificial Intelligence*, pp. 360–371, 2013.

[191] Mehdi Elahi, Nabil El Ioini, Anna Alexander Lambrix and Mouzhi Ge. Exploring personalized university ranking and recommendation. In *Adjunct Publication of the 28th ACM Conference on User Modeling, Adaptation and Personalization*, pp. 6–10, 2020.

[192] Mehdi Elahi, Mouzhi Ge, Francesco Ricci, David Massimo and Shlomo Berkovsky. Interactive food recommendation for groups. In *Poster Proceedings of the 8th ACM Conference on Recommender Systems, RecSys 2014, Foster City, Silicon Valley, CA, USA, October 6–10, 2014*, pp. 1, 2014.

[193] Mehdi Elahi, Reza Hosseini, Mohammad H. Rimaz, Farshad B. Moghaddam and Christoph Trattner. Visually-aware video recommendation in the cold start. In *Proceedings of the 31st ACM Conference on Hypertext and Social Media*, pp. 225–229, 2020.

[194] Mehdi Elahi, Dietmar Jannach, Lars Skjærven, Erik Knudsen, Helle Sjøvaag, Kristian Tolonen, Øyvind Holmstad, Igor Pipkin, Eivind Throndsen, Agnes Stenbom et al. Towards responsible media recommendation.

[195] Mehdi Elahi, Danial Khosh Kholgh, Mohammad Sina Kiarostami, Sorush Saghari, Shiva Parsa Rad and Marko Tkalcic. Investigating the impact of recommender systems on user-based and item-based popularity bias. *Information Processing & Management*, 58: 102655, 2021.

[196] Mehdi Elahi, Francesco Ricci and Neil Rubens. Adapting to natural rating acquisition with combined active learning strategies. In *ISMIS'12: Proceedings of the 20th International Conference on Foundations of Intelligent Systems*, pp. 254–263, Berlin, Heidelberg, 2012. Springer-Verlag.

[197] Mehdi Elahi, Francesco Ricci and Neil Rubens. Active learning in collaborative filtering recommender systems. In *E-Commerce and Web Technologies*, pp. 113–124. Springer International Publishing, 2014.

[198] Mehdi Elahi, Francesco Ricci and Neil Rubens. Active learning strategies for rating elicitation in collaborative filtering: A system-wide perspective. *ACM Transactions on Intelligent Systems and Technology*, 5(1): 2014.

[199] Manuel Enrich, Matthias Braunhofer and Francesco Ricci. Cold-start management with cross-domain collaborative filtering and tags. In *Proceedings of the 14th International Conference E-Commerce and Web Technologies*, pp. 101–112, 2013.

[200] Sheena Erete, Emily Ryou, Geoff Smith, Khristina Marie Fassett and Sarah Duda. Storytelling with data: Examining the use of data by non-profit organizations. In *Proceedings of the 19th ACM Conference on Computer-Supported Cooperative Work & Social Computing*, pp. 1273–1283. ACM, 2016.

[201] Gunes Erkan and Dragomir R. Radev. Lexrank: Graph-based lexical centrality as salience in text summarization. *Journal of Artificial Intelligence Research*, 22: 457–479, 2004.

[202] Liana Ermakova, Jean Valère Cossu and Josiane Mothe. A survey on evaluation of summarization methods. *Information Processing & Management*, 56(5): 1794–1814, 2019.

[203] Allae Erraissi and Abdessamad Belangour. Data sources and ingestion big data layers: meta-modeling of key concepts and features. *International Journal of Engineering & Technology*, 7(4): 3607–3612, 2018.

[204] Loretta Ezeife. *Social Media Strategies for Increasing Sales*. PhD thesis, Walden University, 2017.

[205] Tobias Falke. *Automatic Structured Text Summarization with Concept Maps*. PhD thesis, Technische Universität, 2019.

[206] Chenyou Fan, Zehua Zhang and David J. Crandall. Deepdiary: Lifelogging image captioning and summarization. *Journal of Visual Communication and Image Representation*, 55: 40–55, 2018.

[207] Helia Farhood, Xiangjian He, Wenjing Jia, Michael Blumenstein and Hanhui Li. Counting people based on linear, weighted, and local random forests. In *2017 International Conference on Digital Image Computing: Techniques and Applications (DICTA)*, pp. 1–7. IEEE, 2017.

[208] Helia Farhood, Stuart Perry, Eva Cheng and Juno Kim. 3d point cloud reconstruction from a single 4d light field image. In *Optics, Photonics and Digital Technologies for Imaging Applications VI*, volume 11353, page 1135313. International Society for Optics and Photonics, 2020.

[209] Helia Farhood, Stuart Perry, Eva Cheng and Juno Kim. Enhanced 3d point cloud from a light field image. *Remote Sensing*, 12(7): 1125, 2020.

[210] Atefeh Farzindar and Guy Lapalme. Legal text summarization by exploration of the thematic structure and argumentative roles. In *Text Summarization Branches Out*, pp. 27–34, 2004.

[211] Mohamed Abdel Fattah and Fuji Ren. Ga, mr, ffnn, pnn and gmm based models for automatic text summarization. *Computer Speech & Language*, 23(1): 126–144, 2009.

[212] Marat Fayzullin, V.S. Subrahmanian, Massimiliano Albanese, Carmine Cesarano and Antonio Picariello. Story creation from heterogeneous data sources. *Multimedia Tools and Applications*, 33(3): 351–377, 2007.

[213] Alexander Felfernig and Robin Burke. Constraint-based recommender systems: Technologies and research issues. In *Proceedings of the 10th International Conference on Electronic Commerce*, ICEC'08, pp. 3:1–3:10, New York, NY, USA, 2008. ACM.

[214] Pedro F. Felzenszwalb, Ross B. Girshick, David McAllester and Deva Ramanan. Object detection with discriminatively trained part-based models. *IEEE Transactions on Pattern Analysis and Machine Intelligence*, 32(9): 1627–1645, 2009.

[215] Guozhong Feng, Jianhua Guo, Bing-Yi Jing and Lizhu Hao. A bayesian feature selection paradigm for text classification. *Information Processing & Management*, 48(2): 283–302, 2012.

[216] Ignacio Fernández-Tobías, Matthias Braunhofer, Mehdi Elahi, Francesco Ricci and Iván Cantador. Alleviating the new user problem in collaborative filtering by exploiting personality information. *User Modeling and User-Adapted Interaction*, 26(2-3): 221–255, 2016.

[217] Rafael Ferreira, Frederico Freitas, Luciano de Souza Cabral, Rafael Dueire Lins, Rinaldo Lima, Gabriel França, Steven J. Simske and Luciano Favaro. A context based text summarization system. In *2014 11th IAPR International Workshop on Document Analysis Systems*, pp. 66–70. IEEE, 2014.

[218] Xavier Ferrer, Tom van Nuenen, Jose M. Such, Mark Coté and Natalia Criado. Bias and discrimination in ai: A cross-disciplinary perspective. *IEEE Technology and Society Magazine*, 40(2): 72–80, 2021.

[219] David A. Ferrucci. Introduction to 'this is watson'. *IBM Journal of Research and Development*, 56(3.4), 2012.

[220] Bruce Ferwerda, Markus Schedl and Marko Tkalcic. Predicting personality traits with instagram pictures. In *Proceedings of the 3rd Workshop on Emotions and Personality in Personalized Systems 2015*, pp. 7–10, 2015.

[221] Bruce Ferwerda, Markus Schedl and Marko Tkalčič. Personality & Emotional states: Understanding users' music listening needs. In *Extended Proceedings of the 23rd International Conference on User Modeling, Adaptation and Personalization (UMAP)*, Dublin, Ireland, June–July 2015.

[222] Katja Filippova, Enrique Alfonseca, Carlos A. Colmenares, Łukasz Kaiser and Oriol Vinyals. Sentence compression by deletion with lstms. In *Proceedings of the 2015 Conference on Empirical Methods in Natural Language Processing*, pp. 360–368, 2015.

[223] Juliana Freire, David Koop, Emanuele Santos and Cláudio T. Silva. Provenance for computational tasks: A survey. *Computing in Science and Engg.*, 10: 11–21, May 2008.

[224] André Freitas and Edward Curry. Big data curation. In *New Horizons for a Data-Driven Economy*, pp. 87–118. Springer, 2016.

[225] Jill Freyne and Shlomo Berkovsky. Intelligent food planning: Personalized recipe recommendation. In *IUI*, pp. 321–324. ACM, 2010.

[226] Daniel Gallego, Wolfgang Woerndl and Gabriel Huecas. Evaluating the impact of proactivity in the user experience of a context-aware restaurant recommender for android smartphones. *Journal of Systems Architecture*, 59(9): 748–758, 2013.

[227] Mahak Gambhir and Vishal Gupta. Recent automatic text summarization techniques: A survey. *Artificial Intelligence Review*, 47(1): 1–66, 2017.

[228] Michael Gamon, Anthony Aue, Simon Corston-Oliver and Eric Ringger. Pulse: Mining customer opinions from free text. In *International Symposium on Intelligent Data Analysis*, pp. 121–132. Springer, 2005.

[229] Kavita Ganesan, ChengXiang Zhai and Jiawei Han. Opinosis: A graph based approach to abstractive summarization of highly redundant opinions. 2010.

[230] Kavita Ganesan, ChengXiang Zhai and Evelyne Viegas. Micropinion generation: An unsupervised approach to generating ultra-concise summaries of opinions. In *Proceedings of the 21st International Conference on World Wide Web*, pp. 869–878, 2012.

[231] Huiji Gao, Jiliang Tang, Xia Hu and Huan Liu. Exploring temporal effects for location recommendation on location-based social networks. In

Proceedings of the 7th ACM Conference on Recommender Systems, pp. 93–100, 2013.

[232] Yang Gao, Christian M. Meyer and Iryna Gurevych. April: Interactively learning to summarise by combining active preference learning and reinforcement learning. *arXiv preprint arXiv:1808.09658*, 2018.

[233] Yang Gao, Christian M. Meyer, Mohsen Mesgar and Iryna Gurevych. Reward learning for efficient reinforcement learning in extractive document summarisation. *arXiv preprint arXiv:1907.12894*, 2019.

[234] Francisco García-Sánchez, Ricardo Colomo-Palacios and Rafael Valencia-García. A social-semantic recommender system for advertisements. *Information Processing and Management*, 57(2), Mar. 2020.

[235] Venkata Rama Kiran Garimella, Abdulrahman Alfayad and Ingmar Weber. Social media image analysis for public health. In *Proceedings of the 2016 CHI Conference on Human Factors in Computing Systems*, pp. 5543–5547, 2016.

[236] Mouzhi Ge, Mehdi Elahi, Ignacio Fernaández-Tobías, Francesco Ricci and David Massimo. Using tags and latent factors in a food recommender system. In *Proceedings of the 5th International Conference on Digital Health 2015, DH'15*, pp. 105–112, New York, NY, USA, 2015. ACM, ACM.

[237] Tao Ge, Wenzhe Pei, Heng Ji, Sujian Li, Baobao Chang and Zhifang Sui. Bring you to the past: Automatic generation of topically relevant event chronicles. In *Proceedings of the 53rd Annual Meeting of the Association for Computational Linguistics and the 7th International Joint Conference on Natural Language Processing (Volume 1: Long Papers)*, pp. 575–585, 2015.

[238] David Gewirtz. Volume, velocity, and variety: Understanding the three v's of big data. *ZDnet available at https://www. zdnet. com/article/volume-velocityand-variety-understanding-the-three-vs-of-big-data*, 2018.

[239] Seyed Mohssen Ghafari, Amin Beheshti, Aditya Joshi, Cécile Paris, Adnan Mahmood, Shahpar Yakhchi and Mehmet A. Orgun. A survey on trust prediction in online social networks. *IEEE Access*, 8: 144292–144309, 2020.

[240] Samira Ghodratnama. Towards personalized and human-in-the-loop document summarization. *arXiv e-prints, pages arXiv–2108*, 2021.

[241] Samira Ghodratnama, Amin Beheshti, Mehrdad Zakershahrak and Fariborz Sobhanmanesh. Extractive document summarization based on dynamic feature space mapping. *IEEE Access*, 8: 139084–139095, 2020.

[242] Samira Ghodratnama, Amin Beheshti, Mehrdad Zakershahrak and Fariborz Sobhanmanesh. Intelligent narrative summaries: From indicative to informative summarization. *Big Data Research*, 26: 100257, 2021.

[243] Samira Ghodratnama, Mehrdad Zakershahrak and Amin Beheshti. Summary2vec: Learning semantic representation of summaries for healthcare analytics. In *2021 International Joint Conference on Neural Networks (IJCNN)*, pp. 1–8, 2021.

[244] Samira Ghodratnama, Mehrdad Zakershahrak and Fariborz Sobhanmanesh. Adaptive summaries: A personalized concept-based summarization approach by learning from users' feedback. In *International Conference on Service-Oriented Computing*, pp. 281–293. Springer, 2020.

[245] Samira Ghodratnama, Mehrdad Zakershahrak and Fariborz Sobhanmanesh. Am i rare? An intelligent summarization approach for identifying hidden anomalies. In *International Conference on Service-Oriented Computing*, pp. 309–323. Springer, 2020.

[246] Jennifer Gillenwater, Alex Kulesza and Ben Taskar. Discovering diverse and salient threads in document collections. In *Proceedings of the 2012 Joint Conference on Empirical Methods in Natural Language Processing and Computational Natural Language Learning*, pp. 710–720, 2012.

[247] Michael Gillhofer and Markus Schedl. Iron Maiden While Jogging, Debussy for Dinner? An analysis of music listening behavior in context. In *Proceedings of the 21st International Conference on MultiMedia Modeling (MMM)*, Sydney, Australia, January 2015.

[248] Kevin Gimpel, Nathan Schneider, Brendan O'Connor, Dipanjan Das, Daniel Mills, Jacob Eisenstein, Michael Heilman, Dani Yogatama, Jeffrey Flanigan and Noah A. Smith. Part-of-speech tagging for twitter: Annotation, features, and experiments. Technical report, Carnegie-Mellon Univ Pittsburgh Pa School of Computer Science, 2010.

[249] Ross Girshick. Fast r-cnn. In *Proceedings of the IEEE International Conference on Computer Vision*, pp. 1440–1448, 2015.

[250] Jennifer Golbeck, Cristina Robles, Michon Edmondson and Karen Turner. Predicting personality from twitter. In *2011 IEEE Third International Conference on Privacy, Security, Risk and Trust and 2011 IEEE Third International Conference on Social Computing*, pp. 149–156. IEEE, 2011.

[251] Saurabh Goorha and Lyle Ungar. Discovery of significant emerging trends. In *Proceedings of the 16th ACM SIGKDD International Conference on Knowledge Discovery and Data Mining*, pp. 57–64, 2010.

[252] Siddharth Gopal and Yiming Yang. Multilabel classification with meta-level features. In *Proceedings of the 33rd International ACM SIGIR Conference on Research and Development in Information Retrieval*, pp. 315–322, 2010.

[253] Samuel D. Gosling, Adam A. Augustine, Simine Vazire, Nicholas Holtzman and Sam Gaddis. Manifestations of personality in online social networks: Self-reported facebook-related behaviors and observable profile information. *Cyberpsychology, Behavior, and Social Networking*, 14(9): 483–488, 2011.

[254] Samuel D. Gosling, Sam Gaddis, Simine Vazire et al. Personality impressions based on facebook profiles. *Icwsm*, 7: 1–4, 2007.

[255] David Gotz and Zhen Wen. Behavior-driven visualization recommendation. In *Proceedings of the 14th International Conference on Intelligent User Interfaces*, pp. 315–324, 2009.

[256] Amit Goyal, Francesco Bonchi and Laks V.S. Lakshmanan. A data-based approach to social influence maximization. *arXiv preprint arXiv:1109.6886*, 2011.

[257] Ziyu Guan, Can Wang, Jiajun Bu, Chun Chen, Kun Yang, Deng Cai and Xiaofei He. Document recommendation in social tagging services. In *Proceedings of the 19th International Conference on World Wide Web*, pp. 391–400, 2010.

[258] Sushmita Guha, Paul Harrigan and Geoff Soutar. Linking social media to customer relationship management (crm): A qualitative study on smes. *Journal of Small Business & Entrepreneurship*, 30(3): 193–214, 2018.

[259] Serkan Günal, Semih Ergin, MBilginer Gülmezoğlu and Ö Nezih Gerek. On feature extraction for spam e-mail detection. In *International Workshop on Multimedia Content Representation, Classification and Security*, pp. 635–642. Springer, 2006.

[260] Cong Guo, Bei Li and Xinmei Tian. Flickr group recommendation using rich social media information. *Neurocomputing*, 204: 8–16, 2016.

[261] Guibing Guo, Jie Zhang and Daniel Thalmann. Merging trust in collaborative filtering to alleviate data sparsity and cold start. *Knowledge-Based Systems*, 57: 57–68, Feb 2014.

[262] Guibing Guo, Jie Zhang and Neil Yorke-Smith. A novel recommendation model regularized with user trust and item ratings. *IEEE Transactions on Knowledge and Data Engineering*, 28(7): 1607–1620, Jul 2016.

[263] Vishal Gupta and Gurpreet Singh Lehal. A survey of text summarization extractive techniques. *Journal of Emerging Technologies in Web Intelligence*, 2(3): 258–268, 2010.

[264] Tural Gurbanov and Francesco Ricci. Action prediction models for recommender systems based on collaborative filtering and sequence mining hybridization. In *Proceedings of the Symposium on Applied Computing, SAC'17*, pp. 1655–1661, New York, NY, USA, 2017. ACM.

[265] Robert H. Guttman, Alexandros G. Moukas and Pattie Maes. Agent-mediated electronic commerce: A survey. *Knowl. Eng. Rev.*, 13(2): 147–159, July 1998.

[266] Ido Guy. Social recommender systems. In *Recommender Systems Handbook*, pp. 511–543. Springer, 2015.

[267] Hakan Hacigümüs, Sharad Mehrotra and Balakrishna R. Iyer. Providing database as a service. In *ICDE*, pp. 29–38, 2002.

[268] Aria Haghighi and Lucy Vanderwende. Exploring content models for multi-document summarization. In *Annual Conference of the Association for Computational Linguistics*, 2009.

[269] Alon Y. Halevy, Michael J. Franklin and David Maier. Principles of dataspace systems. In *PODS*, pp. 1–9, 2006.

[270] Shanmugasundaram Hariharan, Thirunavukarasu Ramkumar and Rengaramanujam Srinivasan. Enhanced graph based approach for multi-document summarization. *The International Arab Journal of Information Technology*, 10: 4, July 2013.

[271] Shanmugasundaram Hariharan and Rengaramanujam Srinivasan. Studies on graph based approaches for single and multi-document summarizations. *International Journal of Computer Theory and Engineering*, 1: 5, 2009.

[272] Negar Hariri, Bamshad Mobasher and Robin Burke. Context-aware music recommendation based on latenttopic sequential patterns. In *Proceedings of the Sixth ACM Conference on Recommender Systems*, pp. 131–138. ACM, 2012.

[273] Zellig S. Harris. Distributional structure. *Word*, 10(2-3): 146–162, 1954.

[274] Khalid Haruna, Maizatul Akmar Ismail, Suhendroyono Suhendroyono, Damiasih Damiasih, Adi Cilik Pierewan, Haruna Chiroma and Tutut Herawan. Context aware recommender system: A review of recent developmental process and future research direction. *Applied Sciences*, 7(2): 1211–1221, 2017.

[275] Bilal Hawashin, Mohammad Lafi, Tarek Kanan and Ayman Mansour. An efficient hybrid similarity measure based on user interests for recommender systems. *Expert Systems*, pp. e12471, 2019.

[276] Naieme Hazrati and Mehdi Elahi. Addressing the new item problem in video recommender systems by incorporation of visual features with restricted boltzmann machines. *Expert Systems*, 38(3): e12645, 2021.

[277] Tom Heath and Christian Bizer. Linked data: Evolving the web into a global data space. *Synthesis Lectures on the Semantic Web: Theory and Technology*, 1(1): 1–136, 2011.

[278] Jee-Uk Heu, Iqbal Qasim and Dong-Ho Lee. Fodosu: Multi-document summarization exploiting semantic analysis based on social folksonomy. *Information Processing & Management*, 51(1), 2015.

[279] Paul Heymann, Georgia Koutrika and Hector Garcia-Molina. Can social bookmarking improve web search? In *Proceedings of the 2008 International Conference on Web Search and Data Mining*, pp. 195–206, 2008.

[280] Thomas Hoffman. Probabilistic latent semantic indexing. In *Proceedings of the 22nd Annual ACM Conference on Research and Development in Information Retrieval, 1999*, pp. 50–57, 1999.

[281] Thomas Hofmann. Probabilistic latent semantic indexing. In *Proceedings of the 22nd Annual International ACM SIGIR Conference on Research and Development in Information Retrieval*, pp. 50–57, 1999.

[282] Matthieu Hog. *Light Field Editing and Rendering*. PhD thesis, Rennes 1, 2018.

[283] David A. Holland, Uri Braun, Diana Maclean, Kiran-Kumar Muniswamy-Reddy and Margo I. Seltzer. Choosing a data model and query language for provenance. In *Second International Provenance and Annotation Workshop (IPAW'08)*, 2008.

[284] Jacob Honer, Aiden Fadool and Juyang Weng. User flagging for posts at 3dtube. org: the first social platform for 3d-exclusive contents. In *2020 Seventh International Conference on Social Networks Analysis, Management and Security (SNAMS)*, pp. 1–6. IEEE, 2020.

[285] Liangjie Hong and Brian D. Davison. Empirical study of topic modeling in twitter. In *Proceedings of the First Workshop on Social Media Analytics*, pp. 80–88, 2010.

[286] Andreas Hotho, Andreas Nürnberger and Gerhard Paaß. A brief survey of text mining. In *Ldv Forum*, 20: 19–62. Citeseer, 2005.

[287] Eduard Hovy, Chin-Yew Lin et al. Automated text summarization in summarist. *Advances in Automatic Text Summarization*, 14: 81–94, 1999.

[288] Jian Hu, Lujun Fang, Yang Cao, Hua-Jun Zeng, Hua Li, Qiang Yang and Zheng Chen. Enhancing text clustering by leveraging wikipedia semantics. In *Proceedings of the 31st Annual International ACM SIGIR Conference on Research and Development in Information Retrieval*, pp. 179–186, 2008.

[289] Minqing Hu and Bing Liu. Mining and summarizing customer reviews. In *Proceedings of 10th ACM SIGKDD International Conference on Knowledge Discovery and Data Mining*, pp. 168–177, 2004.

[290] Minqing Hu and Bing Liu. Mining and summarizing customer reviews. In *Proceedings of the Tenth ACM SIGKDD International Conference on Knowledge Discovery and Data Mining*, pp. 168–177, 2004.

[291] Po Hu, Minlie Huang, Peng Xu, Weichang Li, Adam K. Usadi and Xiaoyan Zhu. Generating breakpoint-based timeline overview for news topic retrospection. In *2011 IEEE 11th International Conference on Data Mining*, pp. 260–269. IEEE, 2011.

[292] Rong Hu and Pearl Pu. A comparative user study on rating vs. personality quiz based preference elicitation methods. In *Proceedings of the 14th International Conference on Intelligent User Interfaces*, IUI'09, pp. 367–372, New York, NY, USA, 2009. ACM.

[293] Rong Hu and Pearl Pu. A study on user perception of personality-based recommender systems. In Paul De Bra, Alfred Kobsa and David N. Chin (eds.). *UMAP*, volume 6075 of *Lecture Notes in Computer Science*, pp. 291–302. Springer, 2010.

[294] Rong Hu and Pearl Pu. Enhancing collaborative filtering systems with personality information. In *Proceedings of the Fifth ACM Conference on Recommender Systems*, RecSys'11, pp. 197–204, New York, NY, USA, 2011. ACM.

[295] Xia Hu and Huan Liu. Text analytics in social media. In *Mining Text Data*, pp. 385–414. Springer, 2012.

[296] Yifan Hu, Yehuda Koren and Chris Volinsky. Collaborative filtering for implicit feedback datasets. In *Proceedings of the 2008 Eighth IEEE International Conference on Data Mining*, ICDM'08, pp. 263–272, Washington, DC, USA, 2008. IEEE Computer Society.

[297] Shiu-Li Huang. Designing utility-based recommender systems for E-commerce: Evaluation of preference-elicitation methods. *Electron. Commer. Rec. Appl.*, 10(4): 398–407, July 2011.

[298] Martin Husák, Jana Komárková, Elias Bou-Harb and Pavel Čeleda. Survey of attack projection, prediction, and forecasting in cyber security. *IEEE Communications Surveys & Tutorials*, 21(1): 640–660, 2018.

[299] Muhammad Imran, Ferda Ofli, Doina Caragea and Antonio Torralba. Using AI and social media multimodal content for disaster response and management: Opportunities, challenges, and future directions, 2020.

[300] Rizwana Irfan, Christine K. King, Daniel Grages, Sam Ewen, Samee U. Khan, Sajjad A. Madani, Joanna Kolodziej, Lizhe Wang, Dan Chen, Ammar Rayes et al. A survey on text mining in social networks. *The Knowledge Engineering Review*, 30(2): 157–170, 2015.

[301] Aaron Isaksen, Leonard McMillan and Steven J. Gortler. Dynamically reparameterized light fields. In *Proceedings of the 27th Annual Conference on Computer Graphics and Interactive Techniques*, pp. 297–306, 2000.

[302] Mohsen Jamali and Martin Ester. TrustWalker: a random walk model for combining trust-based and item-based recommendation. In *Proceedings of the 15th ACM SIGKDD International Conference on Knowledge Discovery and Data Mining—KDD'09*, pp. 397–406, New York, New York, USA, 2009. ACM Press.

[303] Dietmar Jannach, Markus Zanker, Alexander Felfernig and Gerhard Friedrich. *Recommender Systems: An Introduction.* Cambridge University Press, 2010.

[304] Zanker M., Flfering A., Jannach D. and Friedfrich G. *Recommender Systems: An Introduction.* Cambridge University Press, 2011.

[305] Dureen Jayaram, Ajay K. Manrai and Lalita A. Manrai. Effective use of marketing technology in eastern Europe: Web analytics, social media, customer analytics, digital campaigns and mobile applications. *Journal of Economics, Finance and Administrative Science*, 20(39): 118–132, 2015.

[306] M.Z.H. Jesmeen, J. Hossen, S. Sayeed, C.K. Ho, K. Tawsif, Armanur Rahman and E.M.H. Arif. A survey on cleaning dirty data using machine learning paradigm for big data analytics. *Indonesian Journal of Electrical Engineering and Computer Science*, 10(3): 1234–1243, 2018.

[307] Karel Ježek and Josef Steinberger. Automatic text summarization (the state of the art 2007 and new challenges). In *Proceedings of Znalosti*, pp. 1–12. Citeseer, 2008.

[308] Ming Ji, Yizhou Sun, Marina Danilevsky, Jiawei Han and Jing Gao. Graph regularized transductive classification on heterogeneous information networks. In *Joint European Conference on Machine Learning and Knowledge Discovery in Databases*, pp. 570–586. Springer, 2010.

[309] CuiQing Jiang, Kun Liang, Hsinchun Chen and Yong Ding. Analyzing market performance via social media: A case study of a banking industry crisis. *Science China Information Sciences*, 57(5): 1–18, 2014.

[310] Feng Jin, Minlie Huang and Xiaoyan Zhu. A query-specific opinion summarization system. In *2009 8th IEEE International Conference on Cognitive Informatics*, pp. 428–433. IEEE, 2009.

[311] Kanika Jindal and Rajni Aron. A systematic study of sentiment analysis for social media data. *Materials Today: Proceedings*, 2021.

[312] Hongyan Jing. Sentence reduction for automatic text summarization. In *Sixth Applied Natural Language Processing Conference*, pp. 310–315, 2000.

[313] Oliver P. John and Sanjay Srivastava. The big five trait taxonomy: History, measurement, and theoretical perspectives. In: *Handbook of Personality: Theory and Research*, 1999. vol. 2, pp. 102 to 138.

[314] Nicolas Jones, Armelle Brun and Anne Boyer. Comparisons instead of ratings: Towards more stable preferences. In *Proceedings of the 2011 IEEE/ WIC/ACM International Conferences on Web Intelligence and Intelligent Agent Technology—Volume 01*, WI-IAT'11, pp. 451–456, Washington, DC, USA, 2011. IEEE Computer Society.

[315] Steve Jones, Stephen Lundy and Gordon W. Paynter. Interactive document summarisation using automatically extracted keyphrases. In *Proceedings of the 35th Annual Hawaii International Conference on System Sciences*, pp. 1160–1169. IEEE, 2002.

[316] Jungseock Joo and Zachary C. Steinert-Threlkeld. Image as data: Automated visual content analysis for political science. *arXiv preprint arXiv:1810.01544*, 2018.

[317] Anirudh Kadadi, Rajeev Agrawal, Christopher Nyamful and Rahman Atiq. Challenges of data integration and interoperability in big data. In *2014 IEEE International Conference on Big Data (Big Data)*, pp. 38–40. IEEE, 2014.

[318] Saikishore Kalloori, Francesco Ricci and Marko Tkalcic. Pairwise preferences based matrix factorization and nearest neighbor recommendation techniques. In *Proceedings of the 10th ACM Conference on Recommender Systems*, RecSys'16, pp. 143–146, New York, NY, USA, 2016. ACM.

[319] Ahmad Kamal. Review mining for feature based opinion summarization and visualization. *arXiv preprint arXiv:1504.03068*, 2015.

[320] Marius Kaminskas, Francesco Ricci and Markus Schedl. Location-aware music recommendation using auto-tagging and hybrid matching. In *Proceedings of the 7th ACM Conference on Recommender Systems (RecSys)*, Hong Kong, China, October 2013.

[321] Marius Kaminskas, Francesco Ricci and Markus Schedl. Location-aware music recommendation using auto-tagging and hybrid matching. In *Proceedings of the 7th ACM Conference on Recommender Systems*, pp. 17–24. ACM, 2013.

[322] Jaap Kamps, Maarten Marx, Robert J. Mokken and Maarten de Rijke. Using wordnet to measure semantic orientation of adjectives. In *Proceedings of 4th International Conference on Language Resources and Evaluation*, pp. 1115–1118, 2004.

[323] Tapas Kanungo, David M. Mount, Nathan S. Netanyahu, Christine D. Piatko, Ruth Silverman and Angela Y. Wu. An efficient k-means clustering algorithm: Analysis and implementation. *IEEE Transactions on Pattern Analysis and Machine Intelligence*, 24(7): 881–892, 2002.

[324] Andreas M. Kaplan and Michael Haenlein. Users of the world, unite! The challenges and opportunities of social media. *Business Horizons*, 53(1): 59–68, 2010.

[325] Amir Karami, Vishal Shah, Reza Vaezi and Amit Bansal. Twitter speaks: A case of national disaster situational awareness. *Journal of Information Science*, 46(3): 313–324, 2020.

[326] Mozhgan Karimi, Dietmar Jannach and Michael Jugovac. News recommender systems–survey and roads ahead. *Information Processing & Management*, 54(6): 1203–1227, 2018.

[327] Rasoul Karimi, Christoph Freudenthaler, Alexandros Nanopoulos and Lars Schmidt-Thieme. Active learning for aspect model in recommender systems. In *CIDM*, pp. 162–167. IEEE, 2011.

[328] Grigoris Karvounarakis, Zachary G. Ives and Val Tannen. Querying data provenance. In *Proceedings of the 2010 International Conference on Management of Data*, SIGMOD'10, pp. 951–962, 2010.

[329] Faris Kateb and Jugal Kalita. Classifying short text in social media: Twitter as case study. *International Journal of Computer Applications*, 111(9): 1–12, 2015.

[330] Navjot Kaur and Yadwinder Kaur. Object classification techniques using machine learning model. *International Journal of Computer Trends and Technology (IJCTT)*, 18(4), 2014.

[331] Pavlos Kefalas, Panagiotis Symeonidis and Yannis Manolopoulos. Recommendations based on a heterogeneous spatio-temporal social network. *World Wide Web*, 21(2): 345–371, 2018.

[332] Diane Kelly and Jaime Teevan. Implicit feedback for inferring user preference: A bibliography. In *ACM SIGIR Forum*, 37: 18–28. ACM, 2003.

[333] Stephen Kelly, Xiubo Zhang and Khurshid Ahmad. Mining multimodal information on social media for increased situational awareness. 2017.

[334] Remy Kessler, Xavier Tannier, Caroline Hagege, Véronique Moriceau and André Bittar. Finding salient dates for building thematic timelines. In *Association for Computational Linguistics*, pp. 730–739, 2012.

[335] Samina Khalid, Tehmina Khalil and Shamila Nasreen. A survey of feature selection and feature extraction techniques in machine learning. In *2014 Science and Information Conference*, pp. 372–378. IEEE, 2014.

[336] Atif Khan, Naomie Salim and Yogan Jaya Kumar. A framework for multi-document abstractive summarization based on semantic role labelling. *Applied Soft Computing*, 30: 737–747, 2015.

[337] Pooja Kherwa, Arjit Sachdeva, Dhruv Mahajan, Nishtha Pande and Prashast Kumar Singh. An approach towards comprehensive sentimental data analysis and opinion mining. In *2014 IEEE International Advance Computing Conference (IACC)*, pp. 606–612. IEEE, 2014.

[338] Kwangseob Kim and Kiwon Lee. Applicability of kompsat image data in open data cube. *Abstracts of the ICA*, 1: NA–NA, 2019.

[339] Soo-Min Kim and Eduard Hovy. Determining the sentiment of opinions. In *COLING 2004: Proceedings of the 20th International Conference on Computational Linguistics*, pp. 1367–1373, 2004.

[340] Kerstin Klemisch, Ingo Weber and Boualem Benatallah. Context-aware ui component reuse. In *International Conference on Advanced Information Systems Engineering*, pp. 68–83. Springer, 2013.

[341] Kevin Knight and Daniel Marcu. Statistics-based summarization-step one: Sentence compression. *AAAI/IAAI*, 2000: 703–710, 2000.

[342] Kevin Knight and Daniel Marcu. Summarization beyond sentence extraction: A probabilistic approach to sentence compression. *Artificial Intelligence*, 139(1): 91–107, 2002.

[343] Oleksandr Kolomiyets, Steven Bethard and Marie Francine Moens. Extracting narrative timelines as temporal dependency structures. In *Proceedings of the 50th Annual Meeting of the Association for Computational Linguistics (Volume 1: Long Papers)*, pp. 88–97, 2012.

[344] Nicholas Kong and Maneesh Agrawala. Graphical overlays: Using layered elements to aid chart reading. *IEEE Transactions on Visualization and Computer Graphics*, 18(12): 2631–2638, 2012.

[345] Yehuda Koren. Factorization meets the neighborhood: A multifaceted collaborative filtering model. In *KDD'08: Proceeding of the 14th ACM SIGKDD International Conference on Knowledge Discovery and Data Mining*, pp. 426–434, New York, NY, USA, 2008. ACM.

[346] Yehuda Koren. Collaborative filtering with temporal dynamics. *Commun. ACM*, 53(4): 89–97, April 2010.

[347] Yehuda Koren and Robert Bell. Advances in collaborative filtering. In Francesco Ricci, Lior Rokach, Bracha Shapira and Paul Kantor (eds.). *Recommender Systems Handbook*, pp. 145–186. Springer Verlag, 2011.

[348] Yehuda Koren and Robert Bell. Advances in collaborative filtering. In *Recommender Systems Handbook*, pp. 77–118. Springer, 2015.

[349] Yehuda Koren, Robert Bell and Chris Volinsky. Matrix factorization techniques for recommender systems. *Computer*, 42(8): 30–37, 2009.

[350] Michal Kosinski, David Stillwell and Thore Graepel. Private traits and attributes are predictable from digital records of human behavior. *Proceedings of the National Academy of Sciences*, pp. 2–5, March 2013.

[351] Julia Kreutzer, Shahram Khadivi, Evgeny Matusov and Stefan Riezler. Can neural machine translation be improved with user feedback? *arXiv preprint arXiv:1804.05958*, 2018.

[352] Julia Kreutzer, Artem Sokolov and Stefan Riezler. Bandit structured prediction for neural sequence-to-sequence learning. *arXiv preprint arXiv:1704.06497*, 2017.

[353] Krish Krishnan. *Data Warehousing in the Age of Big Data*. Newnes, 2013.

[354] Wojciech Kryściński, Romain Paulus, Caiming Xiong and Richard Socher. Improving abstraction in text summarization. *arXiv preprint arXiv:1808.07913*, 2018.

[355] Lun-Wei Ku, Yu-Ting Liang, Hsin-Hsi Chen et al. Opinion extraction, summarization and tracking in news and blog corpora. In *AAAI Spring Symposium: Computational Approaches to Analyzing Weblogs*, volume 100107, pp. 1–167, 2006.

[356] Hannu Kukka, Minna Pakanen, Mahmoud Badri and Timo Ojala. Immersive street-level social media in the 3d virtual city: Anticipated user experience and conceptual development. In *Proceedings of the 2017 ACM Conference*

on *Computer Supported Cooperative Work and Social Computing*, pp. 2422–2435, 2017.

[357] Girish Kulkarni, Visruth Premraj, Vicente Ordonez, Sagnik Dhar, Siming Li, Yejin Choi, Alexander C. Berg and Tamara L. Berg. Babytalk: Understanding and generating simple image descriptions. *IEEE Transactions on Pattern Analysis and Machine Intelligence*, 35(12): 2891–2903, 2013.

[358] Vipin Kumar and Rohan Mirchandani. Increasing the roi of social media marketing. *MIT Sloan Management Review*, 54(1): 55, 2012.

[359] Linda S.L. Lai and Wai Ming To. Content analysis of social media: A grounded theory approach. *Journal of Electronic Commerce Research*, 16(2): 138, 2015.

[360] Cait Lamberton and Andrew T. Stephen. A thematic exploration of digital, social media, and mobile marketing: Research evolution from 2000 to 2015 and an agenda for future inquiry. *Journal of Marketing*, 80(6): 146–172, 2016.

[361] Carolin Lawrence and Stefan Riezler. Counterfactual learning from human proofreading feedback for semantic parsing. *arXiv preprint arXiv:1811.12239*, 2018.

[362] Dawn Lawrie, W. Bruce Croft and Arnold Rosenberg. Finding topic words for hierarchical summarization. In *Proceedings of the 24th Annual International ACM SIGIR Conference on Research and Development in Information Retrieval*, pp. 349–357, 2001.

[363] Alejandro Valerio David Leake. Jump-starting concept map construction with knowledge extracted from documents. In *In Proceedings of the Second International Conference on Concept Mapping (CMC)*. Citeseer, 2006.

[364] Kathy Lee, Diana Palsetia, Ramanathan Narayanan, Md Mostofa Ali Patwary, Ankit Agrawal and Alok Choudhary. Twitter trending topic classification. In *2011 IEEE 11th International Conference on Data Mining Workshops*, pp. 251–258. IEEE, 2011.

[365] Yeha Lee, Hun-young Jung, Woosang Song and Jong-Hyeok Lee. Mining the blogosphere for top news stories identification. In *Proceedings of the 33rd International ACM SIGIR Conference on Research and Development in Information Retrieval*, pp. 395–402, 2010.

[366] Taras Lehinevych, Nikolaos Kokkinis-Ntrenis, Giorgos Siantikos, A. Seza Dogruöz, Theodoros Giannakopoulos and Stasinos Konstantopoulos. Discovering similarities for content-based recommendation and browsing in multimedia collections. In *Signal-Image Technology and Internet-Based Systems (SITIS), 2014 Tenth International Conference on*, pp. 237–243. IEEE, 2014.

[367] Xiaojiang Lei, Xueming Qian and Guoshuai Zhao. Rating prediction based on social sentiment from textual reviews. *IEEE Transactions on Multimedia*, 18(9): 1910–1921, 2016.

[368] Cane Wing-ki Leung, Stephen Chi-fai Chan and Fu-lai Chung. Integrating collaborative filtering and sentiment analysis: A rating inference approach. In *Proceedings of the ECAI 2006 Workshop on Recommender Systems*, pp. 62–66. ACM, 2006.

[369] Anton Leuski, Chin-Yew Lin and Eduard Hovy. ineats: Interactive multi-document summarization. In *The Companion Volume to the Proceedings of 41st Annual Meeting of the Association for Computational Linguistics*, pp. 125–128, 2003.

[370] Marc Levoy, Billy Chen, Vaibhav Vaish, Mark Horowitz, Ian McDowall and Mark Bolas. Synthetic aperture confocal imaging. *ACM Transactions on Graphics (ToG)*, 23(3): 825–834, 2004.

[371] Daifeng Li, Bing He, Ying Ding, Jie Tang, Cassidy Sugimoto, Zheng Qin, Erjia Yan, Juanzi Li and Tianxi Dong. Community-based topic modeling for social tagging. In *Proceedings of the 19th ACM International Conference on Information and Knowledge Management*, pp. 1565–1568, 2010.

[372] Jiwei Li and Claire Cardie. Timeline generation: Tracking individuals on twitter. In *Proceedings of the 23rd International Conference on World Wide Web*, pp. 643–652, 2014.

[373] Qing Li and Byeong Man Kim. An approach for combining content-based and collaborative filters. In *Proceedings of the Sixth International Workshop on Information Retrieval with Asian Languages - Volume 11*, AsianIR'03, pages 17–24, Stroudsburg, PA, USA, 2003. Association for Computational Linguistics.

[374] Guoqiong Liao, Shan Jiang, Zhiheng Zhou, Changxuan Wan and Xiping Liu. Poi recommendation of location-based social networks using tensor factorization. In *2018 19th IEEE international conference on mobile data management (MDM)*, pp. 116–124. IEEE, 2018.

[375] Elizabeth D. Liddy. Natural language processing. 2001.

[376] Kar Wai Lim, Changyou Chen and Wray Buntine. Twitter-network topic model: A full bayesian treatment for social network and text modeling. *arXiv preprint arXiv:1609.06791*, 2016.

[377] Chin-Yew Lin. Rouge: A package for automatic evaluation of summaries. *Text Summarization Branches Out*, 2004.

[378] Chin-Yew Lin and Eduard Hovy. Identifying topics by position. In *Fifth Conference on Applied Natural Language Processing*, pp. 283–290, 1997.

[379] Cindy Xide Lin, Bo Zhao, Qiaozhu Mei and Jiawei Han. Pet: A statistical model for popular events tracking in social communities. In *Proceedings of the 16th ACM SIGKDD International Conference on Knowledge Discovery and Data Mining*, pp. 929–938, 2010.

[380] Hui Lin and Jeff Bilmes. A class of submodular functions for document summarization. In *Association for Computational Linguistics: Human Language Technologies*, pp. 510–520, 2011.

[381] Lu Lin, Jianxin Li, Richong Zhang, Weiren Yu and Chenggen Sun. Opinion mining and sentiment analysis in social networks: A retweeting structure-aware approach. In *2014 IEEE/ACM 7th International Conference on Utility and Cloud Computing*, pp. 890–895. IEEE, 2014.

[382] Greg Linden, Brent Smith and Jeremy York. Amazon.com recommendations: item-to-item collaborative filtering. *IEEE Internet Computing*, 7(1): 76–80, Jan 2003.

[383] Greg Linden, Brent Smith and Jeremy York. Amazon.com recommendations: Item-to-item collaborative filtering. *IEEE Internet Computing*, 7(1): 76–80, January 2003.

[384] Bin Liu and Hui Xiong. Point-of-interest recommendation in location based social networks with topic and location awareness. In *Proceedings of the 2013 SIAM International Conference on Data Mining*, pp. 396–404. SIAM, 2013.

[385] Leqi Liu, Daniel Preotiuc-Pietro, Zahra Riahi Samani, Mohsen E. Moghaddam and Lyle Ungar. Analyzing personality through social media profile picture choice. In *Proceedings of the International AAAI Conference on Web and Social Media*, volume 10, 2016.

[386] Li Liu, Wanli Ouyang, Xiaogang Wang, Paul Fieguth, Jie Chen, Xinwang Liu and Matti Pietikäinen. Deep learning for generic object detection: A survey. *International Journal of Computer Vision*, 128(2): 261–318, 2020.

[387] Wei Liu, Dragomir Anguelov, Dumitru Erhan, Christian Szegedy, Scott Reed, Cheng-Yang Fu and Alexander C. Berg. Ssd: Single shot multibox detector. In *European Conference on Computer Vision*, pp. 21–37. Springer, 2016.

[388] Xiaojiang Liu, Zaiqing Nie, Nenghai Yu and Ji-Rong Wen. Biosnowball: Automated population of wikis. In *ACM SIGKDD International Conference on Knowledge Discovery and Data Mining*, 2010.

[389] Yan Liu, Alexandru Niculescu-Mizil and Wojciech Gryc. Topic-link lda: Joint models of topic and author community. In *Proceedings of the 26th Annual International Conference on Machine Learning*, pp. 665–672, 2009.

[390] Yang Liu. Fine-tune bert for extractive summarization. *arXiv preprint arXiv:1903.10318*, 2019.

[391] Elena Lloret, Ester Boldrini, Tatiana Vodolazova, Patricio Martínez-Barco, Rafael Munoz and Manuel Palomar. A novel concept-level approach for ultra-concise opinion summarization. *Expert Systems with Applications*, 42(20): 7148–7156, 2015.

[392] Elena Lloret and Manuel Palomar. Analyzing the use of word graphs for abstractive text summarization. In *Proceedings of the First International Conference on Advances in Information Mining and Management, Barcelona, Spain*, pp. 61–6, 2011.

[393] Bianca E. Lopez, Nicholas R. Magliocca and Andrew T. Crooks. Challenges and opportunities of social media data for socio-environmental systems research. *Land*, 8(7): 107, 2019.

[394] Pasquale Lops, Marco De Gemmis and Giovanni Semeraro. Content-based recommender systems: State of the art and trends. In *Recommender Systems Handbook*, pp. 73–105. Springer, 2011.

[395] David G. Lowe. Distinctive image features from scale-invariant keypoints. *International Journal of Computer Vision*, 60(2): 91–110, 2004.

[396] Hans Peter Luhn. A statistical approach to mechanized encoding and searching of literary information. *IBM Journal of Research and Development*, 1(4): 309–317, 1957.

[397] Hans Peter Luhn. The automatic creation of literature abstracts. *IBM Journal of Research and Development*, 2(2): 159–165, 1958.

[398] Wenjuan Luo, Fuzhen Zhuang, Qing He and Zhongzhi Shi. Exploiting relevance, coverage, and novelty for query-focused multi-document summarization. *Knowledge-Based Systems*, 46: 33–42, 2013.

[399] Chih-Chao Ma. A guide to singular value decomposition for collaborative filtering. *Computer*, 42: 30–37, 2009.

[400] Hao Ma, Dengyong Zhou, Chao Liu, Michael R. Lyu and Irwin King. Recommender systems with social regularization. In *Proceedings of the Fourth ACM International Conference on Web Search and Data Mining—WSDM'11*, pp. 287, New York, New York, USA, 2011. ACM Press.

[401] Kazuki Maeno, Hajime Nagahara, Atsushi Shimada and Rin-ichiro Taniguchi. Light field distortion feature for transparent object recognition. In *Proceedings of the IEEE Conference on Computer Vision and Pattern Recognition*, pp. 2786–2793, 2013.

[402] Bernardo Magnini and Carlo Strapparava. Improving user modelling with content-based techniques. In *User Modeling 2001*, pp. 74–83. Springer, 2001.

[403] Shrabanti Mandal, Girish Kumar Singh and Anita Pal. Pso-based text summarization approach using sentiment analysis. In *Computing, Communication and Signal Processing*, pp. 845–854. Springer, 2019.

[404] Masoud Mansoury, Himan Abdollahpouri, Mykola Pechenizkiy, Bamshad Mobasher and Robin Burke. Feedback loop and bias amplification in recommender systems. In *Proceedings of the 29th ACM International Conference on Information & Knowledge Management (CIKM'20)*, pp. 2145–2148, 2020.

[405] Dragos Margineantu, Weng-Keen Wong and Denver Dash. Machine learning algorithms for event detection. *Machine Learning*, 79(3): 257, 2010.

[406] Erwin Marsi, Emiel Krahmer, Iris Hendrickx and Walter Daelemans. On the limits of sentence compression by deletion. In *Empirical Methods in Natural Language Generation*, pp. 45–66. Springer, 2009.

[407] Paolo Massa and Paolo Avesani. Trust-aware collaborative filtering for recommender systems. In *On the Move to Meaningful Internet Systems 2004: CoopIS, DOA, and ODBASE, {OTM} Confederated International Conferences, Agia Napa, Cyprus, October 25–29, 2004, Proceedings, Part {I}*, 2004.

[408] Paolo Massa and Paolo Avesani. Trust-aware recommender systems. In *Proceedings of the 2007 ACM Conference on Recommender Systems— RecSys'07*, 2007.

[409] David Massimo, Mehdi Elahi, Mouzhi Ge and Francesco Ricci. Item contents good, user tags better: Empirical evaluation of a food recommender system. In *Proceedings of the 25th Conference on User Modeling, Adaptation and Personalization*, pp. 373–374. ACM, 2017.

[410] David Massimo, Mehdi Elahi and Francesco Ricci. Learning user preferences by observing user-items interactions in an iot augmented space. In *Adjunct Publication of the 25th Conference on User Modeling, Adaptation and Personalization*, pp. 35–40, 2017.

[411] Judith Masthoff. Group recommender systems: aggregation, satisfaction and group attributes. In *Recommender Systems Handbook*, pp. 743–776. Springer, 2015.

[412] Andreea Mătăcuţă and Cătălina Popa. Big data analytics: Analysis of features and performance of big data ingestion tools. *Informatica Economica*, 22(2): 25–34, 2018.

[413] Yasuko Matsubara, Yasushi Sakurai, B. Aditya Prakash, Lei Li and Christos Faloutsos. Rise and fall patterns of information diffusion: Model and implications. In *Proceedings of the 18th ACM SIGKDD International Conference on Knowledge Discovery and Data Mining*, pp. 6–14, 2012.

[414] Masakazu Matsugu, Katsuhiko Mori, Yusuke Mitari and Yuji Kaneda. Subject independent facial expression recognition with robust face detection using a convolutional neural network. *Neural Networks*, 16(5-6): 555–559, 2003.

[415] Franco Mawad, Marcela Trías, Ana Giménez, Alejandro Maiche and Gastón Ares. Influence of cognitive style on information processing and selection of yogurt labels: Insights from an eye-tracking study. *Food Research International*, 74: 1–9, 2015.

[416] Andrew McCallum, Kamal Nigam et al. A comparison of event models for naive bayes text classification. In *AAAI-98 Workshop on Learning for Text Categorization*, volume 752, pp. 41–48. Citeseer, 1998.

[417] Andrew McCallum, Xuerui Wang and Natasha Mohanty. Joint group and topic discovery from relations and text. In *ICML Workshop on Statistical Network Analysis*, pp. 28–44. Springer, 2006.

[418] Brian McFee and Gert Lanckriet. Hypergraph models of playlist dialects. In *Proceedings of the 13th International Society for Music Information Retrieval Conference (ISMIR)*, Porto, Portugal, 2012.

[419] Kathleen McKeown and Dragomir R. Radev. Generating summaries of multiple news articles. In *Proceedings of the 18th Annual International ACM SIGIR Conference on Research and Development in Information Retrieval*, pp. 74–82, 1995.

[420] Miller McPherson, Lynn Smith-Lovin and James M. Cook. Birds of a feather: Homophily in social networks. *Annual Review of Sociology*, 27(1): 415–444, Aug 2001.

[421] Yogesh Kumar Meena, Peeyush Dewaliya and Dinesh Gopalani. Optimal features set for extractive automatic text summarization. In *2015 Fifth International Conference on Advanced Computing & Communication Technologies*, pp. 35–40. IEEE, 2015.

[422] Yogesh Kumar Meena and Dinesh Gopalani. Analysis of sentence scoring methods for extractive automatic text summarization. In *Proceedings of the 2014 International Conference on Information and Communication Technology for Competitive Strategies*, pp. 1–6, 2014.

[423] Ninareh Mehrabi, Fred Morstatter, Nripsuta Saxena, Kristina Lerman and Aram Galstyan. A survey on bias and fairness in machine learning. *CoRR*, abs/1908.09635, 2019.

[424] Parth Mehta and Prasenjit Majumder. Effective aggregation of various summarization techniques. *Information Processing & Management*, 54(2): 145–158, 2018.

[425] Marcelo Mendoza, Barbara Poblete and Carlos Castillo. Twitter under crisis: Can we trust what we rt? In *Proceedings of the First Workshop on Social Media Analytics*, pp. 71–79, 2010.

[426] Martha Mendoza, Susana Bonilla, Clara Noguera, Carlos Cobos and Elizabeth León. Extractive single-document summarization based

on genetic operators and guided local search. *Expert Systems with Applications*, 41(9): 4158–4169, 2014.

[427] Xinfan Meng, Furu Wei, Xiaohua Liu, Ming Zhou, Sujian Li and Houfeng Wang. Entity-centric topic-oriented opinion summarization in twitter. In *Proceedings of the 18th ACM SIGKDD International Conference on Knowledge Discovery and Data Mining*, pp. 379–387, 2012.

[428] Yishu Miao and Phil Blunsom. Language as a latent variable: Discrete generative models for sentence compression. *arXiv preprint arXiv:1609.07317*, 2016.

[429] Othon Michail. An introduction to temporal graphs: An algorithmic perspective. *Internet Mathematics*, 12(4): 239–280, 2016.

[430] Stuart E. Middleton, Nigel R. Shadbolt and David C. De Roure. Ontological user profiling in recommender systems. *ACM Transactions on Information Systems (TOIS)*, 22(1): 54–88, 2004.

[431] Rada Mihalcea and Paul Tarau. Textrank: Bringing order into text. In *Proceedings of the 2004 Conference on Empirical Methods in Natural Language Processing*, pp. 404–411, 2004.

[432] Tomas Mikolov, Ilya Sutskever, Kai Chen, Greg S. Corrado and Jeff Dean. Distributed representations of words and phrases and their compositionality. *NIPS*, 26: 3111–3119, 2013.

[433] Paolo Missier, Norman W. Paton and Khalid Belhajjame. Fine-grained and efficient lineage querying of collection-based workflow provenance. In *EDBT*, pp. 299–310, 2010.

[434] Tom Mitchell. Machine learning. 1997.

[435] Theophano Mitsa. *Temporal Data Mining*. CRC Press, 2010.

[436] I.C. Mogotsi. Christopher d. manning, prabhakar raghavan, and hinrich schütze: Introduction to information retrieval, 2010.

[437] Muhidin Mohamed and Mourad Oussalah. Srl-esa-textsum: A text summarization approach based on semantic role labeling and explicit semantic analysis. *Information Processing & Management*, 56(4): 1356–1372, 2019.

[438] Raymond J. Mooney and Loriene Roy. Content-based book recommending using learning for text categorization. In *Proceedings of the Fifth ACM Conference on Digital Libraries*, pp. 195–204. ACM, 2000.

[439] Jyoti Sunil More and Chelpa Lingam. A SI model for social media influencer maximization. *Applied Computing and Informatics*, 15(2): 102–108, 2019.

[440] Luc Moreau, Juliana Freire, Joe Futrelle, Robert McGrath, Jim Myers and Patrick Paulson. The open provenance model. 2007.

[441] Mohammed Elsaid Moussa, Ensaf Hussein Mohamed and Mohamed Hassan Haggag. A survey on opinion summarization techniques for social media. *Future Computing and Informatics Journal*, 3(1): 82–109, 2018.

[442] Cataldo Musto, Fedelucio Narducci, Pasquale Lops, Giovanni Semeraro, Marco de Gemmis, Mauro Barbieri, Jan Korst, Verus Pronk and Ramon Clout. Enhanced semantic tv-show representation for personalized electronic program guides. In *User Modeling, Adaptation, and Personalization*, pp. 188–199. Springer, 2012.

[443] Naresh Kumar Nagwani and Shrish Verma. A frequent term and semantic similarity based single document text summarization algorithm. *International Journal of Computer Applications*, 17: 2, March 2011.

[444] Preslav Nakov, Alan Ritter, Sara Rosenthal, Fabrizio Sebastiani and Veselin Stoyanov. Semeval-2016 task 4: Sentiment analysis in twitter. In *Proceedings of the 10th International Workshop on Semantic Evaluation, SemEval@NAACL-HLT 2016, San Diego, CA, USA, June 16–17, 2016*, pp. 1–18, 2016.

[445] Ramesh Nallapati, Ao Feng, Fuchun Peng and James Allan. Event threading within news topics. In *The thirteenth ACM International Conference on Information and Knowledge Management*, 2004.

[446] Ramesh Nallapati, Feifei Zhai and Bowen Zhou. Summarunner: A recurrent neural network based sequence model for extractive summarization of documents. In *Thirty-First AAAI Conference on Artificial Intelligence*, 2017.

[447] Ramesh M. Nallapati, Amr Ahmed, Eric P. Xing and William W. Cohen. Joint latent topic models for text and citations. In *Proceedings of the 14th ACM SIGKDD International Conference on Knowledge Discovery and Data Mining*, pp. 542–550, 2008.

[448] Frank Namugera, Ronald Wesonga and Peter Jehopio. Text mining and determinants of sentiments: Twitter social media usage by traditional media houses in uganda. *Computational Social Networks*, 6(1): 1–21, 2019.

[449] Shashi Narayan, Shay B. Cohen and Mirella Lapata. Ranking sentences for extractive summarization with reinforcement learning. In *Proceedings of the 2018 Conference of the North American Chapter of the Association for Computational Linguistics: Human Language Technologies, Volume 1 (Long Papers)*, pp. 1747–1759, 2018.

[450] Masumi Narita, Kazuya Kurokawa and Takehito Utsuro. A web-based english abstract writing tool using a tagged ej parallel corpus. In *LREC*, 2002.

[451] Nagarajan Natarajan, Donghyuk Shin and Inderjit S. Dhillon. Which app will you use next? Collaborative filtering with interactional context. In *Proceedings of the 7th ACM Conference on Recommender Systems*, pp. 201–208. ACM, 2013.

[452] Catalin Negru, Florin Pop, Mariana Mocanu and Valentin Cristea. Storage solution of spatial-temporal data for water monitoring infrastructures used in smart cities. In *2017 21st International Conference on Control Systems and Computer Science (CSCS)*, pp. 617–621. IEEE, 2017.

[453] Julia Neidhardt, Rainer Schuster, Leonhard Seyfang and Hannes Werthner. Eliciting the users' unknown preferences. In *Proceedings of the 8th ACM Conference on Recommender Systems*, pp. 309–312. ACM, 2014.

[454] Ren Ng. *Digital Light Field Photography*. Stanford University, 2006.

[455] Muon Nguyen, Thanh Ho and Phuc Do. Social networks analysis based on topic modeling. In *The 2013 RIVF International Conference on Computing & Communication Technologies-Research, Innovation, and Vision for Future (RIVF)*, pp. 119–122. IEEE, 2013.

[456] Thao Nguyen, Eun-Ae Park, Jiho Han, Dong-Chul Park and Soo-Young Min. Object detection using scale invariant feature transform. In *Genetic and Evolutionary Computing*, pp. 65–72. Springer, 2014.

[457] Thien Hai Nguyen, Kiyoaki Shirai and Julien Velcin. Sentiment analysis on social media for stock movement prediction. *Expert Systems with Applications*, 42(24): 9603–9611, 2015.

[458] Ian Soboroff, Charles Nicholas and Charles K. Nicholas. Combining content and collaboration in text filtering. In *In Proceedings of the IJCAIÕ 99 Workshop on Machine Learning for Information Filtering*, pp. 86–91, 1999.

[459] Joseph D. Novak, D. Bob Gowin and Gowin D. Bob. *Learning How to Learn*. Cambridge University Press, 1984.

[460] Maria Augusta S.N. Nunes. *Recommender Systems based on Personality Traits: Could Human Psychological Aspects Influence the Computer Decision-making Process?* VDM Verlag, 2009.

[461] Douglas W. Oard, Jinmook Kim et al. Implicit feedback for recommender systems. In *Proceedings of the AAAI Workshop on Recommender Systems*, pp. 81–83, 1998.

[462] Brendan O'Connor, Michel Krieger and David Ahn. Tweetmotif: Exploratory search and topic summarization for twitter. In *Fourth International AAAI Conference on Weblogs and Social Media*, 2010.

[463] Ana Oliveira, Francisco Câmara Pereira and Amílcar Cardoso. Automatic reading and learning from text. In *Proceedings of the International Symposium on Artificial Intelligence (ISAI)*. Citeseer, 2001.

[464] Constantin Orasan and Laura Hasler. Computer-aided summarisation-what the user really wants. In *LREC*, pp. 1548–1551, 2006.

[465] N.A. Osman, S.A.M. Noah and M. Darwich. Contextual sentiment based recommender system to provide recommendation in the electronic product domain. *International Journal of Machine Learning and Computing*, 9(4): 425–431, 2019.

[466] David Alfred Ostrowski. Using latent dirichlet allocation for topic modelling in twitter. In *Proceedings of the 2015 IEEE 9th International Conference on Semantic Computing (IEEE ICSC 2015)*, pp. 493–497. IEEE, 2015.

[467] Edgar Osuna, Robert Freund and Federico Girosit. Training support vector machines: An application to face detection. In *Proceedings of IEEE Computer Society Conference on Computer Vision and Pattern Recognition*, pp. 130–136. IEEE, 1997.

[468] Rania Othman, Rami Belkaroui and Rim Faiz. Customer opinion summarization based on twitter conversations. In *Proceedings of the 6th International Conference on Web Intelligence, Mining and Semantics*, pp. 1–10, 2016.

[469] You Ouyang, Wenjie Li and Qin Lu. An integrated multi-document summarization approach based on word hierarchical representation. In *Proceedings of the ACL-IJCNLP 2009 Conference Short Papers*, pp. 113–116, 2009.

[470] Paul Over, Hoa Dang and Donna Harman. Duc in context. *Information Processing & Management*, 43(6): 1506–1520, 2007.

[471] Mark O'connor, Dan Cosley, Joseph A. Konstan and John Riedl. Polylens: A recommender system for groups of users. In *ECSCW 2001*, pp. 199–218. Springer, 2001.

[472] Turney P. Thumbs up or thumbs down? Semantic orientation applied to unsupervised classification of reviews. In *Proceedings of the 40th Annual Meeting of the Association for Computational Linguistics (ACL)*, pp. 417–424, 2002.

[473] Roberto Pagano, Paolo Cremonesi, Martha Larson, Balázs Hidasi, Domonkos Tikk, Alexandros Karatzoglou and Massimo Quadrana. The contextual turn: From context-aware to context-driven recommender systems. In *Proceedings of the 10th ACM Conference on Recommender Systems*, pp. 249–252, 2016.

[474] Bo Pang, Lillian Lee and Shivakumar Vaithyanathan. Thumbs up? Sentiment classification using machine learning techniques. *arXiv preprint cs/0205070*, 2002.

[475] Jordi Paniagua and Juan Sapena. Business performance and social media: Love or hate? *Business Horizons*, 57(6): 719–728, 2014.

[476] Jaehui Park, Tomohiro Fukuhara, Ikki Ohmukai, Hideaki Takeda and Sanggoo Lee. Web content summarization using social bookmarks: A new approach for social summarization. In *Proceedings of the 10th ACM Workshop on Web Information and Data Management*, pp. 103–110, 2008.

[477] Daraksha Parveen, Hans-Martin Ramsl and Michael Strube. Topical coherence for graph-based extractive summarization. In *Proceedings of the 2015 Conference on Empirical Methods in Natural Language Processing*, pp. 1949–1954, 2015.

[478] Ramakanth Pasunuru and Mohit Bansal. Multi-reward reinforced summarization with saliency and entailment. *arXiv preprint arXiv:1804.06451*, 2018.

[479] Darshna Patel, Saurabh Shah and Hitesh Chhinkaniwala. Fuzzy logic based multi document summarization with improved sentence scoring and redundancy removal technique. *Expert Systems with Applications*, 134: 167–177, 2019.

[480] Priyanka Patel and Khushali Mistry. A review: Text classification on social media data. *IOSR Journal of Computer Engineering*, 17(1): 80–84, 2015.

[481] Ajeet Ram Pathak, Manjusha Pandey and Siddharth Rautaray. Topic-level sentiment analysis of social media data using deep learning. *Applied Soft Computing*, 108: 107440, 2021.

[482] Romain Paulus, Caiming Xiong and Richard Socher. A deep reinforced model for abstractive summarization. In *International Conference on Learning Representations*, 2018.

[483] Michael J. Pazzani. A framework for collaborative, content-based and demographic filtering. *Artif. Intell. Rev.*, 13(5-6): 393–408, December 1999.

[484] Michael J. Pazzani and Daniel Billsus. The adaptive web. *Chapter Content-based Recommendation Systems*, pp. 325–341. Springer-Verlag, Berlin, Heidelberg, 2007.

[485] Flávio Martins, Filipa Peleja, João Magalhães and Pedro Dias. A recommender system for the tv on the web: Integrating unrated reviews and movie ratings. *Multimedia Systems*, 19(6): 543–558, 2013.

[486] Jeffrey Pennington, Richard Socher and Christopher Manning. Glove: Global vectors for word representation. In *Proceedings of the 2014 Conference on Empirical Methods in Natural Language Processing (EMNLP)*, pp. 1532–1543, 2014.

[487] Maria S. Pera and Yiu-Kai Ng. A group recommender for movies based on content similarity and popularity. *Information Processing & Management*, 49(3): 673–687, 2013.

[488] Person. Definition of fashion, 2019.

[489] Tuan-Anh Nguyen Pham, Xutao Li, Gao Cong and Zhenjie Zhang. A general graph-based model for recommendation in event-based social networks. In *2015 IEEE 31st International Conference on Data Engineering*, pp. 567–578. IEEE, 2015.

[490] Viet-Quoc Pham, Tatsuo Kozakaya, Osamu Yamaguchi and Ryuzo Okada. Count forest: Co-voting uncertain number of targets using random forest for crowd density estimation. In *Proceedings of the IEEE International Conference on Computer Vision*, pp. 3253–3261, 2015.

[491] Xuan-Hieu Phan, Le-Minh Nguyen and Susumu Horiguchi. Learning to classify short and sparse text & web with hidden topics from large-scale data collections. In *Proceedings of the 17th International Conference on World Wide Web*, pp. 91–100, 2008.

[492] B. Joseph Pine II and James H. Gilmore. *The Experience Economy*. Harvard Business School Press. Boston, Massachusetts, 1999.

[493] G. Preethi, P. Venkata Krishna, Mohammad S. Obaidat, Vankadara Saritha and Sumanth Yenduri. Application of deep learning to sentiment analysis for recommender system on cloud. In *2017 International Conference on Computer, Information and Telecommunication Systems (CITS)*, pp. 93–97. IEEE, 2017.

[494] V. Priya and K. Umamaheswari. Enhanced continuous and discrete multi objective particle swarm optimization for text summarization. *Cluster Computing*, 22(1): 229–240, 2019.

[495] Xiaojia Pu, Rong Jin, Gangshan Wu, Dingyi Han and Gui-Rong Xue. Topic modeling in semantic space with keywords. In *Proceedings of the 24th ACM International Conference on Information and Knowledge Management, CIKM 2015, Melbourne, VIC, Australia, October 19–23, 2015*, pp. 1141–1150, 2015.

[496] J. Puttamadegowda and S.C. Prasannakumar. White blood cell sementation using fuzzy c means and snake. In *2016 International Conference on Computation System and Information Technology for Sustainable Solutions (CSITSS)*, pp. 47–52. IEEE, 2016.

[497] Iqbal Qasim, Jin-Woo Jeong, Jee-Uk Heu and Dong-Ho Lee. Concept map construction from text documents using affinity propagation. *Journal of Information Science*, 39(6): 719–736, 2013.

[498] Vahed Qazvinian, Dragomir Radev and Arzucan Özgür. Citation summarization through keyphrase extraction. In *COLING 2010*, pp. 895–903, 2010.

[499] Daniele Quercia, Michal Kosinski, David Stillwell and Jon Crowcroft. Our twitter profiles, our selves: Predicting personality with twitter. In *2011 IEEE Third International Conference on Privacy, Security, Risk and Trust*

and 2011 IEEE Third International Conference on Social Computing, pp. 180–185. IEEE, 2011.

[500] Dragomir R. Radev, Sasha Blair-Goldensohn and Zhu Zhang. Experiments in single and multidocument summarization using mead. In *First Document Understanding Conference*, page 1À8. Citeseer, 2001.

[501] Dragomir R. Radev, Eduard Hovy and Kathleen McKeown. Introduction to the special issue on summarization. *Computational Linguistics*, 28(4): 399–408, 2002.

[502] Kanagasabai Rajaraman and Ah-Hwee Tan. Knowledge discovery from texts: A concept frame graph approach. In *Proceedings of the Eleventh International Conference on Information and Knowledge Management*, pp. 669–671, 2002.

[503] Thanawin Rakthanmanon, Eamonn J. Keogh, Stefano Lonardi and Scott Evans. Time series epenthesis: Clustering time series streams requires ignoring some data. In *2011 IEEE 11th International Conference on Data Mining*, pp. 547–556. IEEE, 2011.

[504] David Ramamonjisoa, Riki Murakami and Basabi Chakraborty. Comments analysis and visualization based on topic modeling and topic phrase mining. In *The Third International Conference on E-technologies and Business on the Web (EBW2015)*, p. 1, 2015.

[505] Al Mamunur Rashid, Istvan Albert, Dan Cosley, Shyong K. Lam, Sean M. Mcnee, Joseph A. Konstan and John Riedl. Getting to know you: Learning new user preferences in recommender systems. In *Proceedings of the 2002 International Conference on Intelligent User Interfaces, IUI 2002*, pp. 127–134. ACM Press, 2002.

[506] Lawrence H. Reeve, Hyoil Han and Ari D. Brooks. The use of domain-specific concepts in biomedical text summarization. *Information Processing & Management*, 43(6): 1765–1776, 2007.

[507] Chenghui Ren, Eric Lo, Ben Kao, Xinjie Zhu and Reynold Cheng. On querying historical evolving graph sequences. *VLDB*, 4(11): 727–737, 2011.

[508] Zhaochun Ren, Shangsong Liang, Edgar Meij and Maarten de Rijke. Personalized time-aware tweets summarization. In *Proceedings of the 36th International ACM SIGIR Conference on Research and Development in Information Retrieval*, pp. 513–522, 2013.

[509] Sahin Renckes, Huseyin Polat and Yusuf Oysal. A new hybrid recommendation algorithm with privacy. *Expert Systems*, 29(1): 39–55, 2012.

[510] Steffen Rendle, Christoph Freudenthaler, Zeno Gantner and Lars Schmidt-Thieme. Bpr: Bayesian personalized ranking from implicit feedback. In *Proceedings of the Twenty-fifth Conference on Uncertainty in Artificial Intelligence*, UAI'09, pp. 452–461, Arlington, Virginia, United States, 2009. AUAI Press, AUAI Press.

[511] Peter J. Rentfrow and Samuel D. Gosling. The do re mi's of everyday life: The structure and personality correlates of music preferences. *Journal of Personality and Social Psychology*, 84(6): 1236–1256, 2003.

[512] Peter J. Rentfrow, Samuel D. Gosling et al. The do re mi's of everyday life: The structure and personality correlates of music preferences. *Journal of Personality and Social Psychology*, 84(6): 1236–1256, 2003.

[513] L. Resende. Handling heterogeneous data sources in a SOA environment with service data objects (SDO). In *SIGMOD Conference*, pp. 895–897, 2007.

[514] Paul Resnick, Neophytos Iacovou, Mitesh Suchak, Peter Bergstrom, and John Riedl. Grouplens: An open architecture for collaborative filtering of netnews. In *Proceedings of the 1994 ACM Conference on Computer Supported Cooperative Work*, CSCW'94, pp. 175–186, New York, NY, USA, 1994. ACM.

[515] Nabi Rezvani, Amin Beheshti and Alireza Tabebordbar. Linking textual and contextual features for intelligent cyberbullying detection in social media. In *MoMM'20: The 18th International Conference on Advances in Mobile Computing and Multimedia, Chiang Mai, Thailand, November 30–December 2, 2020*, pp. 3–10. ACM, 2020.

[516] Francesco Ricci and Quang Nhat Nguyen. Acquiring and revising preferences in a critique-based mobile recommender system. *Intelligent Systems, IEEE*, 22(3): 22–29, 2007.

[517] Francesco Ricci, Lior Rokach and Bracha Shapira. Introduction to recommender systems handbook. In Francesco Ricci, Lior Rokach, Bracha Shapira and Paul B. Kantor (eds.). *Recommender Systems Handbook*, pp. 1–35. Springer Verlag, 2011.

[518] Francesco Ricci, Lior Rokach and Bracha Shapira. Introduction to recommender systems handbook. In Francesco Ricci, Lior Rokach, Bracha

Shapira and Paul Kantor (eds.). *Recommender Systems Handbook*, pp. 1–35. Springer Verlag, 2011.

[519] Francesco Ricci, Lior Rokach and Bracha Shapira. Recommender Systems: Introduction and Challenges. In *Recommender Systems Handbook*, volume 54, pages 1–34. Springer US, Boston, MA, 2015.

[520] Francesco Ricci, Lior Rokach and Bracha Shapira. Recommender systems: Introduction and challenges. In *Recommender Systems Handbook*, pp. 1–34. Springer US, 2015.

[521] Francesco Ricci, Lior Rokach, Bracha Shapira and Paul B. Kantor. *Recommender Systems Handbook*. Springer, 2011.

[522] Cody Rioux, Sadid A. Hasan and Yllias Chali. Fear the reaper: A system for automatic multi-document summarization with reinforcement learning. In *Proceedings of the 2014 Conference on Empirical Methods in Natural Language Processing (EMNLP)*, pp. 681–690, 2014.

[523] Alan Ritter, Sam Clark, Mausam and Oren Etzioni. Named entity recognition in tweets: An experimental study. In *Proceedings of the 2011 Conference on Empirical Methods in Natural Language Processing, EMNLP 2011, 27–31 July 2011, John McIntyre Conference Centre, Edinburgh, UK, A Meeting of SIGDAT, a Special Interest Group of the ACL*, pp. 1524–1534, 2011.

[524] Vala Ali Rohani, Shahid Shayaa and Ghazaleh Babanejaddehaki. Topic modeling for social media content: A practical approach. In *2016 3rd International Conference on Computer and Information Sciences (ICCOINS)*, pp. 397–402. IEEE, 2016.

[525] Daniel M. Romero, Brendan Meeder and Jon Kleinberg. Differences in the mechanics of information diffusion across topics: Idioms, political hashtags, and complex contagion on twitter. In *Proceedings of the 20th International Conference on World Wide Web*, pp. 695–704, 2011.

[526] Alexandra Roshchina. *TWIN Personality-based Recommender System*. Institute of Technology Tallaght, Dublin, 2012.

[527] Craig Ross, Emily S. Orr, Mia Sisic, Jaime M. Arseneault, Mary G. Simmering and R. Robert Orr. Personality and motivations associated with facebook use. *Computers in Human Behavior*, 25(2): 578–586, 2009.

[528] Neil Rubens, Mehdi Elahi, Masashi Sugiyama and Dain Kaplan. Active learning in recommender systems. In *Recommender Systems Handbook—*

Chapter 24: Recommending Active Learning, pp. 809–846. Springer US, 2015.

[529] Thomas D. Ruder, Gary M. Hatch, Garyfalia Ampanozi, Michael J. Thali and Nadja Fischer. Suicide announcement on facebook. *Crisis*, 2011.

[530] Alexander M. Rush, Sumit Chopra and Jason Weston. A neural attention model for abstractive sentence summarization. *arXiv preprint arXiv:1509.00685*, 2015.

[531] Seonggi Ryang and Takeshi Abekawa. Framework of automatic text summarization using reinforcement learning. In *Proceedings of the 2012 Joint Conference on Empirical Methods in Natural Language Processing and Computational Natural Language Learning*, pp. 256–265, 2012.

[532] Naidila Sadashiv and S.M. Dilip Kumar. Cluster, grid and cloud computing: A detailed comparison. In *2011 6th International Conference on Computer Science & Education (ICCSE)*, pp. 477–482. IEEE, 2011.

[533] Mehran Sahami, Susan Dumais, David Heckerman and Eric Horvitz. A bayesian approach to filtering junk e-mail. In *Learning for Text Categorization: Papers from the 1998 Workshop*, volume 62, pp. 98–105. Citeseer, 1998.

[534] Tirath Prasad Sahu and Sanjeev Ahuja. Sentiment analysis of movie reviews: A study on feature selection & classification algorithms. In *2016 International Conference on Microelectronics, Computing and Communications (MicroCom)*, pp. 1–6. IEEE, 2016.

[535] Mohammad Aidil Shah Sajat, Habibah Hashim and Nooritawati Md Tahir. Detection of human bodies in lying position based on aggregate channel features. In *2020 16th IEEE International Colloquium on Signal Processing & Its Applications (CSPA)*, pp. 313–317. IEEE, 2020.

[536] Takeshi Sakaki, Makoto Okazaki and Yutaka Matsuo. Earthquake shakes twitter users: Real-time event detection by social sensors. In *Proceedings of the 19th International Conference on World Wide Web*, pp. 851–860, 2010.

[537] Sherif Sakr. *Big Data 2.0 Processing Systems: A Systems Overview*. Springer Nature, 2020.

[538] Jesus M. Sanchez-Gomez, Miguel A. Vega-Rodríguez and Carlos J. Pérez. Extractive multi-document text summarization using a multi-objective

artificial bee colony optimization approach. *Knowledge-Based Systems*, 159: 1–8, 2018.

[539] Jesus M. Sanchez-Gomez, Miguel A. Vega-Rodríguez and Carlos J. Pérez. Experimental analysis of multiple criteria for extractive multi-document text summarization. *Expert Systems with Applications*, 140: 112904, 2020.

[540] Yogesh Sankarasubramaniam, Krishnan Ramanathan and Subhankar Ghosh. Text summarization using wikipedia. *Information Processing & Management*, 50(3): 443–461, 2014.

[541] Sunita Sarawagi. *Information Extraction*. Now Publishers Inc, 2008.

[542] Kamal Sarkar. Using domain knowledge for text summarization in medical domain. *International Journal of Recent Trends in Engineering*, 1(1): 200, 2009.

[543] Anish Das Sarma, Xin (Luna) Dong and Alon Y. Halevy. Data modeling in dataspace support platforms. In *Conceptual Modeling: Foundations and Applications*, pp. 122–138, 2009.

[544] Badrul Sarwar, George Karypis, Joseph Konstan and John Riedl. Item-based collaborative filtering recommendation algorithms. In *Proceedings of the 10th International Conference on World Wide Web*, pp. 285–295. ACM, 2001.

[545] W. Earl Sasser and Frederick F. Reichheld. Zero defections: Quality comes to services. *Harvard Business Review*, 68(5): 105–111, 1990.

[546] Markus Schedl, Peter Knees and Fabien Gouyon. New paths in music recommender systems research. In *Proceedings of the 11th ACM Conference on Recommender Systems (RecSys 2017)*, Como, Italy, September 2017.

[547] Markus Schedl, Hamed Zamani, Ching-Wei Chen, Yashar Deldjoo and Mehdi Elahi. Current challenges and visions in music recommender systems research. *International Journal of Multimedia Information Retrieval*, 7(2): 95–116, 2018.

[548] Francesco Schiliro, Amin Beheshti, Samira Ghodratnama, Farhad Amouzgar, Boualem Benatallah, Jian Yang, Quan Z. Sheng, Fabio Casati and Hamid Reza Motahari-Nezhad. icop: Iot-enabled policing processes. In *Service-Oriented Computing—ICSOC 2018 Workshops—ADMS, ASOCA, ISYyCC, CloTS, DDBS, and NLS4IoT, Hangzhou, China, November 12–15, 2018*,

Revised Selected Papers, volume 11434 of *Lecture Notes in Computer Science*, pp. 447–452. Springer, 2018.

[549] Robert Schima, Hannes Mollenhauer, Görres Grenzdörffer, Ines Merbach, Angela Lausch, Peter Dietrich and Jan Bumberger. Imagine all the plants: Evaluation of a light-field camera for on-site crop growth monitoring. *Remote Sensing*, 8(10): 823, 2016.

[550] Fabrizio Sebastiani. Machine learning in automated text categorization. *ACM Computing Surveys (CSUR)*, 34(1): 1–47, 2002.

[551] Fabrizio Sebastiani and Andrea Esuli. Sentiwordnet: A publicly available lexical resource for opinion mining. In *Proceedings of the 5th International Conference on Language Resources and Evaluation*, pp. 417–422, 2006.

[552] Abigail See, Peter J. Liu and Christopher D. Manning. Get to the point: Summarization with pointer-generator networks.

[553] Dafna Shahaf and Carlos Guestrin. Connecting the dots between news articles. In *Proceedings of the 16th ACM SIGKDD International Conference on Knowledge Discovery and Data Mining*, pp. 623–632, 2010.

[554] Dafna Shahaf, Carlos Guestrin and Eric Horvitz. Metro maps of science. In *Proceedings of the 18th ACM SIGKDD International Conference on Knowledge Discovery and Data Mining*, pp. 1122–1130, 2012.

[555] Dafna Shahaf, Carlos Guestrin and Eric Horvitz. Trains of thought: Generating information maps. In *Proceedings of the 21st International Conference on World Wide Web*, pp. 899–908, 2012.

[556] Claude E. Shannon. A mathematical theory of communication. *The Bell System Technical Journal*, 27(3): 379–423, 1948.

[557] Ori Shapira, Hadar Ronen, Meni Adler, Yael Amsterdamer, Judit Bar-Ilan and Ido Dagan. Interactive abstractive summarization for event news tweets. In *Proceedings of the 2017 Conference on Empirical Methods in Natural Language Processing: System Demonstrations*, pp. 109–114, 2017.

[558] Rajesh Shardan and Uday Kulkarni. Implementation and evaluation of evolutionary connectionist approaches to automated text summarization. 2010.

[559] Beaux Sharifi, Mark-Anthony Hutton and Jugal Kalita. Summarizing microblogs automatically. In *Human Language Technologies: The 2010*

Annual Conference of the North American Chapter of the Association for Computational Linguistics, pp. 685–688, 2010.

[560] Himanshu Sharma, Manmohan Agrahari, Sujeet Kumar Singh, Mohd Firoj and Ravi Kumar Mishra. Image captioning: A comprehensive survey. In *2020 International Conference on Power Electronics & IoT Applications in Renewable Energy and its Control (PARC)*, pp. 325–328. IEEE, 2020.

[561] Chao Shen, Fei Liu, Fuliang Weng and Tao Li. A participant-based approach for event summarization using twitter streams. In *Proceedings of the 2013 Conference of the North American Chapter of the Association for Computational Linguistics: Human Language Technologies*, pp. 1152–1162, 2013.

[562] Dou Shen, Jian-Tao Sun, Hua Li, Qiang Yang and Zheng Chen. Document summarization using conditional random fields. In *IJCAI*, volume 7, pp. 2862–2867, 2007.

[563] Yu Shen, Tingjie Lv, Xia Chen and Yidi Wang. A collaborative filtering based social recommender system for e-commerce. *International Journal of Simulation: Systems, Science and Technology*, 17(22): 91–96, 2016.

[564] Kate Sherren, John R. Parkins, Michael Smit, Mona Holmlund and Yan Chen. Digital archives, big data and image-based culturomics for social impact assessment: Opportunities and challenges. *Environmental Impact Assessment Review*, 67: 23–30, 2017.

[565] Stuart M. Shieber and Yves Schabes. Synchronous tree-adjoining grammars. 1991.

[566] Jyoti Shokeen and Chhavi Rana. A study on features of social recommender systems. *Artificial Intelligence Review*, 53(2): 965–988, 2020.

[567] Heung-Yeung Shum, Xiao-dong He and Di Li. From eliza to xiaoice: Challenges and opportunities with social chatbots. *Frontiers of Information Technology & Electronic Engineering*, 19(1): 10–26, 2018.

[568] Börkur Sigurbjörnsson and Roelof Van Zwol. Flickr tag recommendation based on collective knowledge. In *Proceedings of the 17th International Conference on World Wide Web*, pp. 327–336, 2008.

[569] Catarina Silva and Bernardete Ribeiro. The importance of stop word removal on recall values in text categorization. In *Proceedings of the*

International Joint Conference on Neural Networks, 2003, volume 3, pp. 1661–1666. IEEE, 2003.

[570] Artem Sokolov, Julia Kreutzer, Stefan Riezler and Christopher Lo. Stochastic structured prediction under bandit feedback. In *Advances in Neural Information Processing Systems*, pp. 1489–1497, 2016.

[571] Wei Song, Lim Cheon Choi, Soon Cheol Park and Xiao Feng Ding. Fuzzy evolutionary optimization modeling and its applications to unsupervised categorization and extractive summarization. *Expert Systems with Applications*, 38(8): 9112–9121, 2011.

[572] Virach Sornlertlamvanich, Eakasit Pacharawongsakda and Thatsanee Charoenporn. Understanding social movement by tracking the keyword in social media. *Proceedings of Multiple Approaches Lexicon (MAPLEX)*, 2015.

[573] Kamal Nigam t Andrew McCallum St. Learning to classify text from labeled and unlabeled documents. 1998.

[574] Anna Stavrianou, Periklis Andritsos and Nicolas Nicoloyannis. Overview and semantic issues of text mining. *ACM Sigmod Record*, 36(3): 23–34, 2007.

[575] Ben Steichen and Bo Fu. Towards adaptive information visualization-a study of information visualization aids and the role of user cognitive style. *Frontiers in Artificial Intelligence*, 2: 22, 2019.

[576] Josef Steinberger and Karel Ježek. Evaluation measures for text summarization. *Computing and Informatics*, 28(2): 251–275, 2012.

[577] David H. Stern, Ralf Herbrich and Thore Graepel. Matchbox: Large scale online bayesian recommendations. In *Proceedings of the 18th International Conference on World Wide Web*, WWW'09, pp. 111–120, New York, NY, USA, 2009. ACM.

[578] Mark Steyvers and Tom Griffiths. Probabilistic topic models. In *Handbook of Latent Semantic Analysis*, pp. 439–460. Psychology Press, 2007.

[579] Michael Stonebraker, Daniel Bruckner, Ihab F. Ilyas, George Beskales, Mitch Cherniack, Stanley B. Zdonik, Alexander Pagan and Shan Xu. Data curation at scale: The data tamer system. In *CIDR 2013, Sixth Biennial Conference on Innovative Data Systems Research, Asilomar, CA, USA, January 6–9, 2013, Online Proceedings*, 2013.

[580] Xiaoyuan Su and Taghi M. Khoshgoftaar. A survey of collaborative filtering techniques. *Adv. in Artif. Intell.*, 2009: 4:2–4:2, January 2009.

[581] V. Subramaniyaswamy and R. Logesh. Adaptive knn based recommender system through mining of user preferences. *Wireless Personal Communications*, 97(2): 2229–2247, 2017.

[582] Fabian M. Suchanek, Gjergji Kasneci and Gerhard Weikum. Yago: A core of semantic knowledge. In *Proceedings of the 16th international conference on World Wide Web*, pp. 697–706, 2007.

[583] Fabian M. Suchanek and Gerhard Weikum. Knowledge bases in the age of big data analytics. *Proceedings of the VLDB Endowment*, 7(13): 1713–1714, 2014.

[584] Amr Suleiman and Vivienne Sze. Energy-efficient hog-based object detection at 1080hd 60 fps with multi-scale support. In *2014 IEEE Workshop on Signal Processing Systems (SiPS)*, pp. 1–6. IEEE, 2014.

[585] Farhana Sultana, Abu Sufian and Paramartha Dutta. A review of object detection models based on convolutional neural network. *Intelligent Computing: Image Processing Based Applications*, pp. 1–16, 2020.

[586] N. Sumith, B. Annappa and Swapan Bhattacharya. Influence maximization in large social networks: Heuristics, models and parameters. *Future Generation Computer Systems*, 89: 777–790, 2018.

[587] Chris Sumner, Alison Byers and Matthew Shearing. Determining personality traits & privacy concerns from facebook activity. *Black Hat Briefings*, 11(7): 197–221, 2011.

[588] Yizhou Sun, Jiawei Han, Jing Gao and Yintao Yu. itopicmodel: Information network-integrated topic modeling. In *2009 Ninth IEEE International Conference on Data Mining*, pp. 493–502. IEEE, 2009.

[589] Russell Swan and James Allan. Automatic generation of overview timelines. In *Proceedings of the 23rd Annual International ACM SIGIR Conference on Research and Development in Information Retrieval*, pp. 49–56, 2000.

[590] Alireza Tabebordbar, Amin Beheshti and Boualem Benatallah. Conceptmap: A conceptual approach for formulating user preferences in large information spaces. In *Web Information Systems Engineering—WISE 2019—20th International Conference, Hong Kong, China, November 26–30, 2019, Proceedings*, volume 11881 of *Lecture Notes in Computer Science*, pp. 779–794. Springer, 2019.

[591] Alireza Tabebordbar, Amin Beheshti, Boualem Benatallah and Moshe Chai Barukh. Adaptive rule adaptation in unstructured and dynamic environments. In *Web Information Systems Engineering—WISE 2019— 20th International Conference, Hong Kong, China, November 26–30, 2019, Proceedings*, volume 11881 of *Lecture Notes in Computer Science*, pp. 326–340. Springer, 2019.

[592] Alireza Tabebordbar, Amin Beheshti, Boualem Benatallah and Moshe Chai Barukh. Feature-based and adaptive rule adaptation in dynamic environments. *Data Sci. Eng.*, 5(3): 207–223, 2020.

[593] Kou Takahashi, Takao Miura and Isamu Shioya. Hierarchical summarizing and evaluating for web pages. In *EROW*, 2007.

[594] Ikbal Taleb, Rachida Dssouli and Mohamed Adel Serhani. Big data preprocessing: A quality framework. In *2015 IEEE International Congress on Big Data*, pp. 191–198. IEEE, 2015.

[595] Jiliang Tang, Xia Hu and Huan Liu. Social recommendation: A review. *Social Network Analysis and Mining*, 3(4): 1113–1133, 2013.

[596] Lei Tang and Huan Liu. Relational learning via latent social dimensions. In *Proceedings of the 15th ACM SIGKDD International Conference on Knowledge Discovery and Data Mining*, pp. 817–826, 2009.

[597] Nan Tang. Big data cleaning. In *Asia-Pacific Web Conference*, pp. 13–24. Springer, 2014.

[598] Xuning Tang and Christopher C. Yang. Tut: A statistical model for detecting trends, topics and user interests in social media. In *Information and Knowledge Management*, pp. 972–981, 2012.

[599] Hristina Tankovska. Global Twitter user distribution by gender. https:// www.statista.com/statistics/828092/distribution-of-users-on-twitter-worldwide-gender/, June 2021.

[600] Chun-Yuen Teng, Yu-Ru Lin and Lada A. Adamic. Recipe recommendation using ingredient networks. In *Proceedings of the 4th Annual ACM Web Science Conference*, pp. 298–307. ACM, 2012.

[601] Ya-Wen Teng, Chih-Hua Tai, Philip S. Yu and Ming-Syan Chen. Modeling and utilizing dynamic influence strength for personalized promotion. In *Proceedings of the 2015 IEEE/ACM International Conference on Advances in Social Networks Analysis and Mining 2015*, pp. 57–64, 2015.

[602] Stefan Thomas, Christian Beutenmüller, Xose de la Puente, Robert Remus and Stefan Bordag. ExB text summarizer. In *Proceedings of the 16th Annual Meeting of the Special Interest Group on Discourse and Dialogue*, pp. 260–269, Prague, Czech Republic, September 2015. Association for Computational Linguistics.

[603] Hao Tian and Peifeng Liang. Improved recommendations based on trust relationships in social networks. *Future Internet*, 9(1): 9, 2017.

[604] Marko Tkalcic, Andrej Kosir and Jurij Tasic. The ldos-peraff-1 corpus of facial-expression video clips with affective, personality and user-interaction metadata. *Journal on Multimodal User Interfaces*, 7(1-2): 143–155, 2013.

[605] Marko Tkalcic, Matevz Kunaver, Andrej Košir and Jurij Tasic. Addressing the new user problem with a personality based user similarity measure. In *Proceedings of the 1st International Workshop on Decision Making and Recommendation Acceptance Issues in Recommender Systems*, p. 106, 2011.

[606] Christoph Trattner and David Elsweiler. Food recommender systems: Important contributions, challenges and future research directions. *arXiv preprint arXiv:1711.02760*, 2017.

[607] Michele Trevisiol, Luca Chiarandini and Ricardo Baeza-Yates. Buon appetito: Recommending personalized menus. In *Proceedings of the 25th ACM Conference on Hypertext and Social Media*, pp. 327–329. ACM, 2014.

[608] Raphaël Troncy. Linking entities for enriching and structuring social media content. In *WWW*, pp. 597–597, 2016.

[609] Hong-Linh Truong and Schahram Dustdar. On analyzing and specifying concerns for data as a service. In *APSCC*, pp. 87–94, 2009.

[610] Peter D. Turney. Thumbs up or thumbs down? Semantic orientation applied to unsupervised classification of reviews. *arXiv preprint cs/0212032*, 2002.

[611] Johan Ugander, Brian Karrer, Lars Backstrom and Cameron Marlow. The anatomy of the facebook social graph. *CoRR*, abs/1111.4503, 2011.

[612] Alper Kursat Uysal and Serkan Gunal. The impact of preprocessing on text classification. *Information Processing & Management*, 50(1): 104–112, 2014.

[613] Natalia Vanetik and Marina Litvak. Multilingual summarization with polytope model. In *Proceedings of the 16th Annual Meeting of the Special Interest Group on Discourse and Dialogue*, pp. 227–231, Prague, Czech Republic, September 2015. Association for Computational Linguistics.

[614] Vasudeva Varma, Litton J. Kurisinkel and Priya Radhakrishnan. Social media summarization. In *A Practical Guide to Sentiment Analysis*, pp. 135–153. Springer, 2017.

[615] Konstantinos N. Vavliakis, Andreas L. Symeonidis and Pericles A. Mitkas. Event identification in web social media through named entity recognition and topic modeling. *Data & Knowledge Engineering*, 88: 1–24, 2013.

[616] Marta Vicente, Óscar Alcón and Elena Lloret. The University of Alicante at MultiLing 2015: Approach, results and further insights. In *Proceedings of the 16th Annual Meeting of the Special Interest Group on Discourse and Dialogue*, pp. 250–259, Prague, Czech Republic, September 2015. Association for Computational Linguistics.

[617] Jorge Villalon and Rafael A. Calvo. Concept extraction from student essays, towards concept map mining. In *2009 Ninth IEEE International Conference on Advanced Learning Technologies*, pp. 221–225. IEEE, 2009.

[618] João Vinagre, Alípio Mário Jorge and João Gama. Online bagging for recommender systems. *Expert Systems*, 35(4): e12303, 2018.

[619] Kobkrit Viriyayudhakorn, Susumu Kunifuji and Mizuhito Ogawa. A comparison of four association engines in divergent thinking support systems on wikipedia. In *Knowledge, Information, and Creativity Support Systems*, pp. 226–237. Springer, 2011.

[620] Nam Vo, Nathan Jacobs and James Hays. Revisiting im2gps in the deep learning era. In *Proceedings of the IEEE International Conference on Computer Vision*, pp. 2621–2630, 2017.

[621] Tatiana Vodolazova, Elena Lloret, Rafael Muñoz and Manuel Palomar. Extractive text summarization: Can we use the same techniques for any text? In *International conference on Application of Natural Language to Information Systems*, pp. 164–175. Springer, 2013.

[622] Xiaojun Wan. Towards a unified approach to simultaneous single-document and multi-document summarizations. In *Proceedings of*

the 23rd International Conference on Computational Linguistics, pp. 1137–1145. Association for Computational Linguistics, 2010.

[623] Chong Wang, David Blei and David Heckerman. Continuous time dynamic topic models. *arXiv preprint arXiv:1206.3298*, 2012.

[624] Fu Lee Wang, Christopher C. Yang and Xiaodong Shi. Multi-document summarization for terrorism information extraction. In *International Conference on Intelligence and Security Informatics*, pp. 602–608. Springer, 2006.

[625] Jiannan Wang and Nan Tang. Towards dependable data repairing with fixing rules. In *Proceedings of the 2014 ACM SIGMOD International Conference on Management of Data*, pp. 457–468, 2014.

[626] Lizhe Wang, Rajiv Ranjan, Jinjun Chen and Boualem Benatallah. *Cloud Computing: Methodology, Systems, and Applications*. CRC Press, Taylor and Francis Group, In Print (anticipated hardcopy publication date), January 15 2012.

[627] Lichuan Wang, Xianyi Zeng, Ludovic Koehl and Yan Chen. Intelligent fashion recommender system: Fuzzy logic in personalized garment design. *IEEE Transactions on Human-Machine Systems*, 45(1): 95–109, 2014.

[628] Lu Wang, Hema Raghavan, Claire Cardie and Vittorio Castelli. Query-focused opinion summarization for user-generated content. *arXiv preprint arXiv:1606.05702*, 2016.

[629] Lu Wang, Hema Raghavan, Vittorio Castelli, Radu Florian and Claire Cardie. A sentence compression based framework to query-focused multidocument summarization. *arXiv preprint arXiv:1606.07548*, 2016.

[630] Shuai Wang, Xiang Zhao, Bo Li, Bin Ge and Daquan Tang. Integrating extractive and abstractive models for long text summarization. In *2017 IEEE International Congress on Big Data (Big Data Congress)*, pp. 305–312. IEEE, 2017.

[631] Suhang Wang, Jiliang Tang, Charu C. Aggarwal and Huan Liu. Linked document embedding for classification. In *Proceedings of the 25th ACM International Conference on Information and Knowledge Management, CIKM 2016, Indianapolis, IN, USA, October 24–28, 2016*, pp. 115–124, 2016.

[632] Xinxi Wang, David Rosenblum and Ye Wang. Context-aware mobile music recommendation for daily activities. In *Proceedings of the 20th ACM*

International Conference on Multimedia, pp. 99–108, Nara, Japan, 2012. ACM.

[633] Xinxi Wang, Yi Wang, David Hsu and Ye Wang. Exploration in interactive personalized music recommendation: A reinforcement learning approach. *ACM Transactions on Multimedia Computing, Communications, and Applications (TOMM)*, 11: 1–22, 2014.

[634] Xufei Wang, Lei Tang, Huiji Gao and Huan Liu. Discovering overlapping groups in social media. In *2010 IEEE International Conference on Data Mining*, pp. 569–578. IEEE, 2010.

[635] Yibo Wang, Mingming Wang and Wei Xu. A sentiment-enhanced hybrid recommender system for movie recommendation: A big data analytics framework. *Wireless Communications and Mobile Computing, 2018*, 2018.

[636] Yuanyuan Wang, Stephen Chi-Fai Chan and Grace Ngai. Applicability of demographic recommender system to tourist attractions: A case study on trip advisor. In *Proceedings of the The 2012 IEEE/WIC/ACM International Joint Conferences on Web Intelligence and Intelligent Agent Technology - Volume 03*, WI-IAT'12, pp. 97–101, Washington, DC, USA, 2012. IEEE Computer Society.

[637] Jonathan J. Webster and Chunyu Kit. Tokenization as the initial phase in nlp. In *COLING 1992 Volume 4: The 14th International Conference on Computational Linguistics*, 1992.

[638] Jian Wei, Jianhua He, Kai Chen, Yi Zhou and Zuoyin Tang. Collaborative filtering and deep learning based recommendation system for cold start items. *Expert Systems with Applications*, 69: 29–39, 2017.

[639] Yandong Wen, Zhifeng Li and Yu Qiao. Latent factor guided convolutional neural networks for age-invariant face recognition. In *Proceedings of the IEEE Conference on Computer Vision and Pattern Recognition*, pp. 4893–4901, 2016.

[640] Robert West, Ryen W. White and Eric Horvitz. From cookies to cooks: Insights on dietary patterns via analysis of web usage logs. In *Proceedings of the 22nd International Conference on World Wide Web*, pp. 1399–1410. International World Wide Web Conferences Steering Committee, 2013.

[641] Tom White. *Hadoop: The Definitive Guide*. O'Reilly Media, original edition, June 2009.

[642] Brett Wilkinson and Paul Calder. Augmented reality for the real world. In *International Conference on Computer Graphics, Imaging and Visualisation (CGIV'06)*, pp. 452–457. IEEE, 2006.

[643] Kristian Woodsend and Mirella Lapata. Automatic generation of story highlights. In *Proceedings of the 48th Annual Meeting of the Association for Computational Linguistics*, pp. 565–574. Association for Computational Linguistics, 2010.

[644] Chih-Wen Wu. The performance impact of social media in the chain store industry. *Journal of Business Research*, 69(11): 5310–5316, 2016.

[645] Gaochang Wu, Belen Masia, Adrian Jarabo, Yuchen Zhang, Liangyong Wang, Qionghai Dai, Tianyou Chai and Yebin Liu. Light field image processing: An overview. *IEEE Journal of Selected Topics in Signal Processing*, 11(7): 926–954, 2017.

[646] Shaomei Wu, Jake M. Hofman, Winter Mason and Duncan J. Watts. Who says what to whom on twitter. In *Proceedings of the 20th International Conference on World Wide Web*, 2011.

[647] Yuxiang Wu and Baotian Hu. Learning to extract coherent summary via deep reinforcement learning. In *Thirty-Second AAAI Conference on Artificial Intelligence*, 2018.

[648] Sander Wubben, E.J. Krahmer, A.P.J. van den Bosch and Suzan Verberne. Abstractive compression of captions with attentive recurrent neural networks. 2016.

[649] Jiacheng Xu and Greg Durrett. Neural extractive text summarization with syntactic compression. In *Proceedings of the 2019 Conference on Empirical Methods in Natural Language Processing and the 9th International Joint Conference on Natural Language Processing (EMNLP-IJCNLP)*, pp. 3283–3294, 2019.

[650] Yichao Xu, Hajime Nagahara, Atsushi Shimada and Rin-ichiro Taniguchi. Transcut: Transparent object segmentation from a light-field image. In *Proceedings of the IEEE International Conference on Computer Vision*, pp. 3442–3450, 2015.

[651] Shahpar Yakhchi, Amin Beheshti, Seyed Mohssen Ghafari, Mehmet A. Orgun and Guanfeng Liu. Towards a deep attention-based sequential recommender system. *IEEE Access*, 8: 178073–178084, 2020.

[652] Rui Yan, Liang Kong, Congrui Huang, Xiaojun Wan, Xiaoming Li and Yan Zhang. Timeline generation through evolutionary trans-temporal summarization. In *Proceedings of the 2011 Conference on Empirical Methods in Natural Language Processing*, pp. 433–443, 2011.

[653] Rui Yan, Xiaojun Wan, Jahna Otterbacher, Liang Kong, Xiaoming Li and Yan Zhang. Evolutionary timeline summarization: A balanced optimization framework via iterative substitution. In *Proceedings of the 34th International ACM SIGIR Conference on Research and Development in Information Retrieval*, pp. 745–754, 2011.

[654] Bo Yang, Yu Lei, Jiming Liu and Wenjie Li. Social collaborative filtering by trust. *IEEE Transactions on Pattern Analysis and Machine Intelligence*, 39(8): 1633–1647, 2016.

[655] Bo Yang, Yu Lei, Jiming Liu and Wenjie Li. Social collaborative filtering by trust. *IEEE Transactions on Pattern Analysis and Machine Intelligence*, 39(8): 1633–1647, Aug 2017.

[656] Bo Yang, Tao Mei, Xian-Sheng Hua, Linjun Yang, Shi-Qiang Yang and Mingjing Li. Online video recommendation based on multimodal fusion and relevance feedback. In *Proceedings of the 6th ACM International Conference on Image and Video Retrieval*, pp. 73–80. ACM, 2007.

[657] Christopher C. Yang and Fu Lee Wang. Fractal summarization: Summarization based on fractal theory. In *Proceedings of the 26th Annual International ACM SIGIR Conference on Research and Development in Informaion Retrieval*, pp. 391–392, 2003.

[658] Jaewon Yang and Jure Leskovec. Patterns of temporal variation in online media. In *Proceedings of the Fourth ACM International Conference on Web Search and Data Mining*, pp. 177–186, 2011.

[659] Jian Yang, Yongping Tang and Amin Beheshti. Design methodology for service-based data product sharing and trading. In *Next-Gen Digital Services. A Retrospective and Roadmap for Service Computing of the Future - Essays Dedicated to Michael Papazoglou on the Occasion of His 65th Birthday and His Retirement*, volume 12521 of *Lecture Notes in Computer Science*, pp. 221–235. Springer, 2021.

[660] Shuang-Hong Yang, Alek Kolcz, Andy Schlaikjer and Pankaj Gupta. Largescale high-precision topic modeling on twitter. In *Proceedings of the 20th ACM SIGKDD International Conference on Knowledge Discovery and Data Mining*, pp. 1907–1916, 2014.

[661] Becatien Yao, Aleksan Shanoyan, Hikaru Hanawa Peterson, Cheryl Boyer and Lauri Baker. The use of new-media marketing in the green industry: Analysis of social media use and impact on sales. *Agribusiness*, 35(2): 281–297, 2019.

[662] Ting Yao, Yingwei Pan, Yehao Li, Zhaofan Qiu and Tao Mei. Boosting image captioning with attributes. In *Proceedings of the IEEE International Conference on Computer Vision*, pp. 4894–4902, 2017.

[663] Mao Ye, Peifeng Yin, Wang-Chien Lee and Dik-Lun Lee. Exploiting geographical influence for collaborative point-of-interest recommendation. In *Proceedings of the 34th International ACM SIGIR Conference on Research and Development in Information Retrieval*, pp. 325–334, 2011.

[664] Dawei Yin, Zhenzhen Xue, Liangjie Hong and Brian D. Davison. A probabilistic model for personalized tag prediction. In *Proceedings of the 16th ACM SIGKDD International Conference on Knowledge Discovery and Data Mining*, pp. 959–968, 2010.

[665] Jie Yin, Sarvnaz Karimi, Andrew Lampert, Mark Cameron, Bella Robinson and Robert Power. Using social media to enhance emergency situation awareness. In *Twenty-fourth International Joint Conference on Artificial Intelligence*, 2015.

[666] Zhijun Yin, Rui Li, Qiaozhu Mei and Jiawei Han. Exploring social tagging graph for web object classification. In *Proceedings of the 15th ACM SIGKDD International Conference on Knowledge Discovery and Data Mining*, pp. 957–966, 2009.

[667] Eman M.G. Younis. Sentiment analysis and text mining for social media microblogs using open source tools: An empirical study. *International Journal of Computer Applications*, 112(5), 2015.

[668] Naitong Yu, Jie Zhang, Minlie Huang and Xiaoyan Zhu. An operation network for abstractive sentence compression. In *Proceedings of the 27th International Conference on Computational Linguistics*, pp. 1065–1076, 2018.

[669] Hadi Zare, Mina Abd Nikooie Pour and Parham Moradi. Enhanced recommender system using predictive network approach. *Physica A: Statistical Mechanics and its Applications*, 520: 322–337, Apr 2019.

[670] Mohammad Reza Zarei and Mohammad Reza Moosavi. A memory-based collaborative filtering recommender system using social ties. In *4th International Conference on Pattern Recognition and Image Analysis*,

IPRIA 2019, pp. 263–267. Institute of Electrical and Electronics Engineers Inc., Mar 2019.

[671] Apostolos V. Zarras, Panos Vassiliadis and Ioannis Dinos. Keep calm and wait for the spike! insights on the evolution of amazon services. In *Advanced Information Systems Engineering—28th International Conference, CAiSE 2016, Ljubljana, Slovenia, June 13–17, 2016. Proceedings*, pp. 444–458, 2016.

[672] Zheng-Jun Zha, Xian-Sheng Hua, Tao Mei, Jingdong Wang, Guo-Jun Qi and Zengfu Wang. Joint multi-label multi-instance learning for image classification. *In 2008 IEEE Conference on Computer Vision and Pattern Recognition*, pp. 1–8. IEEE, 2008.

[673] Ke Zhai, Jordan Boyd-Graber, Nima Asadi and Mohamad L. Alkhouja. Mr. lda: A flexible large scale topic modeling package using variational inference in mapreduce. In *Proceedings of the 21st International Conference on World Wide Web*, pp. 879–888, 2012.

[674] Cha Zhang and Zhengyou Zhang. A survey of recent advances in face detection. 2010.

[675] Haizheng Zhang, C. Lee Giles, Henry C. Foley and John Yen. Probabilistic community discovery using hierarchical latent gaussian mixture model. In *AAAI*, volume 7, pp. 663–668, 2007.

[676] Xiaozheng Zhang and Yongsheng Gao. Face recognition across pose: A review. *Pattern Recognition*, 42(11): 2876–2896, 2009.

[677] Yin Zhang, Zhixiao Tu and Qian Wang. Temporec: Temporal-topic based recommender for social network services. *Mobile Networks and Applications*, 22(6): 1182–1191, 2017.

[678] Yongfeng Zhang, Guokun Lai, Min Zhang, Yi Zhang, Yiqun Liu and Shaoping Ma. Explicit factor models for explainable recommendation based on phrase-level sentiment analysis. In *Proceedings of the 37th International ACM SIGIR Conference on Research & Development in Information Retrieval*, pp. 83–92, 2014.

[679] Qiankun Zhao, Prasenjit Mitra and Bi Chen. Temporal and information flow based event detection from social text streams. In *AAAI*, volume 7, pp. 1501–1506, 2007.

[680] Xiaojian Zhao, Guangda Li, Meng Wang, Jin Yuan, Zheng-Jun Zha, Zhoujun Li and Tat-Seng Chua. Integrating rich information for

video recommendation with multi-task rank aggregation. In *Proceedings of the 19th ACM International Conference on Multimedia*, pp. 1521–1524. ACM, 2011.

[681] Yang Zhao, Zhiyuan Luo and Akiko Aizawa. A language model based evaluator for sentence compression. In *Proceedings of the 56th Annual Meeting of the Association for Computational Linguistics (Volume 2: Short Papers)*, pp. 170–175, 2018.

[682] Yong Zhao, Yongjun Zhang, Ruzhong Cheng, Daimeng Wei and Guoliang Li. An enhanced histogram of oriented gradients for pedestrian detection. *IEEE Intelligent Transportation Systems Magazine*, 7(3): 29–38, 2015.

[683] Elena Zheleva, John Guiver, Eduarda Mendes Rodrigues and Nataša Milić-Frayling. Statistical Models of Music-listening Sessions in Social Media. In *Proceedings of the 19th International Conference on World Wide Web (WWW)*, pp. 1019–1028, Raleigh, NC, USA, 2010.

[684] Wenchao Zhou, Qiong Fei, Shengzhi Sun, Tao Tao, Andreas Haeberlen, Zachary Ives, Boon Thau Loo and Micah Sherr. NetTrails: A declarative platform for maintaining and querying provenance in distributed systems. In *Demo; Proceedings of the ACM SIGMOD International Conference on Management of Data (SIGMOD'11)*, June 2011.

[685] Yang Zhou, Hong Cheng and Jeffrey Xu Yu. Graph clustering based on structural/attribute similarities. *Proceedings of the VLDB Endowment*, 2(1): 718–729, 2009.

[686] Linhong Zhu, Sheng Gao, Sinno Jialin Pan, Haizhou Li, Dingxiong Deng and Cyrus Shahabi. Graph-based informative-sentence selection for opinion summarization. In *Proceedings of the 2013 IEEE/ACM International Conference on Advances in Social Networks Analysis and Mining*, pp. 408–412, 2013.

[687] Markus Zopf. Estimating summary quality with pairwise preferences. In *Proceedings of the 2018 Conference of the North American Chapter of the Association for Computational Linguistics: Human Language Technologies, Volume 1 (Long Papers)*, pp. 1687–1696, 2018.

[688] Huang Zou, Xinhua Tang, Bin Xie and Bing Liu. Sentiment classification using machine learning techniques with syntax features. In *2015 International Conference on Computational Science and Computational Intelligence (CSCI)*, pp. 175–179. IEEE, 2015.

[689] Zhengxia Zou, Zhenwei Shi, Yuhong Guo and Jieping Ye. Object detection in 20 years: A survey. *arXiv preprint arXiv:1905.05055*, 2019.

[690] Amal Zouaq and Roger Nkambou. Building domain ontologies from text for educational purposes. *IEEE Transactions on Learning Technologies*, 1(1): 49–62, 2008.

[691] Krunoslav Zubrinic, Damir Kalpic and Mario Milicevic. The automatic creation of concept maps from documents written using morphologically rich languages. *Expert Systems with Applications*, 39(16): 12709–12718, 2012.

Index